D1594534

THE
CONTRITE SPIRIT

THE
CONTRITE SPIRIT

HOW THE TEMPLE HELPS US APPLY
CHRIST'S ATONEMENT

BRUCE C. HAFEN

AND

MARIE K. HAFEN

DESERET
BOOK

SALT LAKE CITY, UTAH

Library of Congress Cataloging-in-Publication Data

Hafen, Bruce C., author.

The contrite spirit : how the temple helps us apply Christ's atonement / Bruce C. Hafen and Marie K. Hafen.

pages cm

Includes bibliographical references and index.

ISBN 978-1-62972-158-3 (hardbound : alk. paper)

1. Atonement—The Church of Jesus Christ of Latter-day Saints. 2. Mormon temples. I. Hafen, Marie K., author. II. Title.

BX8643.A85H343 2015

264'.09332—dc23   2015028993

Printed in the United States of America

Publishers Printing, Salt Lake City, UT

10   9   8   7   6   5   4   3   2   1

To

Sarah, Ben, Spencer, Joshua, Eliza, Samuel, and Hannah

Devin, Lauren, Abby, Michael, Anna, Lizzy, Claire, and Emma

Daniel, Chaya, Caleb, Elia, Asher, Micah, Devorah, and Jaren

Lydia, Hannah, Emma, Clark, Kayla, Ellie, and Brigham

Holden, Ethan, Caleb, Eve, Peter, Marie, and Charlie

Madison, Zach, Jacob, Joshua, Kate, and Andrew

Cadence, Oakley, and Scarlett

"And [Elijah] shall plant in the hearts of the children
the promises made to the fathers, and the hearts of the
children shall turn to their fathers."

D&C 2:2

And ye shall offer for a sacrifice unto me a broken heart and a contrite spirit. And whoso cometh unto me with a broken heart and a contrite spirit, him will I baptize with fire and with the Holy Ghost.

3 NEPHI 9:20

CONTENTS

Preface ix

Prologue xiii

PART I: HE PREPARED THE WAY FOR US

1. Clarifying the Atonement Conversation—
   and How the Temple Helps 3

2. The Purpose of Christ's Atonement: Providing for
   Our Growth 22

3. His Atonement: Redeeming Blessings 29

4. His Atonement: Strengthening Blessings 34

5. His Atonement: Perfecting Blessings 46

6. The Temple Ordinances and the Two Priesthoods 53

7. The Temple and the Doctrine of Sacrifice 63

8. The Temple and the Power of Godliness Made Manifest 68

9. The Blessings of Temple Sealings 75

PART II: OUR JOURNEY

10. The Ascending Journey of True Followers—
    Engaging Christ's Atonement 87

11. Waiting Upon the Lord 96

12. Expectations 112

13. Marriage, At-one-ment, and the Temple 128

14. The Temple and the Natural Order of Marriage 142

15. Missionary Work, the Temple, and Real Growth 152

16. Keep the Covenants and the Covenants Will Keep You 167

17. The Reach of the Sealing Power 180

18. Saviors on Mount Zion: Restoring the Generations 193

19. Consecration 204

20. Sanctification 222

21. When "Almost" Is Enough 239

Notes 249

Index 263

PREFACE

This book seeks to complete, or at least to move forward, a project that began twenty-six years ago with the publication of *The Broken Heart: Applying the Atonement to Life's Experiences.* That book tried in an introductory way to explore how the Atonement of Jesus Christ applies to the many human experiences that can cause us to be, or to feel, separated from God.

Those experiences include not only the physical separation caused by death and the spiritual separation caused by our sins; they also include feelings of estrangement from God caused by adversity, by our inadequacies, and by our unintentional mistakes. *At-one-ment* means bringing together that which has been separated, especially separated from God. And, as stated in *The Broken Heart,* the Atonement is not just for sinners. The blessings made possible by the Savior's sacrifice can also heal our other wounds, whether self-inflicted or from sources beyond our control. In addition, those blessings can eventually help us become as He is. Christ is the ultimate source not only of our forgiveness but also of our peace and our perfection.

In the intervening years we have concluded that the exploration of Christ's Atonement begun in *The Broken Heart* cannot be complete without including the temple. So *The Contrite Spirit* will consider the doctrines, principles, ordinances, and covenants of the temple—each a part of what our Father in Heaven has prepared to help us along our journey back to Him. Essential to this journey is a clear understanding of how the Atonement applies to our lives, not only at the beginning of our trek but as we grow beyond our baptism toward spiritual maturity. Also essential is our own contrite spirit, the meek and submissive attitude through which we access all that the Lord has prepared for us. These perspectives can also give new meaning to our participation in temple ordinances.

Part I—"He Prepared the Way for Us"—offers a road map for clarifying some doctrinal perspectives on the Savior's Atonement and on the temple. We can gain much of this clarity by considering the Atonement through the lens of the temple—and by looking at the temple through the lens of the Atonement. Because of its interlocking pieces, we hope this conceptual framework will make more sense if it can first be seen as a whole, rather than being offered piecemeal throughout the book.

Part II—the journey of engaging Christ's Atonement—then illustrates some of the ways in which the teachings of the temple ordinances and the blessings of the Atonement can together help us stretch, grow, and become true followers of the Lord Jesus Christ. In Part II, the doctrines of the Atonement and the temple are not always on center stage but act mostly as a backdrop for personal stories that illustrate how some of the doctrines apply to our daily lives. The entire book is of course a personal expression, not a statement of official Church doctrine.

The past two decades have given us a broader perspective on today's global Church, stirring our admiration for the many Latter-day Saints whose "peaceable walk with the children of men" (Moroni 7:4) shows that living the gospel bears the same rich fruits in any culture or language. Still we write only as part of the mutual trust among all Church members that allows a shared conversation, reflecting our common search to understand how to live the gospel.

The two of us met in 1963 in a religion class at BYU called "Your Religious Problems." We solved our main religious problem when the conversations we began in that class led to our marriage. This book is a collaboration that has grown out of that continued conversation. We continue talking about the gospel and the scriptures as the primary perspective and motivation for nearly every aspect of our lives—whether we are talking about our children and their families, the temple, our friends, the books we read, the questions we have, music, current events, new ideas, young adults, and our experiences with other good people in and out of the Church.

One challenge with a co-authored book is with the "voice"— who is speaking when? Rather than getting bogged down in too many pronouns, we believe the context will show who is speaking. We also hope our individual styles will come through distinctly when they need to. For example, Marie wrote the Prologue, and we co-authored chapters 2 through 5 and chapters 16 through 18. Bruce wrote the first drafts of the other chapters—before Marie waded in to make them fully collaborative, our voices frequently interchanging. In "his" chapters, he is the "I" in any stories or personal reflections. In cases where the voice or the appropriate pronoun is in doubt, we are speaking as a couple.

We are very grateful to several friends for their valuable suggestions on earlier versions of the manuscript: Sarah d'Evegnee, Eric d'Evegnee, Cyril Figuerres, Tom Hafen, Thom Harrison, Martha Johnson, Paul Monson, Allan Rau, Annette Reitano, Noel

Reynolds, Jennifer Usterud, and Emily Utt. We also appreciate the capable advice, experience, and good cheer of the Deseret Book production team—Emily Watts, Richard Erickson, Suzanne Brady, Rachael Ward, and Lisa Roper.

We want to thank the people at Brigham Young University for the invitations to prepare earlier versions of chapters 2 through 5 for the 2014 BYU Women's Conference; of chapters 6 through 9 for the 2014 Sperry Symposium sponsored by BYU Religious Education; and of chapters 13 and 14 for the 2014 Annual International Broadcast of the J. Reuben Clark Law Society.

Finally, we express deepest gratitude for the sacred privilege of serving in the St. George Utah Temple together from 2010 to 2013. There we gained a better sense of why Wilford Woodruff, the first president of that temple, would have said of it: "A few days ago I went into the Cealing room where I often go to Pray, for I Consider there is no spot on this Earth more acceptable than this Temple. . . . Light burst upon my understanding. . . . And . . . I felt like shouting Glory Hallalulah to God and the Lamb."[1]

PROLOGUE

By Marie K. Hafen

O hope of every contrite heart,
O joy of all the meek,
To those who fall, how kind thou art!
How good to those who seek![1]

Looking out our kitchen window, I can see across our neighbor's horse pastures that are surrounded by white rail fences and flanked by the lace of a well-pruned orchard, all held in the lap of Mount Timpanogos. For thirty years, I have loved this scene. It is full of symbols of our Father in Heaven's love for us.

I love watching the irrigation water flow from the upper stream down to the pastures below in gentle but sometimes cutting floods as it works its way to the river. I love watching the fruit trees stirring from the skeletons of winter to the flower vases of spring, which become the fruit bowls of summer that shimmer into the golden glow of autumn. I love watching the snow fall like flakes of mercy on grateful ground. I love watching the horses that have come and gone over the years, some of them well trained, some of them not, all of them with spirits of their own. And I love watching the people who also come and go—with spirits of *their* own.

The whole scene is a lively allegory that sometimes has me feeling as though I'm living *in* the scriptures, seeing for myself why James would have compared the word of God to a bit in a horse's mouth (James 3:3–4) or why Alma would have taught his son Shiblon about moral discipline with the counsel to "bridle all your passions, that ye may be filled with love" (Alma 38:12). I have not ridden many horses myself, but I have watched fine trainers at work for years, and I can tell you that a well-trained horse is a thing of beauty, especially when the horse and rider have come to know and trust each other so well that they move as though they are one.

From all the years of watching from my window, the image of such a finely attuned relationship is saddled with meaning for me. It has become a picture of what true unity can look like, of how a little thing like a bridle can turn the whole of a mighty animal around, and of how visible the joy is—how exhilarating—when the horse and its master are truly one with each other.

And, because of a poem Bruce found some years ago, which we will share near the end of this book, a well-broken horse has also become for us an image of meekness. Think of it, an immense mass of orchestrated muscle moving with both a power that is innate and a grace that is learned. The meekness shows through in the moment this majestic animal, when at full gallop, peaks his velvet ears to catch even the slightest signal from his master to change course or to seize to a submissive stop. Without a stutter, the horse yields to whatever his master commands.

A horse that is well broken is a horse that is well trained. When the Lord asks us for our broken hearts, He is asking, in part, for us to take His word into us, to put His bit in our mouths, to wear His bridle so our ears can become attuned to His voice.

But notice, when the Lord asks for our broken heart, often He also asks for a contrite spirit. As with the Nephites at the temple in the land Bountiful, He commands us, "Come unto me with a broken heart *and* a contrite spirit" (3 Nephi 12:19; emphasis added). That exact phrase, coupling heart and spirit, appears twice in the Old Testament, seven times in the Book of Mormon, and five times in the Doctrine and Covenants. What is He saying by linking them? He doesn't use *or,* as if the conditions were synonymous. In using the word *and* He is telling us something about how the two qualities are companions, how they give meaning to each other, and how together they affect us in ways neither can alone.

Contrition of spirit when added to a state of brokenheartedness moves us toward Christ because we want His help. But without contrition of spirit, the pains of our lives could make us hardhearted and bitter. For example, in the last years of the Book of Mormon, the Nephites were mournful over their condition; but it was not sorrow unto repentance, only lamentation at not being delivered from their enemies or able to find happiness while yet in their sins (see Mormon 2:13–14).

A contrite spirit is eager to repent. It accepts responsibility for its own weakness and choices with a willingness to be corrected and desires to "learn of [Him] and listen to [His] words" (D&C 19:23). The Latin root of the word *contrite* means to wear away, as in rubbing rough edges smooth. Like the well-disciplined horse, a contrite spirit is one that is softening and yielding, learning to be responsive to the Master, submissive to His every command, and willing to sacrifice its own will in faith that His will is for the highest good (see Isaiah 55:9).

A contrite spirit does not hide. It seeks Jesus, compelled by faith in Christ's ability to save and to heal. "Will ye not now return unto me," He pleads, "and repent of your sins, and be converted, that I may heal you?" (3 Nephi 9:13).

If we have a broken heart and a contrite spirit and we keep

our covenants by sacrifice, then the Lord "will cause [us] to bring forth as a very fruitful tree which is planted in a goodly land, by a pure stream, that yieldeth much precious fruit" (D&C 97:8–9). In His next breath, after making such a sublime promise, the Lord commands His people to build a temple—a portal, if you will, that gives us access to such a "goodly land." It is through the sacred patterns of the temple—the multilayered *template*—that He can make a tree of life of each of us.

In the coming chapters, we will explore how a contrite spirit together with a broken heart unlock the blessings of the Atonement that are held in the temple. As I've come to see it, the temple is the place where we covenant to unite our sacrifice with His sacrifice, and in that union—in that becoming one with our Master—our eternal lives are born.

And behold, I have given you the law and the commandments of my Father, that ye shall believe in me, and that ye shall repent of your sins, and come unto me with a broken heart and a contrite spirit . . . , and the law is fulfilled.

3 NEPHI 12:19

Will ye not now return unto me, . . . and be converted, that I may heal you? . . . If ye will come unto me ye shall have eternal life. Behold, mine arm of mercy is extended towards you, and whosoever will come, him will I receive.

3 NEPHI 9:13–14

PART I

HE PREPARED THE WAY FOR US

CHAPTER 1

CLARIFYING THE ATONEMENT CONVERSATION—AND HOW THE TEMPLE HELPS

It is a familiar Sabbath scene: Earnest young men freshly groomed and dressed in white shirts and ties, kneeling over the bread and water they have placed so carefully on the sacrament table. In their newly deepened voices and with as much reverence as they can muster, they speak those ancient prayers. Hushed from singing the sacrament hymn, we in the congregation are further calmed by those precise words and beckoned to bring our hearts to the table—to the altar of sacrifice.

At the sacrament table, as we do at the altars of the temple, we seek to unite—through covenant—our sacrifice with His sacrifice. Over time, as we grow more receptive and the meaning of Christ's sacrifice for us sinks deeper into our souls, we can occasionally hear something almost startlingly new in those short prayers we thought we knew by heart—something that freshens our resolve to be connected with Him more constantly, more clearly, more meekly.

Then one day we might come to feel about the sacrament the way Elder L. Tom Perry felt. As life was slipping from his tall-framed body, he sent a last message to all of us through his fellow

Apostles. Of all else he could have said, with some emotion he gestured to his lips and pled with us to think more about what is really happening in our lives when we pick up the bread and the water, because if we can do that, "something happens." Our thoughtfulness in that moment, he said with a gesture toward his head, "turns us toward the Savior. . . . We need to stay close to Him. . . . Jesus is the Christ, the Savior of the world." He is our hope.[1]

Turning my thoughts toward that hope on such a Sabbath, it lifts my spirit when I see that the sacrament hymn will be one of those that are especially meaningful to me. Something about the moving interplay between the words and the music lets these songs seem fresh to me each time we sing them. I resonate inside, as I do with this one:

> In humility, our Savior, Grant thy Spirit here, we pray.
> As we bless the bread and water, In thy name this holy day
> Let me not forget, O Savior, Thou didst bleed and die for me
> When thy heart was stilled and broken, On the cross at Calvary.
>
> Fill our hearts with sweet forgiving, Teach us tolerance and love.
> Let our prayers find access to thee, In thy holy courts above.
> Then, when we have proven worthy Of thy sacrifice divine,
> Lord, let us regain thy presence; Let thy glory round us shine.[2]

These are the words and the mood of mind and spirit I would like to invoke as we begin now to talk about the meaning behind those sacrament hymns we love to sing. In humility, our Savior, grant thy Spirit here, we pray.

In recent years, we Latter-day Saints have been teaching and testifying much more about the Atonement of Jesus Christ. Between 1971 and 1981, for example, the word *atonement* was used an average of 15 times per year in general conference talks and 40 times per year in *Ensign* articles. By the 1990s, references to *atonement* had roughly tripled, to about 50 per year in conference talks and about 120 times per year in the *Ensign*,[3] and we've all watched that trend increase almost exponentially since then.

This growing attention is evident in many places—in talks by Church leaders, in greater visibility of the subject in Church publications, and in other books, articles, talks, and lessons. We have seen a veritable groundswell among Church members as we increasingly, in Nephi's terms, talk of Christ, rejoice in Christ, preach of Christ, and write of Christ (see 2 Nephi 25:23).

At the level of personal experience, more people are bearing testimony that because they have increased their knowledge of and reliance upon His Atonement, they have discovered the Savior's greater influence in their lives. They speak not only of their having found forgiveness and greater assurance of the Resurrection and life beyond the grave, but, like the faithful woman in the crowd reaching for the Savior's hem, they have also reached Him from the depths of their most personal needs and have been filled with the strength and comfort that only He can give.

I think, for example, of the stake president's wife who suffered constant, sometimes disabling anxiety, primarily due to her assumption that she and her family had to be flawless in every way. She said her increased insight about the Atonement had changed her past thinking and habits, helping her to become both more peaceful and more productively engaged with life around her.

I think of many with whom I have spoken who as children suffered crippling abuses of all kinds. In his or her own way, each has described finding access, even if only gradually, to the Lord's strength as a restoring, healing refuge from what would otherwise have been overwhelming debilitation. They have shared the discovery that, as they have sought Him, His atoning power has brought relief from the darkness and damage inflicted by the sins of others.

I think of friends who, when facing the harsh realities of losing dear relationships, have developed a closer relationship with the Great Healer. And He has helped them soothe and heal the heartache.

I am genuinely grateful for this greater opening of our hearts to Him.

Yet there are a few reasons for us to be cautious about the expanding volume and reach of today's Atonement discussions among the Latter-day Saints. Some of these concerns suggest a possible need for more doctrinal clarity about Atonement-related subjects—and I believe we will find much of that clarity in the temple. Yet I realize that clarification does little for us if it doesn't also help us internalize what our Father in Heaven offers us in these doctrines.

A FEW REASONS FOR CAUTION

A first general caution arises from clues in the way some outside observers of the Church interpret our conversations. For example, Jan Shipps, a non-LDS scholar who is among the most astute and sympathetic observers of the Church, believes that what she calls the increasing "LDS atonement discourse" within the Church has failed "to specify how [Christ's] atoning act is connected to the 'fulness of the Gospel.' Most especially, [LDS] atonement discourse fails to link the atonement to that part of the 'plan of salvation' that includes progression toward godhood."[4]

Our doctrine clearly teaches, however, that the entire purpose of the "perfecting blessings" of Christ's Atonement is to make possible our progression toward becoming like Him. So has Jan Shipps just not read enough about that part of our teachings to be clear about what we believe? It is more likely that, as a scholar, she knows our doctrine well—but based on her considerable observations as a longtime "sojourner" among us, she just doesn't hear many Latter-day Saints clearly expressing an understanding of that doctrine and what it means in their own lives. If so, that is our loss, not her mistake.

Another clue: Evangelical scholar Carl Mosser believes that our increased Atonement discussions are moving Latter-day Saints toward an understanding of the relationship between grace and works (and related ideas) that draws on and is becoming more consistent with Protestant doctrine—especially grace-oriented Evangelical Protestantism.

Thus Mosser applauds the work of LDS writers who he believes "promote an understanding of the relationship between grace and works that is openly modeled" after Evangelical teachings. He interprets this LDS writing as a "move away from" Joseph Smith's teachings about the nature of God and man's capacity to become like God, as Joseph expressed in the King Follett discourse.[5] That observation adds another witness to what Jan Shipps observed about similar issues.

However, in reality the doctrines of the Restoration are significantly different from the Protestant tradition regarding many fundamental principles. We *are* utterly dependent, of course, upon the Lord's grace. Surely and eternally, "it is *by his grace,* and his great condescensions unto the children of men, that we have power . . . [even to come] upon the face of the earth" (Jacob 4:7–9; emphasis added), let alone to have the opportunities of salvation and eternal life. In the most fundamental sense, this universal or unconditional form of grace is never "earned." We never *deserve* it, as if we were entitled to it. If the Lord hadn't extended this level of grace to us in the first place, we would be totally lost, without hope before we could even begin our journey.

Although this is true, there is a second dimension of the Lord's grace that is *not* a free gift. This further level of grace is available only when we meet certain *conditions*—not to satisfy some arbitrary standard of "works" in a mathematical grace-works formula, but for reasons related to the very nature of human growth. For example, forgiveness is conditioned upon our repentance. And the scriptural stories about the Lord's delivering the Israelites or the Nephites from their bondage show that the Savior offers the grace of His strengthening blessings to His people *only as they willingly participate* in their deliverance by keeping their covenants and exerting their own strength to the utmost. As discussed more fully in the next chapters, the conditional nature of this element of grace requires us to engage in the participatory process that results in our personal and spiritual development.

Without our complete engagement, the problem is not that the Lord's grace *won't* help us grow, but that it *can't*. Spiritual strength is like a muscle; it will grow only when it is repeatedly stretched to its outer limits. Were it otherwise, in our pre-earth life our Father could have simply given us enough grace and strength to perfect us instantly, thus skipping the terrible risks and travails of life on earth. But in such a bypass, we would miss out on the experience necessary to comprehend and assimilate the very nature of joy. Without sorrow and opposition, there is no growth. And without growth, there can be no joy.

This reference to personal growth and development is part of a unique but bedrock doctrinal perspective in the restored gospel of Christ—the purpose of the Atonement. That purpose, as part of the Father's eternal plan for us—His provisions for the journey of Christ's followers—is to make possible a mortal experience that allows us to learn and grow through overcoming the oppositions of sometimes miserable experience. Only because of the Atonement can the frequent bitterness of that experience be made sweet—not that Christ completely removes our afflictions, but that, if we follow Him, He interacts with us in ways that make the hard things bearable as He consecrates them for our gain and growth. And the ultimate end of that growth process is to become godlike—exactly as Joseph Smith taught in the King Follett discourse.

Only in the light of seeing our complete and eternal existence—from premortality to mortality to the promises of exaltation—can we appreciate Joseph's optimistic teachings about our potential destiny as children of God. That understanding comes from a much fuller perspective on our origins and our possibilities than the narrow belief of some Christians that we are born inherently evil as part of an *ex nihilo* creation—that is, made from nothing.

Is LDS Atonement discourse really moving away from Joseph Smith's teachings about who we are and what we can become? If it is, that discourse needs our attention—not just to help outsiders understand our doctrine, but especially to help *us* within the Church better understand and live it.

As something of a precedent for outsiders' questions today, I still remember what Kenneth Woodward, the religion editor of *Newsweek* magazine, wrote in a 1980 story called "What Mormons Believe":

"Unlike orthodox Christians, Mormons believe that men are born free of sin and earn their way to godhood by the proper exercise of free will, rather than through the grace of Jesus Christ. Thus Jesus' suffering and death in the Mormon view were brotherly acts of compassion, but they do not atone for the sins of others. For this reason, Mormons do not include the cross in their iconography nor do they place much emphasis on Easter."[6]

I was surprised and troubled that this seasoned religion writer would miss the point of our central doctrine. I was glad when another Church member wrote a published letter expressing the dismay I felt; namely, how could Mr. Woodward have done the extensive research he did (including numerous interviews with Church members) and "come away with the conclusion that Mormons don't believe that the atonement of Christ is efficacious for personal sins."[7]

But then Mr. Woodward replied, "I did read several books of Mormon scripture and theology before writing the article. My intent, however, was *not* to review books but rather to report how representative members of the LDS Church describe and interpret their own traditions. . . . The point is to determine what doctrines of a church are genuinely infused into the lifeblood of its adherents."[8]

It still bothers me that *Newsweek*'s readers were left with a serious misimpression about this key doctrine of the Restoration. But more troubling was the conclusion Mr. Woodward drew from his interviews among Church members—that the doctrines taught in our scriptures were not "genuinely infused into the lifeblood" of our people. To the extent that this is still true, such limited understanding can deny those same people the spiritual reassurance and guidance they may desperately need at pivotal moments in their personal lives.

In recent years, as noted earlier, we have witnessed an increased infusion of the Restoration's teachings about the Savior's Atonement into the lifeblood of the Latter-day Saints. But we are still learning, and observations from outsiders can positively provoke us to avoid further misunderstandings and misapplications of those very teachings today—a concern more about the Church's insiders than about its outsiders.

A second and perhaps related reason for caution is that some of our recent Atonement conversation needs a little more anchoring in our own doctrinal foundations—especially in seeing how Christ's Atonement applies to our experiences *after* baptism. Without clearer ties to those foundations, our repeated references to the Atonement run the risk of becoming too casual and all-inclusive, thus reducing its meaning for us.

For example, during our recent years serving in the St. George Temple, one of our ordinance workers came to express his puzzlement over something he had heard in a Sunday School class in his ward. His teacher had told a story about a little girl who had lost her glasses. She prayed for help and soon found the glasses. The teacher then said, with well-meant sincerity, "Isn't it wonderful that the Atonement helped that child find her glasses?" The temple worker asked me, "Can you tell me what the Atonement has to do with that story?" I said I really couldn't see its role in the story, unless we are ready to interpret every form of divine assistance as somehow coming directly from Christ's Atonement.

Our Heavenly Father's plan of salvation for His children includes at its very center the need for a Savior and for His Atonement. And divine assistance of any kind—including the very existence of the plan—is always a manifestation of our Father's love for us. The Savior's Atonement is the ultimate expression of that love, but not its *only* expression.

On another occasion I heard about someone describing the huge tsunami that devastated several Asian countries a few years ago, resulting in widespread damage and the loss of many lives. In answer to another person's distress about this vast destruction, he said, again with sincerity, "Well, don't be concerned. The

Atonement will take care of all of that." I might have misunderstood, but that observation seems so vague and so easy that it
lacks both understanding and compassion.

I felt a similar concern when I heard a Church member say
that "because Christ suffered, we don't need to." That is of course
a true statement with regard to His suffering as payment for the
sins of those who repent (see D&C 19:16). But the speaker's
context implied that if we really understood the Atonement,
that would relieve us of all other suffering—which could suggest that if we are suffering, we don't understand or have enough
faith in the Atonement. Yet Paul's statements about our entering
into the fellowship of Christ's suffering make it clear that, even
though Christ suffered for our sins, as His disciples we may well
be required to endure other suffering of our own. Repentance, for
example, requires the kind of suffering that Paul called "godly sorrow " (2 Corinthians 7:10). Further, we may need to suffer what
we may feel are undeserved adversities and pains, both to learn
from our own experience and to appreciate more fully what His
suffering means to us (see Romans 8:17–18; Philippians 3:10).

Similar questions can arise when we say that everything that
is unfair about life can be made right by the Atonement. That
is a true statement if we mean that no disadvantage in our life
circumstances will limit our eternal blessings if we accept Christ's
Atonement and live the gospel. The statement is also true if it
means that those who receive the blessings of exaltation will ultimately consider whatever experiences brought them there to have
been fair—in the sense of fully resolving all of their concerns,
whatever they were.

But some of what I've heard people say can convey the broader
implication that somehow the Atonement will bring about some
kind of universal fairness that will correct whatever has seemed

unjust—as broadly and unconditionally as the Resurrection. In reality, some of the problems we face, which may indeed seem unfair to us, might actually be the means by which we can learn what God has sent us here to learn. As the parable of the talents shows, He has blessed each of us with a unique mixture of gifts and limitations, even burdens, in a customized curriculum suited for each individual. And even if the Savior's blessings do help us cope with some perceived unfairness in such a case, it feels like looking beyond the mark to imply that everything really will someday be made "fair"—as in "the same"—for everybody.

In addition, we still need to consider how much of our own uniquely personal initiative is required for the Atonement's blessings to be fully effective in our individual circumstances. And who decides what is fair and what "made right" could mean? Moreover, identifying fairness as an objective of the Atonement simply might not make sense. Because the Lord's mercy is far more than fair, His blessings to us will be infinitely more than we deserve.

I share these examples not because I want to split hairs or quibble about terminology, but because I care so deeply about this core doctrine of the gospel and about our need for its blessings. If we become too casual in the way we talk or think about it, we may not be able to find that help. As President Dieter F. Uchtdorf recently counseled, "The Savior's Atonement cannot become commonplace in our teaching, in our conversation, or in our hearts. It is sacred and holy."[9]

If we let our thoughts and conversations about His Atonement become too much like clichés, that could have the unintended effect of hiding its meaning behind terms that seem so shallow (or so opaque) that few people give them a second thought—let alone a hundred thoughts.

By way of analogy, in Walmart one day I heard over the loud-speakers the melody from a great classical symphony being played by pop instruments as background music for the noise and chatter in the store. That's actually one way to keep people from discovering the power of classical music. When we have heard the "attention Walmart shoppers" version, we can too easily assume that we know the real thing—like comparing the opening sounds of "Chopsticks" with the opening of Beethoven's Fifth Symphony. Each of those pieces of music starts with the same three notes—but the similarity ends there.

A few years ago I was invited to offer some thoughts at an in-service meeting for the seminary and institute teachers in the southwest Utah region. I shared with them some of these concerns about being too casual about Atonement-related discussions to see if they had noticed similar trends. Many of them nodded in agreement. Afterward one of those teachers sent me this note:

> [Some people] reduce the Atonement to a sort of spiritual rabbit's foot [a good luck charm], which assumes that the mere reference to [it] justifies most of their wishes. In the past I have held that any association with the Atonement was helpful. [So] I have been hesitant to counsel [others] to be parsimonious about their references to the Atonement. Recently, [however,] I have thought to be slightly more bold. I have discovered that the misunderstanding of a doctrine is not much better than the rejection of that doctrine.[10]

The reality is, as Elder Tad R. Callister put it, that "the Atonement is not just a prime teaching of the gospel; it is the heart of the gospel. It infuses life into every doctrine, every principle, and every ordinance. . . . No doctrine . . . even approaches the Atonement in importance. . . . It is . . . the keystone of Christianity and the foundation of a spiritual life."[11] Indeed, in a fundamental sense, the Atonement simply *is* the gospel: "This is the gospel . . . that I came into the world to do the will of my Father. . . . And my Father sent me that I might be lifted up upon the cross" (3 Nephi 27:13–14).

Yet precisely because this doctrine has—and should have—such overwhelming magnitude, some of us might inadvertently assume that the Atonement's infinite implications eliminate our need to know and apply the meaning of other key doctrines. Ironically, then, a "spiritual rabbit's foot" approach to this greatest of doctrinal subjects can let it make other essential principles seem redundant instead of breathing life into them.

Someone once said that when your only tool is a hammer, every problem can look like a nail. Such an assumption would not only keep us from learning what other tools are designed to do, it may also cause us to hammer on things that could be more precisely (and better) served with a more precise instrument.

Our appreciation for, and use of, Atonement doctrine can and should *enhance* our understanding of other doctrines, rather than diminish it. Think of the role of the Holy Ghost, priesthood blessings, inspiration, prayer and its processes and answers, the teachings of the temple, and the teachings of Christ from the scriptures across an entire range of subjects. We do have a rich spiritual toolbox, not simply a rich spiritual tool.

In addition, we can create spiritual problems for ourselves if we see the Savior's Atonement in only vague, superficial terms. Among this doctrine's great gifts to us are the perspective, the strength, and the healing it can provide when we encounter life's inevitable sorrows and disappointments. But if we see it in an overly shallow light, that misunderstanding could ironically distance us from Him, causing us to feel disillusionment or even betrayal.

For example, one teacher I know recently wrote two sentences on the board and asked his class of young women and men which one best describes what Christ's Atonement does for us: (1) The Atonement makes us happy, or, (2) The Atonement helps us become like Christ, which makes us happy.

After discussion, his teenage class members could see why believing in only the first sentence could perhaps hurt them spiritually someday—because it can imply that the Atonement somehow lets us skip life's hard parts and unhappy surprises, rather than being the sure yet demanding source that helps consecrate our afflictions for our gain. When the false expectation behind the first sentence becomes fixed in our minds, then any disappointment can make us feel that Jesus has let us down.

One more problem with too-casual Atonement conversation is that it tends to omit references to the "conditions" we must meet to qualify for the Atonement's multiple blessings—such as the condition that we must repent to receive forgiveness. As we will see in the pages that follow, we must meet the Lord's conditions in a variety of ways in order to experience the growth our Father desires for us. Yet the doctrine of grace as taught by some other Christian churches tends to minimize or even disregard the place of conditions in our spiritual growth.

Without question, the Lord *always wants* to grant us grace; in fact, by His very nature He is so "merciful and gracious" that He "delight[s] to honor" us—especially "those who serve [Him] in righteousness" (D&C 76:5). But grace *cannot* be completely free if it is going to benefit us. If we don't reach for His reaching, we will never have enough muscle to move.

So there is a need in the Church for us to become more careful, more reverent, and more doctrinally disciplined in our understanding and our application of what Christ's Atonement means.

As we find the best ways to address that need, the Atonement will actually become a source of greater comfort and greater direction, not less. We will then see its meaning and its influence in full and honest interaction with the most demanding realities of our lives. We will be less tempted to see it as a shortcut around those realities, a notion that we might unintentionally borrow from religious traditions that don't demand the conditions, including the sacrifices required for real growth.

As Elder Neal A. Maxwell put it, "How can you and I really expect to glide naively through life, as if to say, 'Lord, give me experience, but not grief, not sorrow, not pain, not opposition, not betrayal, and certainly not to be forsaken. Keep from me, Lord, all those experiences, which made Thee what Thou art! Then let me come and dwell with Thee and fully share Thy Joy.'"[12]

Again and again the scriptures tell us that "any blessing from God" is conditioned upon "obedience to that law upon which it is predicated" (D&C 130:21). He is therefore "bound when ye do what I say;" but if we don't, "ye have no promise" (D&C 82:10). And "They who have kept the covenant . . . shall obtain mercy" (D&C 54:6). In fact, "all things shall work together for your good"—but only *if* you "remember the covenant wherewith ye have covenanted" (D&C 90:24).

And yet, given our inherent mortal limitations, and given that the Atonement's purpose is to help us grow and develop, there really are times when our best—"almost"—can be enough.[13] That miracle is possible because His grace surpasses by such immeasurable distance any condition required of us to receive it.

Nobody believed more than Brigham Young in the need for self-reliance, yet he said, "We ought not to consider it a hard matter to be faithful to God and keep his commandments, for when we obtain a celestial glory we shall have to explain that it is through the grace of God after all, for the glory far exceeds our suffering in this life."[14]

THE TEMPLE IS AN ANCHOR FOR UNDERSTANDING AND APPLYING CHRIST'S ATONEMENT

As we look for ways to stay grounded, rooted, and established in the Restoration's doctrines and practices regarding the Savior's Atonement, the temple is an invaluable, even essential, resource.

For the reasons stated in this chapter, for several years I had been looking for some additional, doctrinally sound ways to describe more clearly the nature and applications of the Atonement's post-baptism blessings. Then Marie and I were called to the St. George Utah Temple in 2010 to serve as president and matron. And the more time we spent in the light of the temple, the more clearly we could see that the doctrinal structure we were looking for was right there in the temple's ordinances and covenants.

Because of our teaching and learning role in the temple for three years, we began to see more plainly how the temple ordinances, like the ordinances of baptism and the sacrament, are *all* deliberately symbolic both of Christ's atoning sacrifice *and* of the relationship of that sacrifice to our daily lives. As the angel taught Adam and Eve at their altars of sacrifice, "This thing is a similitude of the sacrifice of the Only Begotten. . . . Wherefore, thou shalt do all that thou doest in the name of the Son" (Moses 5:7–8).

We began to realize that our own sacrifices should attempt to echo His, even in small ways. We saw that the doctrines of the temple and the doctrines of the Atonement pour such depth of meaning into each other that they are inextricably linked. As we read key scriptural passages about the temple, we saw more about Christ's Atonement—such as in D&C 84 or D&C 88. And as we studied more about the Atonement, we learned more about the temple—such as in Moses 5 or Alma 12–13. As we looked at the two subjects together, their interactive implications helped us see that the two ultimately merge together at the very center of the Father's plan of salvation.

In the temple baptistry, we saw more about the tie between baptism and Christ's Redemption. In the initiatory ordinances, we saw types and shadows of how the Savior's exaltation is the model for our own cleansing and development toward exaltation in fulfillment of our Father's plan for us. In the endowment, we began to grasp that the story of Adam and Eve is the story of *receiving* and engaging His Atonement. We could see more clearly that the temple's ordinances also include the temple's covenants, and that those covenants are a two-way exchange—our promises to Him and His promises to us—and are embedded in, or part of, the ordinances. With these ideas in our minds, the endowment can teach us how to do all that Adam and Eve did to apply His sacrifice to our own sacrifices, helping us become more as He is. In the sealing rooms, we began to understand that, along with its promises for uniting couples and families, the sealing is also a symbolic opportunity to offer our own broken hearts and contrite spirits—completely and without holding back—to Him and to each other.

The sequence of the ordinances, and even the sequences within many ordinances, such as in the endowment, are like the pieces of a great puzzle. The Lord shows us how to put the pieces together, teaching us how to bring together the process of His *giving* the Atonement with the process of our *receiving* it, as the story of Adam and Eve teaches us. The ultimate promises of the Atonement are eternal life and exaltation, but neither is accessible without the ordinances of the temple. The Lord gave us those ordinances for the express purpose of helping us build a closer relationship with Him—to help us become more like Him.

Moreover, our knowledge of the priesthood, the ordinances, and the covenants of the temple provides a secure foundation and a conceptual and doctrinal framework for understanding Christ's Atonement, thus helping us incrementally to engage its power at higher levels in our lives. Through the temple, the restored gospel offers a complete understanding of true discipleship and what it means to come fully unto Christ in a way that the rest of the Christian world would long to embrace if they only knew about it—but "they know not where to find it" (D&C 123:12).

For example, Allan Rau, an institute teacher and a stake president, shared with us his description of this sequential process:

> It is striking to me how often Christ is connected with covenants in [the Book of Mormon]. The message seems to be that if we desire the blessings Christ has to offer we must become his covenant people. . . . [and] the temple seems to be the logical extension of our covenant relationship with Christ. *While baptism seems to focus on the cleansing of the soul, the temple seems to focus on the development of the soul.* Each covenant provides guidance of what we ought to believe and do in order to become like God. [And] implicit in those covenants is the divine power to achieve what is clearly beyond our natural abilities.[15]

This insight echoes President James E. Faust's comment that the temple ordinances teach us about "the endless potential and development of each human soul."[16]

If we are too casual in approaching this doctrine, or too influenced by the teachings of other Christian churches, we could believe that coming unto Christ simply means confessing our belief in Christ, perhaps repenting of a few sins, and accepting baptism and confirmation. But if that is as high as we climb on our journey of the soul, we will miss the majesty of coming to know Him as He knows us (see 1 Corinthians 13:12) and discovering—through our sometimes heart-wrenching exertion toward Him—the fulness of the godly potential within us. Such is the treasure that awaits within the mountain of the Lord. And such is the reason we should symbolically take off our shoes, as we literally do in the temple, when we speak of Christ's Atonement.

CHAPTER 2

The Purpose of Christ's Atonement: Providing for Our Growth

S peaking of heart-wrenching exertion and taking off our shoes, a determined pioneer girl named Agnes Caldwell and her wise wagon master have something to teach us about climbing the mountain of the Lord.

Agnes was nine years old in October of 1856 when she and the rest of the Willie Handcart Company were wading through the wind-driven snow on the high plains of Wyoming. As they camped for the night at the sixth crossing of the Sweetwater, the snow was getting deeper, their rations were desperately meager, and Rocky Ridge was still ahead. Near sundown the next day, the relief party from the Salt Lake Valley would appear on the western horizon coming toward them.

Before the storm hit, Agnes had been taking each mile of the autumn trail in stride, even the one that had been strewn with rattlesnakes. For that mile, she and her friend Mary had held hands and jumped again and again over the snakes until they were out of danger, mercifully unharmed.

But after days of dragging her nearly frozen feet through the deepening snow, Agnes wasn't skipping anymore. And she was literally starving. The death toll in her company was rising with every passing night. Yet, of the arrival of the relief party, all Agnes records in her understated history is, "It certainly was a relief." And then she describes her own rescue:

> The infirm and the aged were allowed to ride, all able-bodied continued to walk. When the wagons started out, a number of us children decided to see how long we could keep up with the wagons, in hopes of being asked to ride. . . . One by one they all fell out, until I was the last one remaining, so determined was I that I should get a ride.
>
> After what seemed the longest run I ever made before or since, the driver, [Brother] Kimball, called to me, "Say, sissy, would you like a ride?" I answered in my very best manner, "Yes, sir." At this he reached over, [took] my hand, [then clucked] to his horses [which made] me run, with legs that seemed to me could run no farther. On we went [for what] seemed miles. . . . [I thought] he was the meanest man that ever lived or that I had ever heard of, and other things that would not be a credit . . . coming from one so young. Just at what seemed the breaking point, he stopped. Taking a blanket, he wrapped me up and lay me in the bottom of the wagon, warm and comfortable. Here I had time to change my mind, as I surely did, knowing full well [that] by doing this he saved me from freezing [to death].[1]

At first Agnes thought Brother Kimball was "the meanest man that ever lived" because, instead of swinging her up into his wagon as an act of tender mercy, he signaled his team to go faster, forcing her into a run. This run—this *severe mercy*[2]—increased her circulation, which saved her life.

This story has much to teach us about the redeeming and strengthening powers of the Atonement of Jesus Christ. We can see the symbolism: the wilderness strewn with rattlesnakes, the brutal and unexpected blizzard that turned the trail to Zion into a refiner's fire, the young girl with her passion and determination to give the journey everything she had, the wagon master who was loving enough to lend his strength yet wise enough to stretch her to her limits and courageous enough to volunteer for the rescue in the first place. This man didn't *have* to leave the comfort of his home, and this young girl didn't *have* to hang onto his hand when he pressed her to give more. Yes, he saved her life, but *so did she.* To be successful, the rescue effort had to be reciprocal. They both had to give it their all.

Is this a story about mercy? Yes. But we wouldn't usually think of mercy as sometimes being "severe" until we have considered it in the light of what Christ requires of those who desire to be His disciples.

As we've been discussing, these days more Latter-day Saints are using Atonement-related terms in talking about their spiritual experiences. This growing dialogue may be coming out of the muddy trenches of each of our lives and our sometimes desperate need to be assured of God's deliverance. Reaching deeper into the heart of the gospel is exactly what we ought to be doing when the storms are beating us down. But in our searching to explain our experiences, at times we may inadvertently draw one another away from the simple clarity of the restored gospel. This is partly because we share many key words with other Christian churches, for whom the meaning of those words may differ from what we intend. With the increasing amount of our discourse, there seems to be some growing confusion.

One young mother, trying diligently to unravel the confusion for herself, made a list of stories from the Book of Mormon in which God's power delivered or strengthened someone, often miraculously. Going down the list she asked, "When is this the

Atonement's enabling power, when is it priesthood power, or when is it simply an answer to a prayer?" She asked, "Are there situations when we should be calling on one of these powers rather than another one?" The doctrine of how to gain access to the Atonement's blessings was feeling like a riddle to her.

As we come to understand the Atonement's purpose and the nature of its blessings, the Savior's teachings clearly reassure us that He desires to help us lift our burdens. And knowing how He feels about us will increase our own desires to stick with Him no matter what. The better we understand why Christ *offered* Himself for us, the more willing we are to submit to whatever He may *ask* of us.

OUR GROWTH AND THE PURPOSE OF CHRIST'S ATONEMENT

Our earthly story begins with the story of Adam and Eve. A friend once asked, "If Jesus Christ is at the center of the gospel and the temple, why doesn't the endowment teach the story of the life of Christ? What's all this about Adam and Eve?" We have come to believe that while the story of Christ's life is the story of *giving* His Atonement, the story of Adam and Eve is the story of *receiving* His Atonement. And their story is *our* story.

Lehi told his children that if Adam and Eve had remained in the Garden of Eden, they would have known only innocence, and their souls could not have grown and developed. "And they would have had no children; wherefore they would have remained in a state of innocence, having no joy, for they knew no misery." And there's more: "doing no good, for they knew no sin. . . . Adam fell that men might be [mortal]; and men are [mortal], that they might have joy" (2 Nephi 2:23, 25).

So Adam and Eve's Fall was not a disaster, as traditional Christianity teaches. It was a great victory that marked the beginning of this journey we call mortality. When we each set foot on that trail, we begin to learn from daily experience—some of it harsh experience—the difference between evil and good, misery and joy. Yet this earth is not our home. It is as if we are away at school—but on a journey that promises to take us back Home in fulfillment of our Father's plan for our salvation and exaltation. Knowing just that much gives us a unique understanding of who we are, who God is, why we are here, and why we need the Atonement of Jesus Christ.

Let us look then at the overall *purpose* of the Atonement, which grows out of our purpose for coming to earth. That perspective explains why the Lord would at times take us by the hand and stretch us into a run.

The restored gospel gives us an understanding of the purpose of the Savior's grace and His Atonement that is very different from the perspective of other Christian churches. To understand that difference, we should take a brief look at what happened during the Great Apostasy. Since about the fifth century A.D., traditional Christianity has taught—incorrectly—that because of the Fall, we are born with an evil nature. As one well-known Christian creed states, Adam and Eve "by their disobedience lost their purity and happiness, and in consequence of their fall all men have become sinners, totally depraved."[3]

This erroneous idea further implies that our inborn evil nature is the primary cause of human sin. In other words, people sin mostly because they can't help it. In this view, only Christ's grace can overcome our depraved nature, and overcoming that depravity is the main purpose of grace. Only God decides to whom He will extend grace. Being evil, we can't choose it for ourselves. This understanding sees grace as a one-way infusion, not as the two-way interaction it really is.

So we Latter-day Saints have a challenge when we use terms like *grace* and *enabling power*, because those terms, long used by other Christian churches, sometimes proceed from their faulty doctrinal assumptions. Yet the Restoration corrected those doctrines with clarity and light about who we are and why we're on the earth. That clear truth resonates in our hearts every time we sing "O My Father" or "I Am a Child of God,"[4] hymns with echoes of divine parents, of having wandered from another sphere, and of an innate longing for heavenly parents who have not only bodies but also *hearts*—hearts like ours.[5] We came to the earth not as depraved sinners but as innocent beings "trailing clouds of glory"[6] and carrying the seeds of a potentially divine nature.

Modern-day scripture teaches us that we are born neither evil nor good by nature; rather, we are born "whole" (Moses 6:54) or "innocent" (D&C 93:38).[7] Then, in a mortal environment that is desirable in many ways yet is also deliberately subject to death and sinful influences, we will taste some sin and bitterness. This is not because we are inherently bad but because we can't learn to prize the sweet without actually tasting the bitter (see D&C 29:39; Moses 6:54–55). And because the effects of that bitterness may separate us from our Heavenly Father, we need Christ's Atonement to overcome whatever separates us from Him— such as the physical separation caused by death and the spiritual separation caused by our sins. That's what the word means: "at-one-ment," the act of reuniting what has been separated.

In addition, we need the Atonement to help us grow to become like Jesus Christ and our Heavenly Father because we cannot be "with Them" forever in the celestial realm until we are "like Them." In this sense, our immature capacity separates us from Them. So in planning how we could realize our full potential as

His children, our Father lovingly sent us away on a journey that gives us opportunities to mature in ways that can come only from traveling and coping our way through such a world as this one. At birth we are completely innocent, literally babes in the woods. Then as we grow up, like our first parents, we wrestle with such afflictions as sin and misery, and in that wrestling, paradoxically, we can learn what joy means. In that way, our sometimes demanding commitments to our children also help us discover the "joy" part of mortality.

The Savior's Atonement makes that learning process possible by protecting us while we discover through practice what love really is or why wickedness cannot produce happiness (see Alma 41:10). Because of the Atonement, we can learn from our experience without being condemned by it. So the Atonement is not just a doctrine about erasing black marks—it is the core doctrine that allows human development, fulfilling the gospel's overall vision and plan that humans can become like our Heavenly Father, one day having the godly capacity for eternal joy.

CHAPTER 3

HIS ATONEMENT: REDEEMING BLESSINGS

In some way unfathomable to the mortal mind, Jesus the Son of God completed the holy Atonement. Because of His sinless life and His willingness to drink the bitter cup, He was able to atone *unconditionally* for physical death and for Adam and Eve's original sin. He also atoned *conditionally* for our personal sins. *He redeemed us.*

As a solemn dimension of this same act, He also descended below all things so that He, after the manner of the flesh—having Himself experienced every fury of Hell and Darkness—could succor and be with each of us as we drink our own bitter cups. *He strengthens us.*

And then, through this same hallowed, atoning gift, He bestows yet more gifts—including His Godly nature—upon those who faithfully follow Him. *He perfects us.*

As we consider these wondrous gifts in closer detail, let us be clear at the outset that the Atonement of Jesus Christ is a singular, unified concept even while it has layered effects and dimensions. We will look at several of its core layers in an effort to clarify how its blessings apply in the differing circumstances and growth stages of our lives.

By analogy, think about the effects of light on a prism. A beam of light contains all the colors of the rainbow. But when that white beam passes through a prism, the prism reflects or refracts the full spectrum of colors the way sunlight passing through water particles can produce a rainbow. If you hold a piece of crystal up to a light, for example, you can see all the colors or one individual color, depending on the angle of your view and the angle of the light coming into the prism.

In the same way, the white light of the Savior's atoning sacrifice contains, and thus can reflect through a prism, the full spectrum of colors. In speaking here of the blessings of His Atonement, we seek better illumination by focusing on the main colors one at a time. When we then step back to look again at the whole, hopefully our minds and hearts will have greater perspective and appreciation for the full Light of His Atonement.

UNCONDITIONAL REDEEMING BLESSINGS

The Savior's Atonement offers us two different kinds of blessings—two levels of grace: *unconditional* blessings and *conditional* ones. The unconditional gifts of God's mercy and grace are given universally to everyone, blessing all of us endlessly, no matter what we do. The Father's mercy is in some sense the source of all our blessings, starting with His plan for us, the Creation, and our very presence on earth. One LDS woman in New Zealand, for example, expressed the absolute wonder she felt when she realized, "I live in a world where the Master of the Universe—the most powerful being in existence—just happens to know me, to love me, and to care about my eternal happiness. What did I ever do to deserve this? Aside from choosing to come to earth, not one thing."

One supernal unconditional miracle of the Atonement is our being redeemed from death—the universal Resurrection—a gift made possible for each of us by the grace of Christ.[1] Because He is risen, all will rise, and eventually all will kneel to acknowledge who He is.

The Savior's Atonement also paid unconditionally for Adam's original sin. Other Christian churches believe, incorrectly, that each person still needs grace to be cleansed from the "stain" of Adam's Fall, which they believe caused man's nature to be evil. But as the second Article of Faith states, men will be not punished for Adam's transgression. In the Lord's words to Adam, "The Son of God hath atoned for original guilt, wherein the sins of the parents cannot be answered upon the heads of the children, for they are *whole* from the foundation of the world" (Moses 6:54; emphasis added).

These are the unconditional blessings of the Atonement. They come to us all, regardless of our actions and choices.

CONDITIONAL REDEEMING BLESSINGS— FORGIVENESS

In addition to these unconditional blessings, the Savior's Atonement also offers us at least three kinds of *conditional* blessings, which for this discussion are grouped into these categories— we can be *forgiven, strengthened,* and *perfected,* on the condition that we participate fully in each of those processes. This chapter briefly discusses forgiveness as one of the Atonement's redeeming blessings, because forgiveness means redemption from sin.[2] The following two chapters consider more fully the strengthening and perfecting blessings.

The eternal law of *justice* requires payment for our sins. Yet the eternal law of *mercy* allows Christ's suffering to pay justice for those sins—on the condition of our repentance. If we do repent, the grace allowed by the law of mercy makes possible our forgiveness. As we sometimes stumble along, we have a perpetual need to repent and the continual opportunity to learn from our wrong choices and mistakes. This repenting and learning is matched by His constant willingness to forgive.

Our repentance does not repay Christ—in that sense, we don't "earn" His grace. However, as a condition of extending grace to us—and to help us grow—He asks us to undertake a process of change or rehabilitation that begins with forsaking our sins and, with serious sins, confessing them to priesthood leaders. This conditional dimension of grace, then, is a two-way exchange—His grace interacting with our repentance. As we humbly do all within our power, He will help us change, even when we feel shackled by habitual or addictive sins. In such weakness, the continuous power of Christ's Atonement[3] is an especially humbling blessing.

Removing sins and sinful habits from our lives is like removing weeds from a garden. It isn't enough just to *mow* the weeds. If we don't yank them up by the roots, they are still there, even if temporarily not very visible. Getting the weeds completely out requires digging and pulling, sweat, time, and effort—much more effort and discipline than a mere apology or even a confession.

Some young people, for instance, mistakenly assume they can romp in sinful mud until taking a shower of repentance just before being interviewed to receive temple ordinances or for a mission. In the very act of transgression, some plan to repent later—an attitude that mocks the gift of mercy that true repentance allows.

At the same time, some other people may work themselves into a state of exhaustion; after sincere efforts to change, they still feel hopelessly stuck and estranged from God. Sometimes that state of mind results from our inability to make restitution for a serious wrong when we correctly sense that restitution is an essential part of repentance. If we have stolen someone's money, for example, we can return what we took. But if we have stolen someone's virtue, or lost our own, it isn't possible for us to just give it back. Only the Savior can restore what to us is irretrievably lost, although even that process can exact long and painful cooperation on our part. Nonetheless, the Savior has the power to restore every loss, a restoration that is real and lasting. Those who discover this form of their dependence on the grace of Christ also discover the peace of knowing that they do have a personal Savior.

It helps to remember that repenting of our sins is different from paying for them. To repent means to change, not just to suffer—even though repentance often involves the real suffering of godly sorrow. Jesus has the infinite capacity to restore and repay, and He accepts the full burden of paying justice and restoring our spiritual losses. He will do this if and as we accept the personal responsibility to repent by changing our own attitudes, our habits, our minds, perhaps our friends, and certainly our hearts—to the fullest extent of our ability. As we do so, His grace helps to complete our change of heart.

In terms that apply to all of the Atonement's conditional blessings, Nephi said, "It is by grace that we are saved, after all we can do" (2 Nephi 25:23). Some people, perhaps because of an overdeveloped sense of self-reliance, think this means the Lord waits to help us until we have totally spent ourselves. However, placing Nephi's meaning within the Atonement's larger doctrinal context makes clear that *after* in this verse means "along with"— His grace is *with us* before, during, and after we do all we can.

CHAPTER 4

HIS ATONEMENT: STRENGTHENING BLESSINGS

When we take our repentance seriously, we can have the conversion experiences that Alma called the "mighty change of heart" (Alma 5:12–26), which can occur either suddenly or gradually. Thus begins the Atonement's interactive strengthening process, as our obedience interacts with His grace to fuel our spiritual growth. When this happened to King Benjamin's people, they had "no more disposition to do evil, but to do good continually" (Mosiah 5:2). They also made covenants to become "the children of Christ." Because He had "spiritually begotten" them, they were born again (Mosiah 5:7). This mighty change marked the beginning of their great journey of following Him.

This pathway of discipleship begins with the *redeeming blessings* of forgiveness. Then, aided all along the way by the *strengthening blessings,* the child of Christ continues in a lifetime growth process, gradually becoming the mature woman or man of Christ (see Helaman 3:29). Mature followers may then, if they so engage themselves, experience the *perfecting blessings* of becoming Christlike.

These three kinds of blessings all flow from the *relationship*

Christ creates with His disciples through the covenants of baptism and the sacrament. As our lives show that we are sincerely *willing* to take upon us *His name,* always to *remember* Him, and to *keep His commandments,* He keeps His covenant to us—that we will *always* have His Spirit to be with us. Through this close, two-way relationship, the Savior offers us the ongoing assurance of forgiveness, strength, and the continual nourishment of our spirits toward becoming like Him. As we comprehend more of His light, He offers us more because we are able to receive more (see D&C 50:24). This *relationship* is the foundation and the source of the strengthening and perfecting blessings that follow baptism.

Along this pathway, as we yield "to the enticings of the Holy Spirit," we will learn how to put off "the natural man"[1] and *become* "as a child, submissive, meek, humble, patient, full of love, willing to submit to all things" which the Lord sees "fit to inflict upon [us]" (Mosiah 3:19). If, however, we yield to the adversary more than we do to the Spirit, we will become like Adam and Eve's children who "loved Satan more than God" (Moses 5:13). Alma said that pursuing this carnal, sensual, and devilish path will ultimately "subject you to the spirit of the devil," who will "*seal you his*" (Alma 34:35; emphasis added), and then we will be like him—evil . . . and miserable. In contrast to that frightening prospect, if we remain on the covenant path, we have the promise from King Benjamin that Christ will eventually "*seal you his*" (Mosiah 5:15; emphasis added). Then we will be like *Him*—having a divine nature . . . and joy.

Many common experiences illustrate our need for the strengthening blessings along this narrow path, especially when we lose our way or we feel separated from God. Our spiritual progress can be thwarted not only by sin but also by other forces that can affect us the way sin does: feelings of inadequacy, unworthiness, or failure; regret or shame from harm we've caused, including unintended harm; feelings of being distant or estranged from family members or from the Lord's presence. It may be helpful to look at some specific examples of how we can be affected by weaknesses, mistakes, harm to us by others, and adversity—and how He intervenes to help as we do our part.

Weaknesses. Struggling with a sense of weakness as we face life's problems is at the very core of mortality's purpose—both the "necessary weakness inherent in the general human condition" and our "specific, individual weaknesses."[2] So when we notice our weakness or we feel inadequate, that doesn't mean there is something wrong with us. As we come unto Christ, He will actually help us see our weakness more clearly and then help us become stronger and wiser—if we humble ourselves enough to listen to Him: "If men come unto me I will show unto them their weakness. I give unto men weakness that they may be humble; and my grace is sufficient for all men that humble themselves before me; for, if they humble themselves before me, and have faith in me, then will I make weak things become strong unto them" (Ether 12:27).

When we thus find ourselves wrestling with our weaknesses, that could actually mean that we are moving nearer to God, not farther away. Some of the Lord's most stirring promises are spoken to those of us (that would be *all* of us at one time or another) who are simply feeling weak: "He giveth power to the faint; and to them that have no might he increaseth strength. Even the youths shall faint and be weary. . . . But they that wait upon the Lord shall renew their strength; . . . they shall run, and not be weary; and they shall walk, and not faint" (Isaiah 40:29–31).

Mistakes. One of the main reasons we are on this earthly journey is to learn by trial and error to discern the difference between good and evil. More than being here to learn facts, we are here to be schooled in character skills. In order to learn such skills as

playing the piano or riding a bike, for example, we need to practice—and practicing means watching for mistakes and learning
from them. We also learn by practice how to be more patient,
kind, compassionate, and charitable; and often we find ourselves
practicing on each other—we are each other's clinical material.
Knowing that this is how we all learn will help spouses and others
be more patient with one another in our families—the home-
room of the earth school. In short, we've come to earth to learn
about the skills of godliness—a learning process that takes a lifetime of tenacious, trial-and-error practice.

This kind of learning is, by its nature, often messy—that's
just how mistakes often look. Even when we're trying to correct
our errors, we probably won't be looking our best. It is easy to
get discouraged at such times. We may feel that we're continually falling short, missing the mark, and living lives marked more
by failure than by success. Nevertheless, because of the Lord's
Atonement, we can learn from our failed attempts without being
a failure. That insight is central to the reason why we are on the
earth rather than having stayed in a premortal world where we
learned only by theory, not by practice. So it really is true that our
only dumb mistakes are the ones we don't learn from.

At the same time, some of our mistakes are serious ones that
can cause real damage. Still, by definition, an unintentional mistake isn't sinful—so it doesn't require either repentance or forgiveness. Yet a mistake's consequences can look and feel enough like
the consequences of deliberate sin that we might yearn for the
same kind of healing as forgiveness because we don't want to feel
separated from the Lord, or we feel hopeless trauma from having
unwittingly harmed others.

One man, for example, unaware that his child was behind
his car, ran over and killed his own two-year-old in the family

driveway. This was the most devastating experience of this faithful man's life. He blamed himself and felt unworthy before God and with his family. But his mistake was not his fault, and it wasn't a sin. It was an accident. Over time, his covenant-based relationship with the Savior deepened to the depth of his pain, and he began to heal. Through the Lord's strength, he eventually made peace with his despair and self-doubt.

Harm inflicted on us by others. After a Church meeting a few years ago, we met a woman who had been sexually abused as a little girl. She felt betrayed, abandoned, and alone—tormented psychologically and spiritually. "For years," she said, "I have felt unclean and shut out from God's presence. But I didn't sin; I was sinned against. Can the Atonement help me?"

One illustration of our answer to her searching question comes from the story of a man we will call Tyler. He had been an active Church member all of his life, but his childhood had been filled with so many forms of abuse that he couldn't believe the Savior's strengthening promises could possibly apply to him. He was permanently broken, or so he felt. As he began learning that those promises were anchored in the deep roots of the Atonement, he sensed that they were real, but he still thought they were for other people.

Over time, as Tyler considered claiming these blessings for himself, he couldn't get past his belief that the blessings would be tainted by his touch—an unimaginable thought to many people, but one that came from his abusive conditioning. Gradually, and with the help of professional intervention, he unraveled that false belief—and many others—which allowed him to clasp the Lord's hand and engage *His* healing process. Now, as a teacher and a bishop, he is able to share his strength and rock-solid, compassionate faith with those in his care who have also been harmed by the choices of others.

Adversity. Adversity has many faces and sources—from physical afflictions like chronic pain or illness to emotional and spiritual trials like depression, lasting conflicts in close relationships, or questioning of one's faith. And any of these can disrupt or destroy our plans, our peace, and sometimes our sense of purpose.

For example, Allison's family life began with a temple marriage and the blessing of several children. As the children became teenagers, some of them made poor choices that began buffeting their family and straining her marriage. For years their family had tried to do everything "right"—scriptures, prayer, Church, temple, family home evening. Yet, she said, "What I had imagined and hoped for was not happening and I [felt] completely stuck. My frustrated mind cried out to Him, 'I was faithful and you left me anyway. Where is my support when all the fiery darts are being thrown at us?'"

Then, after four years of such dark times, a scripture opened to her that felt like a personal message from the Lord about mercy. "Hope began to again peek through my doubts. That small particle of hope in me stretched heavenward. Was God really merciful? Could I repent [and let] go of my doubting, and again be worthy of His support? I was willing to try."

She worked as hard as she knew how to keep her spiritual commitments and to reach out to her family members in healing ways. The healing didn't happen overnight, but over several years it came in small and simple ways. "Our burden," she said, "is being lifted—one scripture at a time, in a quiet prompting in the temple, as Primary children sing their testimonies, and through the kind words of friends who sometimes have no idea [about] the past heartaches."

After years of exerting herself and continuing to interact with the Lord, Allison describes how her children began to return. "My daughter came into my room, sat on the bed," and "for nearly two hours we talked, laughed, and cried. I had dreamed of moments like this. [From my son] I [now] receive my daily hug, which is expected and initiated by him." To see "the light of Christ again reflected in him" brings "such marvelous, peaceful joy that it far outweighs the sorrow of his past choices." Allison said that she had simply trusted Jesus enough to keep working hard herself. She supplied her desire and her work, and He supplied His strength.[3]

CONDITIONS

Like the redeeming blessings of forgiveness, the strengthening blessings are also conditioned on our doing "all we can do"—for some very good reasons related to the Atonement's purpose of nurturing our personal development. Thus certain basic conditions apply across the full range of our experience.

For example, many scriptural stories show that the Lord strengthens His people because of His covenant relationship with them—which demonstrates that keeping our covenants is a fundamental condition for gaining access to His strengthening grace. When the children of Israel were in Egypt, "God heard their groaning, and [He] *remembered his covenant* with Abraham, with Isaac, and with Jacob" (Exodus 2:24; emphasis added). And God said, "I have seen the affliction of *my* people . . . ; for I know their sorrows" (Exodus 3:7; emphasis added). Then this to Moses after crossing the Red Sea: "Ye have seen what I did unto the Egyptians [now, that's an understatement!], and how I bare you on eagles' wings, and brought you unto myself. Now therefore, *if ye will . . . keep my covenant,* . . . ye shall be unto me . . . an holy nation" (Exodus 19:4–6; emphasis added).

The same covenant language appeared in the Lord's

interaction with Alma's people when Amulon held them captive. "I, the Lord God, do visit my people in their afflictions" (Mosiah 24:14). Note: "my" people, not "the" people—"my" meaning those who had entered into covenants with Him, such as baptism. Further, "lift up your heads and be of good comfort, for I know of the covenant which ye have made unto me; and I will covenant with my people and deliver them out of bondage" (Mosiah 24:13). He keeps His covenant to strengthen us as we try diligently to keep our promises to Him.

However, He may not always deliver us out of bondage—at least not immediately—even if we are faithful. But He will strengthen us so that our burdens feel lighter, often using the burdens to teach us. We can't exactly say that He "atoned for" our burdens, in the sense of paying justice for them as He did for our sins. And it is probably not accurate to say that "the Atonement" itself delivered the people of Moses or Alma—or Allison or Tyler. But His Atonement is what qualifies Christ to enter into a personal, covenant relationship with His faithful followers. Then, through that relationship, *Christ Himself* strengthens them. In His words, "Fear not: for I have *redeemed* thee, . . . [and] thou art *mine*" (Isaiah 43:1; emphasis added). "I will *strengthen* thee; yea, I will help thee" (Isaiah 41:10; emphasis added).

For that reason, whenever we use the word *Atonement* in these pages, we intend that always to mean "the Atonement of Jesus Christ," even if, for ease of communication and to avoid too frequent repetition of His name (see D&C 107:4), we sometimes simply say "the Atonement" or "His Atonement." But we never want to diminish the Source of the Atonement's blessings, which is in the person of Christ and in His covenant relationship with His disciples.

The term *strengthen* in this context is more clear to us than the term *enable*. To *strengthen* means to make or become stronger, which assumes that we are already exerting our agency to do whatever we can. To *enable*, on the other hand, can mean to activate or make operational, which could imply that we lack the will (or the agency) to act righteously by ourselves. Said another way, *strengthen* suggests that the Lord adds His strength to ours, while *enable* could imply that He simply acts for us. Perhaps for this reason, some versions of Protestant theology teach that when God elects to extend grace to a sinner, that person is then freed from his sinful state, and "grace alone enables him freely to will and to do that which is spiritually good."[4]

We don't mean to overdo semantic issues, even when they have doctrinal implications. We recognize that the use of the term *enabling power* is so new in today's LDS vocabulary that many of us may not be quite sure what it means.[5] And in some sense, whatever *enabling* means, if seeking it draws us to the Savior, and that helps lift our burdens, perhaps that's what matters most.

At the same time, the essential place of kept covenants in the preceding stories does show that Christ extends His strengthening power only on certain conditions. We needn't be perfect, but we must strive wholeheartedly. As Jacob put it, "Come [to Him] with full purpose of heart, and *cleave* unto God as he *cleaveth* unto you" (Jacob 6:5; emphasis added). The doctrine that this form of grace is conditional differs from the traditional Protestant idea that grace is always a free gift.[6] But this pattern of two-way, interactive covenants is the Lord's way of encouraging us to do what only we can do—exert ourselves enough to participate meaningfully in the growth process. *Without our exertion, even God can't make us grow, no matter how much grace He extends.* Think of Agnes Caldwell, running. That severe mercy was unbelievably hard for her—but it pulled her into action that only she could exert, and it saved her life.

The scriptures use the term *grace* in a number of strengthening ways, nearly all of them conditioned on our taking some clear, energetic action. Some samples: "Teach ye diligently, and my grace shall attend you" (D&C 88:78). Alma's "priests were not to depend upon the people for their support; but for their labor they were to receive the grace of God" (Mosiah 18:26). And Moroni taught, "If ye shall deny yourselves of all ungodliness, and love God with all your might . . . then is his grace sufficient for you" (Moroni 10:32).

STRENGTHENING BY SUCCORING

Often the Savior *strengthens* us by *succoring* us. He is able to succor us as only He can because of the divine capacity for *empathy* that only He has.

Alma tells us that as part of His Atonement, Christ took upon Himself the "pains" and "infirmities" and "sicknesses of his people" (Alma 7:11–12). At the least, then, we do not suffer alone. And if we are fully engaged, He will also help us lift our burdens. Beyond that, did Alma mean that the Savior somehow "paid" justice for our infirmities the same way He "paid" for our sins? And did Alma mean that Christ *unconditionally* took upon Himself all human misery, thus relieving mankind of all injustice and suffering?

We don't believe so—because these interpretations would work against both the Atonement's reach and its purpose. For example, Alma speaks here of Christ strengthening not all people but "his people." Yet even for His people, He does not always remove their burdens, because that could undermine the process of their coming into their own spiritual maturity. Snatching us completely out of what King Limhi called our "effectual struggle" (Mosiah 7:18) would negate the very reason we came to earth, which is to master the traits of godliness while under intense pressure—the pressure that is required to produce those very traits within us. His grace allows us to be purified and sanctified by that pressure without being crushed by it.

Christ was able to extend the succoring dimension of His grace by "suffering pains and afflictions and temptations of every kind." He did this not to satisfy justice, but so "that he may know according to the flesh *how to succor his people*" (Alma 7:11–12; emphasis added). To *succor* means to help, aid, or give relief in time of need or distress. Thus all who trust God "shall be *supported* in their trials, and their troubles, and their afflictions" (Alma 36:3; emphasis added). Notice, "supported *in*."

After speaking of this succoring, Alma adds in the next verse that Christ also took "upon him the *sins* of his people, *that he might blot out their transgressions*" (Alma 7:13; emphasis added). Thus when He pays for our *sins* and we have repented, His act of mercy satisfies the demands of justice that sins must be paid for—and that *blots out* our transgressions. We are then forgiven, and the Lord will "remember [our sins] no more" (D&C 58:42). However, He experienced our non-sinful pains and infirmities not to satisfy justice and blot them out, but to give Him the empathy that allows Him to truly feel with and "succor his people."

We could miss what this understanding of succoring and grace *offers* us if we don't also grasp what it *asks* of us, and why. It's not that God will simply remove the hard things or take our pain completely away if we just decode the hidden messages or push the right button, such as when the computer screen says, "click here to enable." He asks us to give all we have to the refining process of grace—not to please or appease *Him*, but rather to engage *us*. There's Agnes again.

One of the survivors who had waded with Agnes through the handcart tragedy in Wyoming said, "We became acquainted with

[God] in our extremities. [And] the price we paid to [know Him] was a privilege to pay."[7] Not only can the Savior help us to survive suffering, but when we seek Him while in it, He will make weak things become strong unto us (see Ether 12:27). As our earnest seeking draws us closer to Him, fears become faith and trust, anger melts into meekness, anguish becomes empathy. Line upon line, grace for grace, He causes—if *we* will—the affliction to be consecrated for our gain (see 2 Nephi 2:2).

How does He consecrate our afflictions for our gain? It has something to do with what Elder Neal A. Maxwell called Christ's "earned empathy,"[8] derived from His submitting Himself to all of life's bitterness, descending "below all things" (D&C 88:6). Thus He could know from His own mortal, flesh-and-bones experience how to succor His people.

Perhaps His divine empathy was also, in part, a gift from His Father in answer to His prayer for His disciples: "Father, I pray . . . for all those who . . . believe in me, that I may be in them as thou, Father, art in me, that we may be one" (3 Nephi 19:23).[9] It is as if He were asking the Father to let Him feel with us the way the Father felt with Him. By being *in* us, He can feel with us so completely, so perfectly, as to be "at one" with us in our afflictions. And so He whispers to strengthen and encourage us—and to help us sense the larger purpose of our own refiner's fire—

> *Fear not, I am with thee; oh, be not dismayed.*
> *For I am thy God and will still give thee aid.*
> *I'll strengthen thee, help thee, and cause thee to stand,*
> *Upheld by my righteous, omnipotent hand.*
>
> *When through fiery trials thy pathway shall lie,*
> *My grace, all sufficient, shall be thy supply.*
> *The flame will not hurt thee; I only design*
> *Thy dross to consume and thy gold to refine.*[10]

CHAPTER 5

HIS ATONEMENT: PERFECTING BLESSINGS

The Lord's *perfecting* blessings can endow us with divine qualities, even His divine nature, through a process of becoming holy, like Christ. When He has helped to cleanse us from our earthly stains and has strengthened us through our tribulations to the greatest degree possible, we can become "invested, over a lifetime, with holiness from God."[1] This process is also referred to as sanctification—becoming a Saint.

Of this perfecting process, Moroni wrote these familiar lines: "*If* ye shall deny yourselves of all ungodliness, and love God with all your might, mind, and strength, *then* . . . by his grace ye may be perfect in Christ" (Moroni 10:32; emphasis added). The "if-then" connection here shows that the Lord's perfecting grace is also conditional—*if* we forsake ungodliness and love Him fully, *then* He will endow us with holiness.

Martha Humphreys, an early convert to the Church from Australia, wrote to her antagonistic mother that Martha's past life had been a "wilderness of weeds," but that after she found the gospel, "flowers [began springing] up [everywhere]."[2] The Savior's Atonement helps us both to remove the weeds in our lives and to plant flowers of goodness in their place. Through the interactive miracles of repentance, forgiveness, and grace, Christ works with us to remove our sinful weeds and any other obstacles between us and God. Then He helps us to plant and nourish the seeds of divine qualities like meekness, hope, and charity. The Lord's grace does help these flowers grow. But even then, there may still be a few weeds in our flowers, and a few flowers in our weeds—it's an organic process.

The gift of charity—the capacity to love others as Christ does—is perhaps the clearest example in the scriptures of a Christlike characteristic, thus illustrating how other completing qualities may come to us. Mormon urges, "Pray unto the Father with all the energy of heart, that ye may be filled with this love, which he hath *bestowed* upon *all who are true followers of his Son, Jesus Christ*; . . . that when he shall appear we shall be like him" (Moroni 7:48; emphasis added). Is charity, then, a gift of grace? Yes, it is "bestowed"—it comes from outside us, bestowed by the Holy Ghost (see Moroni 8:25–26).

Is charity also a *conditional* blessing, like many of the blessings of grace? Yes. Mormon tells us that charity is given only to those who meet the condition of having become "true followers" of Jesus. The participation required of us at this higher level asks us to stretch as far as we can. That stretching is one way we do "all we can do" (2 Nephi 25:23) in the interactive process of growing toward sanctification.

We will look more closely later at the conditions required for the sanctification process.[3] In general, at this level of our becoming more holy, the Lord asks us more about the spirit of the law, less about the letter of the law; more about our core internal attitudes, less about a mechanical list of dos and don'ts; more about consecration and sacrifice, less about our activity percentages.

Scriptures that describe the perfecting attributes say they are given to those who are, for example, "meek and lowly in heart" (Alma 37:34), or who yield "their hearts unto God" (Helaman 3:35).

Moroni asks that we "love God with all [our] might" (Moroni 10:32). We must love Him as fully as our limited personal capacity allows, but that doesn't mean we must reach some unreachable level of perfection by ourselves—for finally His grace is sufficient to "perfect" us in the sense of our becoming complete, fully mature in every way.

As we give everything we have to the Lord and He gives us everything He has, together and gradually we replace our noxious weeds with abundant flowers. Mormon describes this complete process beautifully, from the blessings of forgiveness and spiritual strengthening through sanctification and the endowment of charity:

> And the first fruits of repentance is baptism; and baptism cometh by faith unto the fulfilling the commandments; and the fulfilling the commandments bringeth remission of sins; and the remission of sins bringeth meekness and lowliness of heart; and because of meekness and lowliness of heart cometh the visitation of the Holy Ghost, which comforter filleth with hope and perfect love, which love [charity] endureth by diligence unto prayer, until the end shall come, when all the saints [the sanctified] shall dwell with God. (Moroni 8:25–26)

To illustrate how the sanctifying, perfecting blessings can come, we remember Elder Neal A. Maxwell. The quest of his life became his desire to be a true disciple of Jesus Christ. For years he thought about discipleship; he prayed about it, talked about it, and wrote about it. In his later years, he began to see in the lives of others that adversity could be sanctifying. He saw three sources of suffering: our own mistakes, life's natural adversities, and, at times, afflictions that the Lord might "inflict" on us to teach us.

Of the latter category Elder Maxwell wrote, "The very act of choosing to be a disciple . . . can bring to us a certain special suffering. . . . [It is a] dimension that comes with deep discipleship. [Thus] all who will can come to know [what Paul called] 'the fellowship of his sufferings' (Philippians 3:10)."[4] He also wrote the hardest line for all of us: "If we are serious about our discipleship, Jesus will eventually request each of us to do those very things which are the most difficult for us to do."[5]

In 1996, after years of teaching others about these principles, Elder Maxwell was stricken with leukemia at the age of seventy. As he worked to absorb the shock of that news, he said to those who knew the link he saw between discipleship and suffering, "I should have seen it coming." This was what he came to call the "wintry doctrine"[6]—the idea that we can't internalize real consecration without our own "clinical experiences."[7]

During the following eight years until his death in 2004, Elder Maxwell's own empathy toward other people increased. He discovered for himself what he had tried to teach others: The Savior is able to succor us in our afflictions because He has drunk the cup of affliction Himself—earned empathy. And those who knew Elder Maxwell during his own season of the wintry doctrine saw a sanctifying process at work in his life, in his teaching, in his interaction with others, and in his visits to the homes of fellow sufferers. At one point, he sensed the Lord answering his question about why. "I have given you leukemia so that you might teach the people with more authenticity."[8] No wonder Neal Maxwell would feel drawn, as he was, to a phrase like *severe mercy.*

As Elder Maxwell was struggling, he seemed to be discovering through his own experience the connection between charity and affliction—which may well be but two sides of the same coin. Thus those who seek to be Christ's true followers may in their own way need to emulate His sacrificial experience by their own sacrifice, not always through physical pain but also in other ways, at least enough to taste even a little of what His empathy and His charity are like. For only then are we becoming enough like Him to feel His love for others *the way He feels it*—to love "*as I have loved you*" (John 13:34; emphasis added).

Then, when we seek to "mourn with those that mourn" and "comfort those that stand in need of comfort" (Mosiah 18:9), our having known adversity and suffering ourselves will help us convey, to the extent of our capacity, our authentic compassion—our own modest degree of "earned empathy."

Little wonder, then, that Christ will not take away all of our suffering. After all, He said, "those who will not endure chastening [i.e., cleansing, refining, purifying] *cannot* be sanctified" (D&C 101:5; emphasis added). May we not be surprised, and may we not shrink, when we discover, paradoxically, how dear a price we may need to pay to receive the perfecting blessing of charity—which is, finally, a gift of grace.

Those who begin to receive charity will not only sense Christ's love for others, they will also sense His love for *themselves* in a way that assures them beyond any question that—despite their persistent weakness—their sacrifices and their lives are acceptable to Him. We imagine that day as one of the culminating moments of Christ's Atonement for all of us, when we shall be "like him, for we shall see him as he is," and we will be "purified even as he is pure" (Moroni 7:48). The Lord has promised that those whose "hearts are honest, and are broken, and their spirits contrite, and are willing to observe their covenants by sacrifice . . . are *accepted* of me" (D&C 97:8–9; emphasis added). Perhaps that was Lehi's experience when he felt himself "encircled about eternally in the arms of his [Redeemer's] love" (2 Nephi 1:15).

We knew a very faithful older woman in Brisbane, Australia, who was present on a night in 1997 when President Gordon B. Hinckley talked to several thousand Australian Saints in a large stadium. As he concluded, he testified of the Lord's love for them, and he expressed his confidence in them in a way that somehow invited an especially calming spirit to descend. The next day, this sister said to us, "I have never believed that my life could really be acceptable to the Lord. But as President Hinckley spoke to our hearts, I felt for the first time that, despite all of my frailties, the Lord could *accept* me. I was astounded."

Our friend Donna grew up with the girlhood dream of marrying and raising a large family. But that blessing never came. Instead, she spent her adult years serving the people in her ward with unmeasured compassion and counseling disturbed and learning-disabled children in a large school district. She had crippling arthritis and experienced many long, blue days. Yet she always lifted and was lifted by her friends and family. Once, when teaching about Lehi's dream, she said with gentle humor, "I'd put myself in that picture on the strait and narrow path, still holding on to the iron rod, but collapsed from fatigue right on the path." And she never felt that her single life could be acceptable. But in an inspired blessing given just before her death, Donna's home teacher said her life was "acceptable" to the Lord. The Spirit rushed in. Tears came. No word could have meant more to her.

As these two women found, not only will the Lord forgive us and ease our burdens, He will also accept and perfect the honest in heart who observe every sacrifice with a contrite spirit—even when their lives fall short of flawless perfection. The Atonement of Jesus Christ makes this acceptance both real and possible, and

He stretches forth His accepting hands unto us "all the day long" (Jacob 6:4).

The heart of Agnes Caldwell's rescue was in the moment when her hand met the hand of the wagon master in that lifesaving clasp. So it is between each of us and Christ. The redeeming, strengthening, and perfecting blessings of His Atonement cannot be unveiled in us until we willingly reach for His outstretched hand, clasp ours in His, and hang on—no matter how fast we need to run or how fiercely the storm may rage.

CHAPTER 6

THE TEMPLE ORDINANCES AND THE TWO PRIESTHOODS

Just as young Agnes Caldwell found deliverance in the freezing snows of Wyoming, the Lord's chief Apostle, Simon Peter, also came to know the strength of a rescuing clasp amid the white-caps of storming Galilee. In Peter's case, however, the rescuer was no proxy. The Rescuer Himself took Peter's hand and saved him from drowning in fear. And just as the trek west was a sanctifying journey for Agnes, so was Peter's journey a sanctifying one through his own times of wilderness both during and beyond Christ's mortal ministry.

At every opportunity, Jesus was preparing Peter to hold the keys of the priesthood after He took His last steps of ascension to His Father. By the time Peter reached his own inverted crucifixion, Peter the impetuous fisherman had truly become Peter the rock—the first and magnificently mature prophet of the early Christian Church. And his role in the landmark moments of the Restoration tells us that he continues to hold significant responsibilities in the kingdom of God in our dispensation.

For example, in 1829 the Lord revealed that He had given certain keys to Peter, James, and John that would be in effect until the Second Coming (see D&C 7:7). Only a month later, when John the Baptist conferred the Aaronic Priesthood upon Joseph and Oliver, he told them that "he acted under the direction of Peter, James and John, who held the keys of the Priesthood of Melchizedek" (Joseph Smith—History 1:72). Not long afterward, those same three men conferred that higher priesthood upon Joseph and Oliver (see D&C 27:12–13).

Less well known is Peter's intriguing appearance at the Kirtland Temple dedication in 1836, a visit that hints at Peter's role with temples. During the dedication, an angel entered through a window and sat next to Joseph Smith Sr. The Prophet later told the congregation that this angel was Peter, who had been sent as a *messenger* to accept the temple dedication.[1]

Why would the Lord send Peter for that purpose? Perhaps it was because Peter holds the keys for the Melchizedek Priesthood, and the temple ordinances *are* the primary ordinances of that priesthood. Thinking of Peter in this way prompts these further thoughts: The primary ordinances of the Aaronic Priesthood are baptism and the sacrament. Those ordinances are also intertwined with the first principles of the gospel—faith and repentance.

Could there be a similar interactive relationship between the ordinances of the higher priesthood and some set of higher gospel principles?

The primary ordinances of the Melchizedek Priesthood are confirmation, priesthood ordination (for brethren), and the endowment and sealing ordinances of the temple.[2] Those higher ordinances are indeed intertwined with such higher principles and laws as sacrifice and consecration. Our progression from the preparatory priesthood through the levels of the higher priesthood, fueled along the way by the link between ordinances and principles, suggests an ascending pattern that is anchored in the laws of God that govern our spiritual growth.

And we learn this sequential pattern in the temple. The more we live what we learn there, the deeper this temple-template is imprinted upon our lives, which can make a temple of us. "Know ye not that ye are the temple of God?" (1 Corinthians 3:16). As that happens, the same template also applies Christ's Atonement to every stage of our personal development as we, like Adam and Eve, thereby fully *receive and engage* the Atonement and its blessings.

DIFFERENCES BETWEEN THE AARONIC AND MELCHIZEDEK PRIESTHOODS

Whatever Peter's exact duties are, the high priesthood for which he holds keys is clearly related to the higher ordinances of the temple. Only in the ordinances and authority of "this greater priesthood"—the temple ordinances—can "the power of godliness" be "manifest unto men in the flesh" (D&C 84:19–21). We learn from Moses's interaction with the children of Israel what we will miss if we do not receive those blessings of the high priesthood: Moses "sought diligently to sanctify his people that they might behold the face of God; But they hardened their hearts and could not endure his presence; therefore, the Lord . . . swore that they should not enter into his rest" (D&C 84:23–24). And when God took away Moses and the higher priesthood, the people could no longer be sanctified by participating in the higher priesthood's ordinances. Even so, God let them retain the Aaronic Priesthood, signaling that they needed further preparation.

The Lord has explained that the "lesser" or Aaronic Priesthood "holdeth the key of . . . the *preparatory gospel;* Which gospel is the gospel of repentance and of baptism, and the remission of sins, and the law of carnal [or temporal] commandments" (D&C 84:26–27; emphasis added). Moreover, this preparatory priesthood administers the "outward ordinances, the letter of the gospel, [and] the baptism of repentance for the remission of sins" (D&C 107:20). In other words, while yet *outside* the temple, the ordinances of the lesser priesthood prepare us to participate *inside* the temple.

The first principles and ordinances of the gospel—faith, repentance, and baptism—are thus identified with the "preparatory" or "outward" ordinances of the lesser priesthood, in contrast to the "internal," more mature ordinances of the higher priesthood. That higher priesthood holds "the keys of all the *spiritual* blessings of the church" including "the privilege of receiving the mysteries of the kingdom" and becoming worthy and able to enjoy "the communion and presence" of the Father and the Son (D&C 107:18–19; emphasis added). And *such higher principles as sacrifice and consecration are to the higher ordinances what the principles of faith and repentance are to the preparatory ordinances.*

These scriptures about the two priesthoods[3] make this simple point: As essential as are faith, repentance, and baptism—so essential and fundamental that all of us must rely constantly on their power and their blessings—those elements really are "first" or "preparatory." There is more. And we can find key portions of that "more" through the initiatory, endowment, and sealing ordinances—in combination with the higher gospel principles that teach us to practice in our lives what we learn in the temple.

Obedience to the ordinances and principles of the Aaronic Priesthood makes us eligible for individual *salvation*—the threshold entrance into the celestial kingdom. Beyond that, participating in the temple ordinances and keeping our covenants to live the higher principles will then help us qualify for *exaltation* with our families—the highest of the three celestial degrees of glory, where marriage and family relationships continue eternally (see D&C 131:1–4). That is why Brigham Young said that the temple endowment provides "all those ordinances in the house of the Lord, which are necessary" for us to "gain [our] eternal exaltation."[4]

BEYOND BAPTISM: WHAT THE HIGHER ORDINANCES AND PRINCIPLES ADD

We don't always speak of this complete pattern of the two priesthoods as much as we could—or perhaps should—and therefore we risk missing the invitation to ascend the mountain of the Lord.

For example, we teach our missionaries "to invite others to come unto Christ by helping them receive the restored gospel through faith in Jesus Christ and His Atonement, repentance, baptism, receiving the gift of the Holy Ghost, and enduring to the end."[5] And clearly, the principles of faith and repentance are not only "first" in the natural sequence of conversion but also "first" as the foundation for every step of our spiritual growth. These are the principles that allow us to learn and grow continually from all of our experience—a vital, lifelong process made possible by our continued reliance on Christ's Atonement. Indeed, those who "hold out *faithful* to the end" have the promise of eternal life (Mosiah 2:41; emphasis added).

Sometimes, however, we refer to the first principles as if they represented the entire process of discipleship. When we do that, "endure to the end" can sound like an afterthought, as if our baptism and confirmation have hooked us like a trout on God's fishing line, and so long as we don't squirm off the hook, He will reel us safely in. Or some assume that "endure to the end" simply describes the "no worries" stage of life, when our main job is to just enjoy frequent trips to our cozy retirement cottage while refraining from doing anything really bad along the way.

But there *is* more. As President Russell M. Nelson has said, "Enduring to the end . . . means the endowment and sealing ordinances of the holy temple."[6] And Noel and Sydney Reynolds, former president and matron of the Mount Timpanogos Utah Temple, believe that "endure to the end" is a gospel principle that is paired with the temple endowment, just as repentance is paired with baptism. President Reynolds said this is the stage when we decide if we really want to become as the Father and the Son are.[7] Nephi offered a similarly expansive view of "enduring"—we should "*endure to the end, in following the example of the Son of the living God*" (2 Nephi 31:16; emphasis added). The first principles will always be first—yet they are but the foundation for pressing on toward the Christlike life: "Therefore, *not leaving* the principles of the doctrine of Christ, let us *go on unto perfection;* not laying again the foundation of repentance from dead works, and of faith toward God, . . . [and] baptisms" (JST, Hebrews 6:1–2; emphasis added).

Nephi also makes clear that faith, repentance, baptism, and the Holy Ghost are but the entry gate—the trailhead—for our lifelong spiritual journey toward the goal of eternal life. Now we must energetically press forward along the narrow path, seeking hope and charity and feasting, not snacking, on Christ's words, because His words, through the Holy Ghost, "will tell you all things what ye should do" (2 Nephi 32:3).

Tell us what to do? About what?

Nephi said he was not free to explain further what he meant by telling us to feast on Christ's words for more direction. He said, "The Spirit stoppeth mine [further] utterance" about that. He was allowed only to tell us to "pray always," and that we should not "perform any thing unto the Lord" without asking God to "consecrate thy performance unto thee," so that it "may be for the welfare of thy soul" (2 Nephi 32:7–9). One place where we might hear the Savior's words in this way is through the reverent and frequent performance of temple ordinances and temple worship, along with personal revelation.

LIVING THE HIGHER ORDINANCES HELPS US BECOME COMPLETE, AS HE IS

The temple endowment reflects for both men and women the sequential process of spiritual growth that we have seen in the relationship between the lesser and the higher priesthoods. As President David O. McKay said, the endowment represents our "step-by-step ascent into the eternal presence. If our young people could but glimpse it, [this] would be the most powerful spiritual motivation of their lives."[8] As crucial as they are, when we focus mostly on the faith/repentance/baptism steps in that ascent, we are seeing only the first legs of the spiritual climb.

In his classic 1920 sermon on temple worship, for example, Elder John A. Widtsoe said:

> Some people, having obeyed these first principles, believe their work done. They are members of God's chosen people— what more need they? . . . [But] the gift of the Holy Ghost . . . is a promise of growth into a larger life and a larger condition of life. . . . [That] promise of added intelligence is realized in part at least in the worship and ordinances of the temples of the Lord. . . . [Therefore] through obedience to the first principles of the Gospel *and a subsequent blameless life* a person may win salvation. . . . [However,] those who [truly] hunger and thirst for righteousness . . . will advance farther than those who placidly sit by with no driving desire within them. Temple worship is an avenue to *exaltation* in God's kingdom.[9]

Elder Widtsoe thus makes clear that the desire for exaltation asks us to actively *step up,* to grow, moving far beyond just doing nothing harmful.

The theme of lifelong spiritual learning and growth was

absolutely central to Joseph Smith. "When you climb up a ladder," he said, "you must begin at the bottom, and ascend step by step, and so you must begin with the first [principles], and go on until you learn all the principles of exaltation."[10] Thus Joseph prayed at the Kirtland Temple dedication "that all those who shall worship in this house . . . may *grow up in thee, and receive a fulness of the Holy Ghost*" (D&C 109:14–15; emphasis added).

SYMBOLS OF THE ASCENDING JOURNEY IN THE TEMPLE'S PHYSICAL PATTERN

When temple work for the dead was first fully instituted in 1877 in the St. George Temple, temple patrons would take each name through each step in the complete sequence of ordinances, rather than doing only baptisms and confirmations, or only initiatory ordinances, or endowments, or sealings on a given day. The grouping of ordinances into today's typical categories occurred only recently to serve the increasing number of patrons more efficiently; however, the original pattern may have shown more clearly the symbolic nature of the ascending sequence of Aaronic followed by Melchizedek Priesthood ordinances.

In addition, the early temples (in some ways, even as early as the Nauvoo Temple)[11] also followed a symbolically important and ascending room-to-room pattern. Again, the modern practice of combining some of these steps into one or two rooms of the temple is for reasons of practical convenience. The room-to-room approach, however, clarified how the entire pattern of the ordinances reflected the climbing, step-by-step nature of each person's progress and growth through the mortal journey back to the Lord's presence. The use of lighting in the current pattern does keep enough of this symbolism to show that it matters.

In those older temples, in order to complete all of the needed ordinances in their natural sequence, patrons began each set of ordinances in the temple's basement or lower level. Then they walked physically upward (in some cases only slightly, but still upward) from room to room—starting with the baptistry, then up to the creation room, up to the garden room, up to the world room, up to the terrestrial room, up to the celestial room, and finally up to the sealing room. This climb symbolizes the "step-by-step ascent" that President McKay referred to.[12]

And the symbols do teach us. A seasoned architect told us that he received his own endowment in a temple where the ordinance is performed in a single room. But he said he didn't really grasp what the endowment teaches about our life journey until he went to the Salt Lake Temple, which still uses all of the original rooms showing each stage of upward progress.

ADDITIONAL BLESSINGS OF CHRIST'S ATONEMENT THROUGH HIGHER ORDINANCES AND PRINCIPLES

Do the blessings of Christ's Atonement play any role in the post-baptism, Melchizedek Priesthood part of this journey? Or does the Savior just get His followers started on their path with baptism and confirmation and expect them to take the rest of the ascending steps on their own?

Elder David A. Bednar has said that the fruit of the tree in Lehi's dream is a symbol for all of the Atonement's blessings. Elder Bednar then invited us to think of baptism and confirmation as only the gate that puts us on the path toward the tree of life. Then, he wrote, "pressing forward [along the path] and partaking of the fruit of the tree may represent the receiving of *additional ordinances and covenants* whereby the Atonement can become *fully* efficacious in our lives."[13] The natural, even obvious, place for those additional ordinances and covenants is the temple.

This doctrinal pattern suggests how the sequence of Aaronic and Melchizedek Priesthood ordinances—and the principles associated with them—invite us through the complete process of our spiritual growth from salvation to exaltation: baptism, confirmation, the sacrament, receiving the priesthood (for brethren), the initiatory ordinances, the endowment, and the sealing blessings.

Throughout these ascending and sequential steps, we are blessed by the redeeming, strengthening, and perfecting powers of the Atonement. The Savior's *redeeming* blessings connect especially to the first principles and ordinances, even though they play a continual and critical role thereafter. Then His *strengthening* and *perfecting* blessings especially help us after baptism as we move from being forgiven (sometimes repeatedly) through the growing pains of learning from opposition and, eventually, being filled with Christlike love and character. Thus can we "endure to the end, in following the example of the Son of the living God" (2 Nephi 31:16).

Even though the idea of sequential steps helps us to see more clearly the normal process of personal spiritual development, it is also clear that all of these steps, and all of the Atonement's blessings, throughout both priesthoods and all ordinances, work together in the wholeness we call the gospel of Jesus Christ. In addition, they overlap and interact together constantly. We are never "done" with faith or repentance, and we can have access to the Savior's power and blessings continually throughout our journey.

In the analogy of white light passing through a prism, the sequence of the two priesthoods and the temple ordinances is like the gradation of individual colors in the spectrum of the rainbow. As we better understand and live each covenant and each principle—each color in the spectrum—we can better comprehend the whole. As we progress in following the given patterns, we are led incrementally to the Source of all Light. Then we are better able focus our "eye single to [His] glory," until our "whole bodies shall be filled with light" (D&C 88:67).

CHAPTER 7

THE TEMPLE AND THE
DOCTRINE OF SACRIFICE

The role of sacrifice in the temple illustrates how the temple ordinances embody and teach higher Melchizedek-level principles. These ordinances reflect Christ's sacrifice, and they teach us symbolically how our own sacrifices might seek to echo His. As our Primary children sing, "He knows I will follow him, Give all my life to him."[1]

PERFORMING ORDINANCES IN SIMILITUDE
OF CHRIST'S SACRIFICE

When they left the Garden of Eden, Adam and Eve built an altar and offered animal sacrifices. Then an angel came to ask Adam *why* he was offering sacrifices. He answered, "I know not, save the Lord commanded me." The angel told him, "This thing is a similitude of the sacrifice of the Only Begotten" (Moses 5:7). The unblemished lambs they sacrificed pointed them toward the Father's future sacrifice of His Son. The angel then taught Adam and Eve that Christ's sacrifice and the plan of redemption gave meaning and purpose to their entire earthly experience, from their fall from Eden until their mortal death and beyond.

Many of us go to the temple today the way Adam and Eve first offered sacrifices—simply because we are commanded, without knowing why. Simple obedience is certainly better than not performing the ordinances at all. But the Lord who sent that angel must have wanted Adam and Eve to know why they performed the ordinances—and I believe He wants *us* to know why we do.

Are today's temple ordinances also "a similitude of the Only Begotten"? Think of how the temple's altars are—like the altar of Adam and Eve—altars of prayer, sacrifice, and covenant. Think of the elements of sacrifice in all the covenants of the endowment. Since Christ completed His atoning mission, we no longer offer animal sacrifice, but He does invite us to sacrifice in the same way that He taught the Nephites: "Ye shall offer for a sacrifice unto me a broken heart and a contrite spirit" (3 Nephi 9:20).

Animal sacrifice was symbolic of the Father's sacrifice of the Son. But the sacrifice of a broken heart and a contrite spirit symbolizes and emulates the Son's sacrifice of Himself. With great reverence, Elder James E. Talmage wrote that Jesus literally "died of a broken heart."[2] To receive the blessings of His blessed offering, Christ now asks us to offer ourselves—our own broken hearts—as a *personal* sacrifice. Though it be as meager as a widow's mite, our offering is indeed "a similitude" of His sacrificial offering to and for us. As Elder Neal A. Maxwell said, "Real, personal sacrifice never was placing an animal on the altar. Instead, it is a willingness to put the animal *in us* upon the altar and letting it be consumed!"[3]

We promise to sacrifice ourselves in this personal way throughout the temple ordinances. Then we leave the temple and reenter our daily lives, where we try to live the covenants we made at the altars of sacrifice. The Savior's strengthening and perfecting blessings, along with the priesthood power of the temple, can then interact with our moment-to-moment striving, helping us press forward to become more fully consecrated followers of Jesus. As the sixth Lecture on Faith teaches, "A religion that does not require the sacrifice of all things never has power sufficient to produce the faith necessary unto life and salvation."[4]

Each time we make or renew sacrificial covenants, we deepen our resolve to live a more sacrificial life—living outside ourselves in love more fully each day, in similitude of His Great Sacrifice. In the temple, He gives us added light and strength to keep that resolve when we leave the temple. As we then live that way, our discoveries make us better able to comprehend His light. Then, with each new step, our experience takes us to slightly higher ground, from where we can take the next step toward receiving added light in an ever-expanding process: "He that receiveth light, and continueth in God, receiveth more light; and that light groweth brighter and brighter until the perfect day" (D&C 50:24).

We are learning the mysteries of God, but the process isn't that mysterious. It is like going to a music teacher for a lesson and then diligently practicing the next assignment until the next lesson. In each temple tutorial, the Master Teacher discerns and assigns specifically what needs our attention, and we witness physically our willingness to pay attention. The depth of our devotion to Him and the growing rigor of our discipline increase our comprehension of His sacrifice because we are becoming more aware of the price of our own sacrifices and the fruit they produce. Gradually we will realize the promise of being "filled with light" and comprehending "all things," including the mysteries and knowledge of God (D&C 88:67). Therefore, "sanctify yourselves, that your minds become single to God" (D&C 88:68).

MAKING SACRIFICES AND LIVING IN SIMILITUDE—
THE MARRIAGE SEALING

To illustrate more specifically how this process works, consider the sealing ordinance. Not long ago, I was about to seal a young couple in the St. George Temple. I invited them to the altar, and as the groom took the bride by the hand, I realized that they were about to place upon that altar of sacrifice their own broken hearts and contrite spirits—an offering of themselves to each other and to God in emulation of Christ's sacrifice for them. And for what purpose? So that through a lifetime of sacrificing for each other— that is, trying to live as He did—they might *become* ever more as He is.

By seeking to live that way every day, they would each come closer to God, which would also bring them closer to each other. Through their increasing closeness to the Lord, their own energy and discipline would also draw upon the strengthening and perfecting powers He offers them through their covenant relationship with Him as His son and daughter. This way of living the covenants of the sealing ordinance would then sanctify not only their marriage but also their hearts, even their lives.

The more our sacrifices help us find Christ in the temple, the more we will find Him in our lives—and that process will *transform* us over time, preparing us to live one day in the exalted company of those seen in vision by President Joseph F. Smith: "And there were gathered together in one place an innumerable company of the spirits of the just, who had been faithful in the testimony of Jesus while they lived in mortality; And *who had offered sacrifice in the similitude of the great sacrifice of the Son of God,* and had suffered *tribulation* in their Redeemer's name" (D&C 138:12–13; emphasis added).

As this exalted language suggests, those who seek the life of mature discipleship at the Melchizedek Priesthood level are likely to find that the higher principles and covenants of sacrifice are often linked to such related higher principles as suffering, meekness, consecration, and sanctification.[5]

In a sense, the sealing ordinance also invites us into the fellowship of Christ's suffering, as our marriage covenants may at times ask us to suffer—to be afflicted in—one another's afflictions. The children born of that sealing may also bring us into this fellowship, as we may at times endure real anguish in bringing them here, rearing them, and suffering with them through their dark valleys. This sacrificial living of our temple covenants can "bring to us a certain special suffering," and thus a special joy, "that comes with deep discipleship."[6]

CHAPTER 8

THE TEMPLE AND THE POWER OF GODLINESS MADE MANIFEST

Another significant dimension of the higher priesthood's spiritual power is that it holds "the key of the *mysteries* of the kingdom, even the key of the knowledge of God." Therefore, in the temple ordinances, "the *power of godliness* is manifest . . . unto men in the flesh" (D&C 84:19–21; emphasis added). Or, as Truman Madsen put it, the temple offers "the ordinances of godliness."[1] As used here, "godliness" suggests "the state of being like God, of approximating God's nature or qualities."[2]

Joseph Smith urged the Saints to "go on to perfection, and search deeper and deeper into the *mysteries of Godliness*."[3] And President Harold B. Lee said that these mysteries are found in the temple endowment:

> These revelations, which are reserved for and taught only to the faithful Church members in sacred temples, constitute what are called the "mysteries of Godliness." The Lord said He had given to Joseph "the keys of the mysteries, and the revelations which are sealed" (D&C 28:7). As a reward to the faithful, the Lord promised: "And to them will I reveal all mysteries,

yea, all the hidden mysteries of my kingdom from days of old"
(D&C 76:7).[4]

FORSAKING UNGODLINESS

The temple ordinances manifest the power of godliness in
several ways.

First, we can bring one part of the power of *godliness* into our
own lives simply by choosing to deny ourselves of *ungodliness* (see
Moroni 10:32). That choice alone makes us a little more godly.
The choice of self-denial is, as Elder D. Todd Christofferson said
of the choice to repent, "a self-willed change."[5]

This illustrates one way in which all of our temple covenants
can influence the way we choose to live. Trying to offer the attitude of a broken heart and a contrite spirit to our families "in
similitude" of the Savior will encourage us to see our spouses and
our children as He sees them. I still remember the woman, for
example, who patiently helped her husband for years until he
overcame a deep-seated addiction. I asked, "How did you do it?"
She said, "I just tried to see him as the Savior sees him." Trying to
live that way, even when we often fall short, will etch the Lord's
pattern of marriage and family life upon our hearts. And by our
own exertion we will become better companions, better parents,
and better people—just as people who choose to live the Word of
Wisdom will have better health.

GODLINESS THROUGH THE
ATONEMENT'S PERFECTING BLESSINGS

As we deny ourselves of ungodliness and seek to give our
hearts to the Lord (see Moroni 10:32), His perfecting blessings will then help us to become more saintly, even more godly.
King Benjamin taught that we can "becom[e] a saint through
the atonement" (Mosiah 3:19) as the Lord's influence leads us to

develop saintly qualities. The Apostle Peter spoke of this process when he urged us to become "partakers of the divine nature" (2 Peter 1:4).

I once asked a group of temple workers if working in the temple really had helped them to develop greater meekness, humility, love, and submissiveness—qualities that help move us toward a divine nature.[6] Listening to their uplifting personal examples, I asked myself—are these dear people more saintly because they love the temple, or do they love the temple because they are so saintly? That is, are they sanctified *by* the temple or *for* the temple? Both dimensions matter, but our time in the St. George Temple left us with no question—the temple lifted us to find Him and know Him better than before. After all, in the words of President Thomas S. Monson, in the temple we can find "a dimension of spirituality and . . . peace which will transcend any other feeling which could come into the human heart."[7]

As Marie recently related, "As I was walking up to the temple one day, I came upon a grandmotherly woman—one of our temple workers—bending over, tending to the flowers near the front door. She looked up. Her aging face was alive with light— the face of a lifetime of temple worship and [the sacrifices of] temple living. Her countenance enveloped me in the aura of the temple and filled me with the desire to have that same happy holiness in me."[8]

"WITH YOU"—GODLINESS AS BEING WITH CHRIST THROUGH THE ORDINANCES

Further, the power of godliness can enhance and deepen our personal relationship with the Lord simply by drawing us closer to Him, opening our hearts to whatever we most need from Him at a given time. In the temple we are endowed "with *power* from on high" (D&C 95:8; emphasis added). Captain Moroni wrote that his people had gained *power* over their enemies by their faith, their religion, and their *"rites of worship,"* along with their "maintenance of the sacred word of God, to which we owe all our happiness" (Alma 44:5; emphasis added).

Drawing on Moroni's comment about gaining power from rites of worship, BYU professor Daniel Belnap has written that the "power of godliness" may refer to the mental and spiritual state a mortal must be in to interact with divinity. If so, temple ordinances offer not only a *symbolic* way of learning but "an *actual* experience" that makes us more conducive to the Spirit as a means of preparing to enter into God's presence.[9] Joseph Smith once said that knowledge about the purpose of mortality "can only be obtained by experience *through the ordinances of God set forth for that purpose.*"[10]

Speaking of the endowment as given in Nauvoo, Richard Bushman wrote that "the temple's sacred story stabilized and perpetuated Joseph's governing passion," which "was to have his people *experience God.*"[11] That is also why Moses "sought diligently to sanctify his people that they might behold the face of God" (D&C 84:23–24). Apparently both Moses and Joseph wanted for their people what they had experienced themselves.

Joseph Smith offered a similar thought in his translation of the Gospel of Mark in a passage about the sacrament. In the King James Version, Jesus said of the bread, "Take, eat: this is my body." And then of the wine, "This is my blood of the new testament, which is shed for many" (Mark 14:22–24). But in his translation of these verses, Joseph told us that the Savior further said, "This is for you to do in remembrance of my body; for as oft as ye do this ye *will remember* this hour that I was *with you.*" Then, as He offered them the wine, He said, "And *as oft as ye do this ordinance,* ye *will remember me* in this hour that I was with you and drank with you of this cup" (JST, Mark 14:21–24; emphasis added).

He did not say "you *should* remember me" but rather, "you *will* remember me." Perhaps the sacrament and the temple ordinances can somehow quicken our awareness and remove the veil from our eyes and minds to help us realize that He is *with us* in our most trying moments or seasons, just as He was literally with those three men in the furnace of their affliction described in the book of Daniel (see Daniel 3). After all, it is only because He drank *His* bitter cup that the bitter cups of our own sacrifices can be sanctifying to us. Without Him, our sacrifice alone would not sanctify us. Just as grace can be reciprocal, there is a reciprocity of sacrifice. He gives Himself to us; we seek to give ourselves to Him.

The phrase *with you* in these verses took on added meaning for us when we were in Sweden for one of the first international Especially For Youth (EFY) programs. We saw how much the Norwegian, Danish, and Swedish youth loved being *with* each other and *with* their young single adult counselors. Most of them had never spent several days with so many their age who shared their faith. They didn't want to go home. At a concluding fireside, the leaders asked us to take just ten minutes to teach them about the Savior's Atonement.

As the meeting began, we saw banners posted around the large gymnasium, showing their group names from the standard EFY tradition—short scriptural phrases like "Happy Still," "Highly Favored," and "Dreamed a Dream." We decided we should also choose a scriptural name for our two-person group, and our warm feeling about being with them prompted us to choose the name "With You."

But what could we possibly say about the Atonement to

young people in ten minutes? We decided to share our group name as our theme. We told them about our grandson Clark, then just over two years old. As his mother was leaving him with a babysitter one morning, little Clark pleaded, "With you, Mom! With you!" He didn't want to be away from her. Then we said to the EFY youth, that's what the Atonement is about: "with you." When we really come to know Him, we don't want to be away from Him. We want to be *with Him.*

Because of His sacrifice for us, He said I will be "with you" in overcoming your sins. I will be "with you" in the hardest times. "With you" in becoming as I am. Because of Him, we can tell our families and each other, I will be "with you" forever. Our relationship with the Lord through the Atonement and the temple is all about the multiple meanings of "with you": "If you do always remember me ye shall have my spirit to be *with you*" (3 Nephi 18:11; emphasis added). "Ye will remember me in this hour that I was *with you* and drank *with you* of this cup" (JST, Mark 14:21–24; emphasis added).

GODLINESS AND ENTERING INTO
"THE REST OF THE LORD"

The idea that the temple ordinances can bring us into the Lord's presence recalls how He dealt with the Israelites in their hard-heartedness. He declared that they "could not endure his presence; therefore, the Lord" would not allow them to "enter into his rest" (D&C 84:24). Entering into the "rest of the Lord" is a significant, temple-related concept that describes the blessing of advancing from living a kind of worldly or telestial life to living on a higher spiritual plane while still in mortality, as if moving upward from one temple room or sphere to another—even though we may still occasionally stumble.

The prophet Mormon spoke of "the peaceable followers of

Christ" who "have obtained a sufficient hope" that they "can enter into *the rest of the Lord*" (Moroni 7:3; emphasis added). President Joseph F. Smith described "the rest of the Lord" as a deep spiritual peace the Lord bestows on those who have "an invincible determination in their hearts to be steadfast in the truth, and who are treading in humility and righteousness the path" of the "followers of Jesus Christ." These people receive "joy to their hearts" that frees them from "unsettled, restless" feelings of mortal discouragement, "suspicion, unrest, [and] uncertainty." This is not just a hope for the next life. We can receive this tangible "spiritual contentment . . . here upon the earth, from this time forth, now, today."[12]

Alma made it clear that entering into the Lord's rest is not a privilege reserved only for the elect few. In his day, "there were many, exceedingly great many, who were made pure and entered into the rest of the Lord their God." Alma also linked "the rest of the Lord" to *ordinances* while speaking of the higher priesthood: "These ordinances were given . . . that thereby the people might look forward on the Son of God, . . . it being his order." Then he implored all of us to become sufficiently "humble, meek, submissive, patient, full of love and all long-suffering" (there are those same higher level words again) that we too might *"enter into his rest"* (Alma 13:12, 16, 28–29; emphasis added).

All who have been through the temple have enjoyed the "privilege of receiving the mysteries of the kingdom" (D&C 107:19). They can therefore say with Nephi that they have "been highly favored of the Lord in all [their] days; yea, having had a great knowledge of the goodness and the mysteries of God" (1 Nephi 1:1). The powers and mysteries of godliness are not really mysterious, they are just sacred. They are also not complicated, for their most essential meaning is as simple as "with You."

CHAPTER 9

The Blessings
of Temple Sealings

I have not seen a more pure form of joy than in the shining faces of certain brides being sealed in the holy temple—unless perhaps it is in the faces of their mothers. Sometimes the groom's face also shines, especially when he is looking at the bride.

As I met with one couple briefly before going with them to the sealing room, I sensed an unusual degree of spiritual maturity and goodness about them as they talked and glanced at each other on this, their day of days. As they then knelt across the altar to be sealed, I saw the tears well up in the young woman's eyes as she smiled radiantly toward her groom. Both her smile and her tears remained as she listened to the sacred sealing words, while the subtle but knowing expressions on her face reflected the obvious depth of her understanding.

I found myself wondering with admiration how many years these two had waited for each other; what they had given—and given up—to be there; what kind of disappointments and opposition they had weathered; what forbearance, sacrifice, and patience they had paid the price to attain. I felt a sense of privilege, being allowed to see eternity reflect its timeless light in those clear eyes.

I also remember being a visitor in a fast and testimony meeting when a woman I didn't know came to the pulpit. She said this was the first time she had borne her testimony in many years, although she had lived in this ward a long time, and it was evident that she and the ward members knew each other well. She was subdued, gentle, and thoughtful. She said she had been to the temple the previous day for the marriage sealing of her son, and she wanted to express the fulness of her heart. She was able to share only the smallest part of all that she was feeling, all that the day had meant. She noted along the way that she was a single parent, though she didn't say what had happened to her husband.

Afterward she returned to her seat in the row behind us, so we were able to thank her after the meeting for what she shared. She told us then, smiling a little as the tears came again, that the boy she spoke about was her only child. As we parted, I tried to imagine how much meaning had hinged—and will yet hinge—for her on that moment in the temple. She had looked forward to it every day of that boy's life until now, and now she would look back to it without end.

These two experiences are but tiny samples of the many personal images most of us can envision related to temple marriages among the people we know well. And those images form a backdrop now to talk about the sealing blessings of the temple.

The culminating phase of our upward spiritual journey through the Aaronic and Melchizedek Priesthood levels takes us to the summit represented by the temple's sealing power. After we have received all of the other ordinances, our sealings can bless us in multiple ways.

First of all, in moments like those in these two stories, the authority of the sealing power restored in our time by Elijah allows us to be sealed in a marriage union that does promise to be celestial—in both time and quality—*if* we live up to the promise. Only through the power of such a sealing and through our keeping our part of the covenants can we qualify for exaltation in the celestial kingdom. There our sealing will let us experience "eternal increase," having children—and joy in our posterity—after the pattern of our heavenly parents. Without the sealing ordinance, there can be no promise of this godly joy (see D&C 131:2–4).

Second, we can also be sealed to both our children and our parents, either through birth in the covenant or through specific sealing ordinances, live or by proxy. These child-to-parent sealings ensure eternal family bonds. They are also welding links in the great ancestral chain that joins all generations together into the family of God through all dispensations (see D&C 128:18).

This welding together is part of what we might call the individual or personal sealing blessings of the temple—eternal promises regarding our own exaltation[1] that are bestowed by the sealing ordinance in addition to, and in some sense independent of, our sealing to a spouse or family. Elder Carlos E. Asay said that if we remain faithful, the sealing ordinance gives us special, personal blessings "pertaining to the prospects of (1) participating in the first [that is, celestial] resurrection, (2) all the blessings of Abraham, Isaac, and Jacob, and (3) the [exalted] blessings of powers and kingdoms."[2]

I mention these individual sealing blessings not only because their promises are so magnificent but also because I found in the temple that many Church members seem unaware of them. Many people assume that temple sealings are for the sole purpose of sealing spouses and family members to one another. This isn't the setting for a complete discussion of the individual sealing blessings, but here is one illustration: If a father in a temple-sealed family is excommunicated and therefore loses his temple blessings, that obviously cancels the sealings between him and the members of his family, and it cancels his individual sealing promises. However, his cancellation does not disturb the individual sealing promises that remain with his worthy spouse and children.[3]

JESUS CHRIST WILL "SEAL YOU HIS"—
BECOMING SONS AND DAUGHTERS OF GOD

The scriptures speak of another dimension of the sealing power that shows how the ordinances and principles of the two priesthoods lead the Savior's followers through a complete upward sequence that fulfills the Atonement's promise of our at-one-ment with the Lord.

After King Benjamin's people covenanted to become "the children of Christ" (Mosiah 5:7), he exhorted them to retain Christ's name in their hearts and to remain obedient, even "steadfast and immovable." If they would do this, he said, the day would come when Christ "may *seal you his* . . . that ye may have everlasting salvation and eternal life" (Mosiah 5:15; emphasis added). Benjamin's people thus became the children of Christ through the doctrine of adoption. And that lifelong process could one day find its fulfillment in their also being sealed to Him eternally.

This example is consistent with other scriptural references to the concept of adoption. For instance, those who are faithful to the oath and covenant of the two priesthoods are "sanctified by the Spirit" until "they become the [adopted] sons of Moses and of Aaron and the seed of Abraham, . . . and the elect of God," and then "all that my Father hath shall be given" to them (D&C 84:33–38).

Other passages teach about adoption, often tying it to ideas about inheritance. For example, while most of those who join the Church are literally descendants of the house of Israel, faithful people who are not literal descendants may be adopted into the house of Israel by baptism, thereby becoming heirs of Israel's promised blessings.[4]

Perhaps the most significant meaning of adoption is to become "the sons of God": "As many as received him, to them gave he power to become the sons of God" (John 1:12). And Paul said, "Ye have received the Spirit of adoption, whereby we cry, Abba, Father." And if we are God's children in this sense, we are also "heirs of God, and joint-heirs with Christ"—*if*, as Paul added, *it "so be that we suffer with him."* For "I reckon that the sufferings of this present time are not worthy to be compared with the glory which shall be revealed in us" in "the manifestation of *the sons of God*" (Romans 8:14–19; emphasis added).

Elder Bruce R. McConkie summarized what all of this means: "Eternal life or exaltation, is to be like God, to be a son of God, a joint-heir with Christ, receiving, inheriting, and possessing, as he does, the fullness of the kingdom of the Father."[5] Elder McConkie and President Joseph Fielding Smith were particularly explicit in teaching that the temple ordinances, particularly the marriage sealing, are the source of our adoption as sons and daughters of God in this sense.[6]

But haven't we been God's sons and daughters ever since our premortal birth? Yes, He is the father of our spirits. Yet prior to that spirit birth or organizing process, some essence of our being existed coeternally with God: "Man was also in the beginning with God" (D&C 93:29). Then, as Joseph Smith taught, "finding [that] he was in the midst of spirits and glory," God instituted "laws whereby the rest could . . . advance like himself" and "be exalted with himself."[7] As then-Elder Spencer W. Kimball put it, "our spirit matter was eternal and co-existent with God, but it was organized into spirit bodies by our Heavenly Father."[8]

As something of a second stage in our premortal existence, then, we know that "man, as a spirit, was begotten and born of heavenly parents, and reared to maturity in the eternal mansions of the Father."[9] Against this rich but not precisely defined background,[10] God is "not a creator who fashions humans for his own purposes," but is more a "heavenly mentor who . . . endows spirit matter with the form and conditions conducive to . . . full emulation of a perfect Father."[11]

At the same time, only Christ is the Father's natural, physical child in mortality—His unblemished "Only Begotten." So only Jesus is a natural heir to the Father's kingdom. And He invites us to share fully in His inheritance by *adopting us through the act and power of His Atonement.* Therefore, the scriptures say, by and of Christ, the earth's inhabitants can be "begotten sons and daughters unto God" (D&C 76:24).

After becoming Christ's adopted children through baptism, if we remain faithful through the sequence of the remaining principles, covenants, and ordinances of the two priesthoods, we may one day "come unto the Father in [Christ's] name, and in due time receive of [the Father's] fulness" (D&C 93:19). "I . . . am the Firstborn," He said. "And all those who are begotten through me" and remain faithful shall one day receive the Father's fulness and thereby become eternal partakers of Christ's glory as members of "the church of the Firstborn" (D&C 93:21–22). Then Christ will seal us His as sons and daughters of the Father who are joint-heirs with Christ, inheriting all that the Father hath. They have received their exaltation, for "all things are theirs . . . and they are Christ's, and Christ is God's" (D&C 76:59).

In his masterful book on Christ's Atonement, President John Taylor described these links between the Atonement, adoption, and our exaltation. His language speaks of this total process as endowing us not only with the forgiveness made possible by the first principles and ordinances but, beyond that, with the Christlike capacities of godliness:

> It is for the *exaltation of man to this state of superior intelligence* and Godhead that the mediation and atonement of Jesus Christ is instituted; and man is *rendered capable* not only of being a son of man, but also *a son of God, through adoption.* . . . And thus through the atonement of Jesus Christ and the adoption he [or she] is capable of eternal exaltation [and] eternal lives. . . . Through that atonement and the power of the Priesthood associated therewith, they become heirs of God and joint heirs with Jesus Christ, [inheriting] dominions in the eternal worlds [where they] can become the fathers and mothers of lives.[12]

So what *does* it mean that Christ might seal us His? This is one of those sacred doctrines about which we can catch only slight glimpses. It does seem to be part of the fulfillment of our relationship with Him, a personal process that is enhanced and authorized by the sealing ordinances of the temple and linked to the blessings of the Atonement. As Truman Madsen said:

> The answer to "Who am I?" can never be complete unless it answers "Whose am I?" You are the son or daughter of a king. The Father himself. Through the ordinances you are begotten spiritually through his Son. You become heir to his throne. . . . You take his name. To receive him fully is to receive the fullness of his atonement. [D&C 131:5, which speaks of being sealed up to eternal life, is] talking about . . . coming to know by revelation through the power of the Holy Priesthood not only that Jesus is the Christ, but also that a relationship has been forged between you and Jesus Christ. . . . How do you come to know that? I can only tell you that the promise does pertain to the temple. . . .

In some patterns of worship, it is thought that the way to convey proper relationships to God is to cultivate darkness . . . and irrational fear. The testimony of the restored temple is that God the Father and his Son Jesus Christ yearn not to widen that gap, but to close it. In the house of the Lord we may come to him in light, in intimacy, and in holy embrace. . . . The temple is many things: a house of faith, a house of study, [of learning, of order, and glory]. But surrounding all of those it is a house of love. None of us receives enough love in this world, none of us. . . . The Father and the Son call us to come in the spirit of sacrifice and be surrounded by that holy environment which embraces us in love.[13]

The last four chapters have been concerned with how the temple and the Savior's Atonement help us to grow up spiritually, to become sons and daughters of God in the fullest eternal sense, rather than merely enduring. Just as we began these chapters with a reference to Peter, we conclude with another scripture from Peter's life about growing up—a verse that also marked a turning point in my own life nearly forty years ago. I had barely begun what was my dream career: being a full-time law professor at BYU. I was then shocked when Elder Neal A. Maxwell asked me on two weeks' notice in mid-semester to leave my dream job and work for "a year or two" in a new correlation department at Church headquarters.

In my first meeting with the members of the Quorum of the Twelve to whom we reported, I was asked to say a few words. Only recently did I recall again the scripture I quoted on that long-ago day. It was from Christ's final words to Peter: "When thou wast young, thou girdedst thyself, and walkedst whither thou wouldest: but when thou shalt be old [also perhaps meaning fully grown up], another shall gird thee, and carry thee whither thou wouldest not" (John 21:18).

Those words referred to how Peter would die, but for me that day, and now, they also have a more general meaning: We are, most of us, quite full of ourselves when we are young. But when we grow up spiritually, we will, we hope, no longer be so self-absorbed. Rather, perhaps we will then desire to live more outside ourselves and to be carried by Him who prepares a way for us to accomplish what He asks of us (see 1 Nephi 3:7).

I was secretly praying that day that I could grow up enough to accept what felt like an unwanted intrusion into my life plans—an intrusion that essentially continued for the next thirty-eight years. In retrospect, I bear witness that I have been carried and stretched and changed for the better by Him who said those sobering words to Peter. So now I respond to Him in Cordelia's words from *King Lear:* O good Master, "How shall I live and work to match thy goodness? My life will be too short, and every measure fail me."[14]

When we have fully "grown up" through the sequence and ordinances of the two priesthoods, it is true that "another shall gird thee"—He who redeems us, strengthens us, and perfects us. "For he said, *Surely they are my people,* . . . so he was their Saviour. In all their affliction he was afflicted, and . . . in his love and in his pity he redeemed them; and he bare them, and carried them all the days of old" (Isaiah 63:8–9; emphasis added).

If . . . [they] keep the commandments of God he doth nourish them, and strengthen them . . . ; wherefore, he did provide means for us while we did sojourn in the wilderness.

1 NEPHI 17:3

PART II

OUR JOURNEY

CHAPTER 10

The Ascending Journey of True Followers— Engaging Christ's Atonement

In a sweeping scriptural vision that captures the drama of our earthly journey on a large but vivid canvas, the Apostle John gave us his grandly prophetic book of Revelation. Scattered among such symbolic images as seals, beasts, trumpets, angels, and dragons, John focuses on the concept of "overcoming"—a frequent theme in epic tales throughout human history, starting, as we've just seen, with the archetypal story of Adam and Eve.

As suggested in other large-scale personal quests in scripture, history, and literature, our travels through the mortal vale of tears can be laden with both joyous possibilities and fearful opposition. Even as the forces of heaven watch over us and open doors for us, the forces of darkness work to oppose us, sometimes ferociously, dead set against our fulfilling what the Lord sent us here to learn and to become. In many ways, then, the course of the true follower's journey can be defined in terms of *overcoming* whatever obstacles may stand (or be placed) between us and our desired return to God's presence.

TEMPLE ALLUSIONS IN THE VISION OF
JOHN THE REVELATOR

The following samples from John the Revelator speak about "overcoming," with frequent references to Christ's Atonement accompanied by echoes that will sound familiar to those who attend the temple. These verses offer a big-picture, universal perspective on how the cosmic battle between good and evil sets the stage for our individual journeys and for our ultimate destiny as true followers who look to the temple for guidance. Without trying to interpret John's entire vision of the earth's future,[1] we will focus here on terms, images, and events that connect temple-like imagery to the spiritual journey of following the Savior into His realm of eternal glory.

As we consider these verses, we might ask ourselves: Who are the verses talking about? What promises are given to those who "overcome"? What are the opposing forces they must overcome? How or by what resources or power will they overcome? If they are faithful, what is their ultimate destiny?

The people portrayed here are worthy disciples of Jesus Christ who are typically clothed in white robes. John saw them standing together before the throne of God. But he also saw that Satan, the great dragon, was allowed to make war with them, in spite of—or perhaps because of—their faithfulness to Jesus and their testimonies of Him.

> [Those] which have not defiled their garments . . . shall walk with me in white: for they are worthy. (Revelation 3:4)

> And white robes were given unto every one of them. (Revelation 6:11)

> A great multitude . . . stood before the throne, and before the Lamb, clothed with white robes. (Revelation 7:9)

And the dragon was wroth with the woman, and went to make war with the remnant of her seed, which keep the commandments of God, and have the testimony of Jesus Christ. (Revelation 12:17)

Throughout John's vision, he hears the voice of the Lord describe a stirring array of eternal promises to His followers who remain faithful until they prevail over all opposition. Several terms in these verses draw upon familiar scriptural imagery, such as the tree of life from the Garden of Eden; the daily manna that God gave the children of Israel; and the ultimate promise of becoming a son or daughter of God—a reference to the blessings of exaltation.

To him that *overcometh* will I give to eat of the tree of life. (Revelation 2:7; emphasis added to this and all scriptures in this chapter)

He that *overcometh* shall not be hurt of the second death. (Revelation 2:11)

To him that *overcometh* will I give to eat of the hidden manna, and will give him a white stone, and in the stone a new name. (Revelation 2:17)

He that *overcometh,* and keepeth my works unto the end, to him will I give power over the nations. (Revelation 2:26)

He that *overcometh,* the same shall be clothed in white raiment; and I will not blot out his name out of the book of life, but I will confess his name before my Father, and before his angels. (Revelation 3:5)

Him that *overcometh* will I make a pillar in the temple of my God, and he shall go no more out: and I will write upon him the name of my God, . . . and I will write upon him my new name. (Revelation 3:12)

To him that *overcometh* will I grant to sit with me in my throne, *even as I also overcame*, and am set down with my Father in his throne. (Revelation 3:21)

He that *overcometh* shall inherit all things; and I will be his God, and he shall be my son. (Revelation 21:7)

The vision showed John that Christ's true followers would face two general forms of opposition. One form includes many kinds of adversity; John simply called it "great *tribulation*" (Revelation 7:14). The other opposing force is *Satan* himself, who makes war with the Saints of God—especially now that he has "but a short time" (Revelation 12:12) until the time when he "shall not have power over the saints *any more at all*" (D&C 88:114).

What are these which are arrayed in white robes? and whence came they? . . . These are *they which came out of great tribulation*. (Revelation 7:13–14)

And there was war in heaven: Michael and his angels fought against the dragon. . . . And the great dragon was cast out, that old serpent, called the Devil, and Satan, which deceiveth the whole world: he was cast out into the earth, and his angels were cast out with him. (Revelation 12:7–9)

The devil is come down unto you, having great wrath, because he knoweth that he hath but a short time. (Revelation 12:12)

And it was given unto him to make war with the saints. (Revelation 13:7)

Through the combined power of the atoning sacrifice itself—the blood of the Lamb—and their own personal testimony of Jesus, the Lord's people will be given strength to overcome both kinds of opposition.

[They] have washed their robes, and made them white in the blood of the Lamb. Therefore are they before the throne of God, and serve him day and night in his temple: and he that sitteth on the throne shall dwell among them.

They shall hunger no more, neither thirst any more; . . .

For the Lamb which is in the midst of the throne shall feed them, and shall lead them unto living fountains of waters: *and God shall wipe away all tears from their eyes.* (Revelation 7:14–17; Elder Gerrit W. Gong offers the tender addition: *"except the tears of joy."*[2])

And [our brethren] overcame him by the blood of the Lamb, *and by the word of their testimony;* and they loved not their lives unto the death. (Revelation 12:11)

These shall make war with the Lamb, and the Lamb shall *overcome* them: for he is Lord of lords, . . . and they that are with him are called, and chosen, and faithful. (Revelation 17:14)

In a vision that might have been similar to portions of John's vision, Joseph Smith was allowed to see the three degrees of glory, as recorded in section 76 of the Doctrine and Covenants. In the part of Joseph's vision that describes those who inherit the celestial kingdom, he foresaw the glorious destiny of those who *overcome* by remaining true and faithful—in language that speaks with the familiar prophetic tongue used by John the Revelator:

They are they who received the testimony of Jesus, . . . and who *overcome* by faith, and are sealed by the Holy Spirit of promise. . . . They are they who are the church of the Firstborn. . . . Wherefore, all things are theirs, whether life or death, . . . and they are Christ's, and Christ is God's. And they shall *overcome* all things. . . . These are they who are just men made perfect through Jesus the mediator of the new covenant, who wrought out this perfect atonement through the shedding of his own blood. These are they whose bodies are celestial, whose glory is that of the sun, even the glory of God. (D&C 76:51, 53–54, 59–60, 69–70)

The cosmic perspective from John and from Joseph Smith contains enough spiritual energy to let us imagine its personal applications to us, even as they are describing a universal, macro-level vision. One hears in these lines a kind of soaring eloquence that already feels set to celestial music, as the song of redeeming love celebrates the majesty of Christ's triumph over all His enemies—and ours.

HOW ADAM AND EVE OVERCAME TRIBULATION AND THE ADVERSARY

To take one more step that connects His victory to ours, we will apply the general pattern from Revelation to see what and how Adam and Eve "overcame." Their story of receiving and engaging the Atonement shows the way for us to do the same.

Few stories are more widely known than the events, choices, and consequences of the Garden of Eden. But what happened in the Garden was only the beginning of Adam and Eve's journey. Their real growth would come as they lived long enough and well enough in the sometimes muddy fields and thickets of mortality to receive all the ordinances and principles of the two priesthoods and to engage all the blessings of the Savior's Atonement. Their experience sets the pattern for those of us who desire to be true followers of Jesus Christ.

The book of Moses in the Pearl of Great Price gives us the most insight into Adam and Eve's ascending sojourn through which they ultimately overcame the fallen world. A closer look there at their post-Eden lives will deepen our perception of how their story helps us live our story. Their passage through the shadows of separation and their climb toward the Light will lead us as we keep climbing.

Each of us is born into the same fallen conditions into which Adam and Eve were cast as they left the Garden. The Lord's warnings and promises to them also apply to us. While still in the Garden, the Lord warned them that in the world that awaited, they too would face the same two general sources of opposition that John saw in his vision: tribulation and Satan. These forces were not just irritants, but dimensions of their existence that could help them learn what they needed to grasp in order to comprehend the meaning of *joy* and, eventually, celestial life.

Speaking of the tribulation and oppositions of mortality in a fallen world, the Lord warned Adam and Eve, "In sorrow thou shalt bring forth children" (Moses 4:22). Also, "By the sweat of thy face shalt thou eat bread" (Moses 4:25). Further, "Cursed shall be the ground for thy sake" (Moses 4:23). And, "In sorrow shalt thou eat of [the ground] all the days of thy life" (Moses 4:23). This sobering language tells us that much of the adversity we encounter is simply *the way things are* in the mortal environment, placed here not to punish us but to school us.

Their second source of mortal opposition was the maliciously familiar Satan, the destroyer. After the Lord's angel had taught Adam and Eve the purpose of their animal sacrifices, they taught their children the wondrous news of the Redemption, which suddenly gave new meaning to what had happened in Eden and to all of their experience since then. Immediately, however, "Satan came among them," and he "commanded" their children to "believe it not; and they believed it not, and they loved Satan more than God" (Moses 5:13). Satan eventually seduced Cain, who also "loved Satan more than God," into slaying his brother Abel (Moses 5:18).

Dumbstruck and heartbroken, Adam and Eve "mourned before the Lord, because of Cain and his brethren" (Moses 5:27). Nevertheless, they persisted in what they had learned from the

Lord and His angel. So, a day at a time, they worked to overcome the destructive forces of both tribulation and Satan.

To strengthen them in that journey, the Lord taught them the purposes of baptism and the gift of the Holy Ghost, in the larger context of teaching them about "the plan of salvation unto all men, through the blood of mine Only Begotten" (Moses 6:62). The Lord then baptized Adam, both with water and "with fire, and with the Holy Ghost," then ordained him to the Melchizedek Priesthood (Moses 6:64–67). Adam and Eve then had access to the Savior's strengthening blessings—many of them through the ministry of the Holy Ghost, who, they were told, would "abide in" them, providing peace, truth, quickening, and "all power" (Moses 6:61).

It was the *eternal present tense* of the Atonement that allowed all of this to happen many centuries before the physical coming of Christ—who, Adam was told, "shall come in the meridian of time" (Moses 6:62). As King Benjamin would explain many years later, but still before the birth of Christ, "Whosoever should believe that Christ should come, the same might receive remission of their sins, and rejoice with exceedingly great joy, even as though he had already come among them" (Mosiah 3:13).

In addition to the ordinances of baptism and receiving the Holy Ghost, Adam and Eve performed the ordinance of sacrifice. And when the angel explained the meaning of that ordinance, he opened their eyes to "the joy of [their] redemption" (Moses 5:11). Finally, after Adam and Eve had received all of the needed ordinances,[3] and the higher principles of the high priesthood had helped them grow to their full spiritual maturity, they received the higher sanctifying and *perfecting* blessings: "Behold, thou art one in me, a son of God; and thus may all become my sons" (Moses 6:68).

As part of the process of receiving the full blessings of the two priesthoods and of Christ's Atonement, Adam and Eve also gave all of their own strength and testimony to the laborious task of overcoming both tribulation and Satan—for their own sakes and for the sake of their posterity. They taught the gospel and testified to their descendants, "and many [of them] have believed and become the sons of God." Yet personal agency played the same role then as it does now: "Many have believed not, and have perished in their sins" (Moses 7:1).

Adam and Eve thus overcame all the forces of opposition in their lives by combining their own strength with the strength of the Lamb of God. And so will it be for any of us who follow their example. With our first parents' journey as our pattern—against the cosmic backdrop provided by the book of Revelation—we now want to explore what it means to *overcome* in our own daily climb as we seek to engage the full blessings of the Atonement.

The following chapters will focus primarily on the portions of our journey that follow baptism. We will thus have more to say about receiving the *strengthening* and *perfecting* blessings the Savior makes possible than about His *redeeming* blessings. We will talk more about the Melchizedek Priesthood stages of our growth than about the Aaronic Priesthood stages.

We will be looking at key attitudes and experiences that can help us learn and trust and grow—attitudes that help us submit to the Master Teacher. He personally guides us through each bend in the trail, sometimes calling us by name as He motions for us to follow Him. Sometimes He points far ahead then lets us find our way. And sometimes He takes us by the hand when the climb is more than our legs can handle. Our personal journeys will vary greatly from one another, but they will probably all share portions of what Alma and the sons of Mosiah discovered in their "journeyings in the land of Nephi," including "their sufferings in the land, their sorrows, and their afflictions, *and their incomprehensible joy*" (Alma 28:8).

CHAPTER 11

WAITING UPON THE LORD

The journey of a true follower of Christ begins with faith, repentance, and baptism, which create the covenant relationship of our being "spiritually begotten" (Mosiah 5:7) or born again as the children of Christ. The scriptures attest just how personal this relationship is *to Him*. When we obediently accept His Atonement, both its blessings and its conditions, He tenderly extends to us the promise of His strength: "Fear not: for I have redeemed thee, I have called thee by thy name" (Isaiah 43:1). "I am with thee: . . . I will *strengthen* thee; yea, I will help thee; yea, I will uphold thee" (Isaiah 41:10; emphasis added).

After our baptism, the temple covenants intentionally deepen our relationship with the Savior, who offers us more strength as the difficulty of our ascent increases. *Overcoming* the tribulation and opposition we face is much like Moroni's description of conquering his enemies. Of the effect of our temple worship on this ability to overcome, he wrote: It is through "that all-powerful God, who has strengthened our arms that we have gained *power* . . . by our faith . . . *and by our rites [ordinances] of worship*" (Alma 44:5; emphasis added).

Beginning with the Kirtland Temple, the Lord promised "a blessing such as is not known among the children of men" that "shall be poured forth" upon those who receive temple ordinances (D&C 39:15)—for in the temple "you shall be endowed with power from on high" (D&C 38:32). "Yea the hearts of . . . tens of thousands shall greatly rejoice in consequence of the blessings which shall be poured out, and the endowment with which my servants have been endowed in this house" (D&C 110:9).

This endowment of spiritual priesthood power also includes the Lord's personalized responses to Joseph's dedicatory prayer in the Kirtland Temple, which applies to each temple: "That all people who shall enter . . . the Lord's house may feel thy power . . . [and] that thy servants may *go forth from this house armed with thy power*. . . . [That] thou wilt fight for thy people as thou didst in the day of battle. . . . That thy people may not faint in the day of trouble . . . [but be helped] by the power of thy Spirit" (D&C 109:13, 22, 28, 38, 79; emphasis added).

The scriptures are full of candid stories of even the most faithful disciples being stretched to the utmost in their quest to "overcome." The Lord's promised blessings of power and deliverance do come, but in His own way and according to His own timing, not ours. Brokenhearted Joseph, for example, pleaded from the prison-temple of Liberty Jail: "O God, where art thou? . . . How long . . . before thine heart shall be softened ? . . . Let thy hiding place no longer be covered" (D&C 121:1–4).

And after submissive Alma and Amulek had "suffered . . . many days" of imprisonment, mocking, and taunting, they cried out, "How long shall we suffer these great afflictions, O Lord? . . . Give us strength according to our faith which is in Christ, even unto deliverance." Finally, not in *their* time but in *His,* the Lord "granted unto them power" to break the cords that bound them (Alma 14:2–28).

These incidents suggest that no matter how righteous our desires or how much faith we exert when seeking the Lord's strengthening blessings, two issues we can't control are *when* He will strengthen us and *how*. So if we desire to learn how to submit to His "when," He invites us to learn something about "waiting upon the Lord."

WAITING IN THE MODERN AGE

Nobody likes to be kept waiting in today's world, and the marketing strategists know it. In one ad or recorded message after another, sellers soothingly reassure us that our call is *really* important to them; this brief survey will take only eighteen seconds; we can FedEx that order overnight; our electronic plot summary can condense into fifteen minutes what it took Tolstoy nine hundred pages to say in *War and Peace;* and, as if that weren't enough, our patented microwave fireplace is guaranteed to give you a four-hour evening of crackling relaxation in three minutes.

This well-calculated environment fills our ears, our eyes, and the Internet with such constant conviction that most of us subliminally believe we have a constitutional right not to be put off, and each one of us is "special." With our collective expectations set so high, no wonder our stomachs churn with frustration when we can't avoid waiting at a checkout counter, at a red traffic light, for a restaurant table, or for the car to be fixed.

This mentality can make it hard to do things that simply take time—like saving money or growing trees. The adversary gladly exploits our willingness to give up a hoped-for righteous goal in exchange for some immediate gratification. This is especially true when (such as in preserving one's sexual purity), as a matter of clear logic, the "right now" excitement isn't worthy even to be compared with the value of lifelong hopes for the future—like burning a cathedral to fry an egg, as someone said.

One of our family's favorite *Sesame Street* episodes from years ago showed what happened when Cookie Monster won a national quiz show—with the help of Mrs. Cookie Monster, of course. With all America watching, Guy Smiley the announcer said with cheerful gusto, "All right, Mr. and Mrs. Cookie Monster, you have won the quiz show! And now you have your choice of three fabulous prizes. You can have a $500,000 dream home next month, a $50,000 new car next week, or . . . you can have *a cookie right now*! What will it be? You have thirty seconds to decide!"

Mr. and Mrs. Monster intensely debated the pros and cons of each option. And as the TV camera zoomed in close enough to show the little beads of tension-induced sweat on Cookie Monster's furry forehead, a big grin swept across his face and he announced, to no one's surprise, "Cookie!" Somehow it was lost on the poor monster that the dream house would have three ovens and he could have baked all the cookies he wanted.

Joking aside, at times we have no choice but to wait, sometimes for years, sometimes all our mortal lives. If we then have unrealistic expectations about the value of waiting, we can face growing discouragement and even the threat of lost hope.

I once worked with a superb secretary whose young husband had gone "missing in action" during the war in Vietnam. She waited for him with their two small children. The military people were unable to say with confidence whether he had been killed, taken prisoner, or gone missing for some other reason. They just didn't know. Eventually the military officials concluded that he was in fact dead. But during her years of agonized waiting, she learned to concentrate fully on her children's needs. She also managed to finish her education, to find and keep a good job, and in other ways to lead a very productive life. Some people in her situation would themselves have gone "missing in inaction," paralyzed by vexing uncertainty.

In Samuel Beckett's celebrated play *Waiting for Godot,* two men carry on what often sounds like meaningless conversation as they keep waiting, expecting someone named Godot to arrive as promised—but he never comes. Because Beckett believed that life has only the meaning we give it, waiting for what or who never comes was for him a fair representation of mortality. That viewpoint is too pessimistic for us; and yet, much of life really can be what happens to us while we're waiting for something else. So we do need to decide whether our unavoidable waiting will be aimless or purposeful. Some of the people or outcomes for which we most earnestly wait may not be resolved in the short term, but our waiting can still have value, even great meaning— as Elder Brent H. Nielson's family found in praying patiently for his sister's eventual return to the Church, "with continued love, we watched and we waited."[1]

I have not waited for a lost family member in a controversial war. I have not yet suffered or supported a spouse who was suffering from a debilitating chronic disease. My generation has not been driven into an unknown wilderness by enemies or held captive for years by a malicious pharaoh or king. So I can't claim much firsthand understanding about the really hard forms of waiting, even though I have watched a few close friends and relatives courageously endure some of them. What I do know about "waiting upon the Lord" came in what may seem a fairly ordinary way, but it was still full of personal meaning for me, partly because of how it let me "liken [the] scriptures unto [myself] . . . for [my] profit and learning" (1 Nephi 19:23).

I had just come through several intense years in my professional life that had kept me totally preoccupied. I had been given unsought-for responsibility to deal with a steady stream of complexity, which required that I try to help some strong, good people keep from misunderstanding each other. My work assignments were generally worthwhile, but at times my role had me feeling like the "weeping mortar" that oozes from between heavy bricks when they are pressed together.

Then my assignments changed in ways that gave me more flexibility to chart my own course for the next few years. But I was also feeling exhausted, perhaps a little discouraged, and just too spent to have much confidence in my own specific sense of direction. I needed spiritual help, and I was searching for a clearer connection with the Lord.

One grey, chill, early December day, I just blurted out to Marie, "Let's go to Jackson." We had spent the first summer of our marriage working in Jackson Hole, Wyoming, and in later summers we had occasionally returned to the familiar majesty of those mountains. Even though this was early winter, Jackson still felt like the place to go.

The park was quiet, nearly deserted. The morning after our arrival, we drew back the curtains covering our window to see a huge American bald eagle standing on the limb of a large dead tree within a stone's throw of us. We had never seen one of those great birds in the wild at such close range. As depleted as I felt, I found myself identifying a little with the dead tree, and it felt as if the eagle might have landed there just for me. Soon he flapped his mighty wings and lifted off, later returning to the same spot.

Something about the eagle's quiet grandeur prompted a memory from Isaiah. We found the verses and read them aloud, then read them again and again:

Hast thou not heard, that the everlasting God, the Lord
. . . fainteth not, neither is weary? . . . *He giveth power to the
faint; and to them that have no might he increaseth strength.* Even
the youths shall faint and be weary, and the young men shall
utterly fall: But *they that wait upon the Lord shall renew their
strength; they shall mount up with wings as eagles;* they shall run,
and not be weary; and they shall walk, and not faint. (Isaiah
40:28–31; emphasis added)

We weren't quite sure what Isaiah meant about "they that wait
upon the Lord." Was he telling us that we should renew our own
strength because we were waiting in uncertainty, or did he mean
the Lord would strengthen those who wait?

That question took us to the Psalm set to music in
Mendelssohn's *Elijah:* "O *rest* in the Lord, wait *patiently* for him,
and he shall give thee thy heart's desire. . . . Commit thy way
unto him, and trust in him; fret not thyself. . . . Wait patiently for
him" (see also Psalm 37:7). "Rest in the Lord." The phrases were
stirring to us.

The next day I ran across an essay about the unique contributions of Joseph Smith's revealed translation of the Bible. One of
those contributions, something I hadn't noticed before, was about
the youth of Jesus Christ. Normally we just think of Luke 2:52,
that "Jesus increased in wisdom and stature, and in favour with
God and man." But Joseph's translation added: "And it came to
pass that Jesus grew up with his brethren, and waxed strong, and
waited upon the Lord for the time of his ministry to come. And he
served under his father, and he spake not as other men, neither
could he be taught; for he needed not that any man should teach
him. And after many years, the hour of his ministry drew nigh"
(JST, Matthew 3:24–26; emphasis added).

So even Jesus "waited upon the Lord" for years, directed by
the unique tutoring He must have received by serving "under his

father." I couldn't imagine that this meant He just stood around in Joseph's carpenter shop, counting the days. Of course not, because even at age twelve He knew that He "must be about [His] Father's business" (Luke 2:49). Being taught by the Father, He "needed not than any *man* should teach him."

These words led me to remember a scripture I once heard President James E. Faust emphasize: "But ye have an unction from the Holy One . . . [and] the anointing which ye have received of him abideth in you, and ye need not that any man teach you: . . . And even as [the anointing] hath taught you, ye shall abide in him" (1 John 2:20, 27).

Suddenly I got the message. There are times when the Lord can and will teach us very directly—more than any man would teach us. But gaining access to that Source requires us to expand and deepen our spiritual receptivity. This means, more than I had been assuming, that waiting upon the Lord is a very active experience; it is not at all passive.

Marie and I both sensed that this was a time for reaching, stretching, and entering into a renewed relationship with the Lord. In that renewal, we needed both to strengthen ourselves as much as we could and to seek the Lord's strength in fresher, deeper ways. Perhaps this would be a kind of spiritual gestation, like a caterpillar inside a cocoon. That meant we needed to be patient as well as active. What happens in a cocoon is not often visible to outside observers, but inside the cocoon the caterpillar is not just relaxing in cozy warmth. Rather, it is in motion, filled with the subtle but intense energy needed to grow wings.

When our lives don't look very successful from the outside, or when our own plans or dreams seem stagnant, that might be exactly the time to "wait" in motion, like a busy caterpillar, moving, struggling, gaining strength, and growing wings.

Two children were watching a cocoon that had formed on the branch of a bush in their yard. When they noticed that the cocoon itself was moving, they ran to their dad. He explained that perhaps a caterpillar was inside, making the changes needed to become a butterfly. He warned the children, "Don't disturb the cocoon before Mother Nature has finished her work."

But when he was away, the children saw enough struggle in the cocoon that they decided Mother Nature needed some help. So they snipped open one end of the cocoon, and out crawled the little creature, its wings only partly formed—not exactly still a caterpillar, but not yet a butterfly; it was just kind of a "teenager." Maybe that's what can happen if we try too hard to rush natural processes that simply require gestation time—along with continued great energy.

Wanting to increase our gestation energy, we both looked for more scriptures about waiting on the Lord. We were buoyed by reading, "Wait on the Lord: be of good courage, and he shall strengthen thine heart: wait, I say, on the Lord" (Psalm 27:14). "Now, Lord, what wait I for? My hope is in thee" (Psalm 39:7). "My soul waiteth for the Lord more than they that watch for the morning: . . . for with the Lord there is mercy, and with him is plenteous redemption" (Psalm 130:6–7). We began to sense that "waiting" can energize our active, covenant relationship with Him—as we move closer to Him, He will move closer to us. "For the people of the Lord are they who wait for him" (2 Nephi 6:13).

These thoughts encouraged us to search for ways to "wait" more actively. That attitude began to affect the way we prayed and what we prayed for; it gave greater purpose to our fasting, to our temple visits, and to our reading of both scriptures and other books. When we needed to travel, we consciously looked for opportunities to make side trips to places where we might find spiritual renewal, fresh insight, and increased closeness to the Lord.

For example, on a brief trip to St. George, I woke up early one morning thinking about my father, who had died years earlier while working in a nearby canyon that he had considered his refuge, a place of peace and spiritual renewal. I hadn't been there in a long time. As we climbed the sandstone trail surrounded by high red cliffs that caught the early-morning sunlight, I felt unusually close to him. He had placed on the wall of his little cabin there one of his favorite poems. It began, "Oh, God, let this be heaven." One of its lines reads, "[And when I die], just leave me here beside these peaks in this rough western land."[2] I sensed his presence and that of my Heavenly Father, lifting both my eyes and my spirits. I thought of the way my dad had always handled uncertainty and stress in peaceful, constructive ways, and I thought that if he could do that, so could I.

Several weeks later, I was assigned to attend a professional meeting in Europe, and Marie joined me. We consciously added a couple of travel days and asked ourselves where we could go that would help us find the clarity of heart and mind we were looking for. I had earlier read the biographies of Heber C. Kimball and Wilford Woodruff, but we had never seen the places in England that these two considered sacred because of their missionary experiences there. Not far from Preston, as we walked from Chatburn toward Clithero, I thought about Heber Kimball's bone-deep, childlike faith—and how he saw that faith rewarded when those to whom he had brought the gospel poured from their houses and followed him in a farewell of tears. I tried to imagine the spot where he said he had wept in such gratitude that he "had to leave the road three times to go to streams of water to bathe my eyes."[3] It seemed as though we were walking with him along that path. Thinking about him in that way brought back memories of how the Spirit had reassured me in refining, sometimes tearful moments of gratitude in the past. In the serenity of the English countryside, those memories brought needed perspective.

At about this same time, we were introduced to a print of Swiss artist Eugene Burnand's painting of Peter and John, running to the tomb in the early light of Resurrection morning. In John's words, "They ran both together" (John 20:4) until they both reached the sepulchre. The look of fearful but reverent anticipation that Burnand captures on their faces, their eagerness and their clear but guarded desire to hope, made me want to run with them to meet Him. They were not just coming to Christ, they were running to Christ. Burnand's depiction, so filled with motion and emotion, became for us an image of what it means to wait upon the Lord.

After our winter of searching we came into spring feeling spiritually replenished. Our perspective felt restored. We had made no specific plans, but we really had regained the peace we needed to think more clearly about our options and our desires. The warmer days, the bright yellow forsythia, and the wind-brushed air all seemed to say that whatever we felt to do, we would be on more secure footing—enough, we hoped, to run and not be weary, to walk and not faint.

As it turned out, those months of learning about active waiting prepared us to receive a new and unexpected full-time Church assignment that spring, which took us first to Australia and a few years later to Europe.

One of our assignments there was to assist with the open house and dedication of the Helsinki Finland Temple in 2007. As I led one group of guests through the elegant, new, Finnish-styled sanctuary, the group just ahead of us was somehow delayed. So our group needed to wait without speaking in the temple's serene celestial room about ten minutes longer than I had earlier told them to expect. When we then went into a nearby sealing room where we could speak again, I apologized briefly and explained why we had been delayed.

As we concluded our tour and moved back toward the temple's entrance, a kind Finnish LDS woman walked next to me. "Elder Hafen," she whispered with a knowing, thoughtful look on her face, "never apologize to a Finn for silence—especially not for silence in the Lord's house. You need to know that two Finns who are the closest of friends could be on an outdoor walk or just sitting together, with neither one speaking for an hour or two—and they would both be sharing deeply, silently. Just because no one is talking doesn't mean nothing is happening."

Her insight opened my understanding, not only about silence among Finns and silence in the temple, but about the sometimes sacred energy of silently waiting upon the Lord. The words to Sibelius's beloved *Finlandia* hymn begin, "*Be still, my soul: The Lord is on thy side.*"[4] Sometimes we sing from another hymn about being "on the Lord's side." That's good counsel. But sometimes we also need to talk less, wait more, and remember that the Lord is also "on thy side." Perhaps if we could wait with more restraint, we would hear those calming words: "Let your hearts be comforted . . . for all flesh is in mine hands; *be still, and know that I am God*" (D&C 101:16; emphasis added).

Waiting in patient stillness can also create an ideal environment for us to offer the Lord a substantial sacrifice—perhaps of the kind most difficult for us to make. Without our unstinting sacrifice, He may not be able to bless us as generously as He might desire.

In the early 1960s, for example, Elder F. Enzio Busche, then a new convert, was the president of a struggling little branch in the large industrial city of Dortmund, Germany. The branch had Church approval to build its first new chapel, after years of rent- ing uninviting places for their meetings. But they encountered so much prejudice that every door closed against their repeated, prayerful efforts to find a building lot. One city official swore that as long as he was alive, "the Mormons" would never receive ap- proval to build.

Feeling great frustration, Enzio sought counsel from Elder Theodore M. Burton, who was then president of the European Mission. Elder Burton challenged the members "to bring a special sacrifice to the Lord and show how serious we were in our desire to secure a piece of land." He asked them to offer what was for them exceedingly difficult—to "do 100 percent home teaching for several consecutive months." If they would, he "promised that the Lord would provide a miracle."[5] The challenge seemed impos- sible because the members, most of them less active, were spread throughout a hundred distant villages, and the branch had only twelve active priesthood holders. But they cared enough to step up with earnest hearts. In one month, Enzio and his companion visited twenty-eight households.

After a few months, Brother Busche was approached by a complete stranger named Kurt Kauper, who had sought him out to tell him this story: Twenty years earlier, Kurt had been a German prisoner of war in an American prison camp in Florida. The camp's leader was a Mormon, and his humane example had taught Kurt that "anything worthwhile can be obtained only through the sacrifice of being honest, reliable, and caring for oth- ers. He attributed everything he accomplished later to the teach- ings of that LDS prison camp leader."[6]

Kurt had recently had a dream about this camp leader and now "felt compelled to do something to repay" him or his

Church; so he asked what he could possibly do. When Enzio said their greatest need was to find a building site in Dortmund, Kurt smiled and said, "I am the head of the [city's] real estate department. . . . Where do you want to build?"[7] Looking beyond anything Enzio dared to imagine, Kurt proposed a choice location with superb public transport access, an ideal spot for visitors and members alike.

About forty years after this incident, I was assigned to visit the Dortmund stake conference. I had loved this story from Elder Busche but had never seen the building. As we drove up to the stake center, nestled gracefully in one of the city's most beautiful, spacious areas, I couldn't hold back the tears. After confirming that this was indeed the building from the story, I asked the stake members in the Sunday general session how many of them knew the story of how their chapel came to be located there.

To my astonishment, fewer than ten people in a congregation of perhaps a thousand raised their hands. So I told them the Kurt Kauper story, and we talked about the place of sacrifice in our personal "yearning for the living God," the title of Elder Busche's candid biographical account that includes this story. The legacy of their stake teaches vividly that "sacrifice brings forth the blessings of heaven."[8]

In the light of such experiences, I'm more at peace now with waiting on the Lord, when I am thinking of—

- The young man we met on the temple grounds, who comes just to the grounds every few days, where he sits on a bench under the trees and reads his scriptures in the shadows of the temple. He is waiting and preparing to be eligible again to receive his temple recommend.

- Our young adult friends who want to marry but who are still waiting for a special person and for the children they might yet bear—desires they have had all of their lives.

- Adam and Eve, who offered sacrifice for "many days" before "an angel of the Lord appeared unto [them] saying: Why dost thou offer sacrifices . . . ?" (Moses 5:6).

- Our temple worker friend who is terminally ill and was told she had probably four months to live. It's been a year and a half now. As she continues to wait upon the Lord, her spirit keeps climbing even as her earthly body gradually and slowly declines.

- The four-year-old granddaughter who looked at a beautifully lit temple with her family one evening and said aloud, "Someday, when I get bigger, and bigger, and bigger, . . . and bigger, . . . I'm going to get married in *that* temple!"

- The young couple who feel the passion of their love for each other, but they wait, because they have yet great desires to serve full-time missions before their temple marriage.

Still, sometimes we will need to keep waiting longer than we imagined, as did Peter on Galilee, even until the fourth watch: "And when [Christ] had sent them away, he departed into a mountain to pray. And when even was come, the ship was in the midst of the sea, and he . . . saw them toiling in rowing; for the wind was contrary unto them: and about the fourth watch of the night [just before dawn] he cometh unto them, walking upon the sea" (Mark 6:48–50).

Jesus had watched them from afar, toiling and rowing against the contrary winds. But He didn't come to them for hours. What was He waiting for? Perhaps He was waiting for His disciples to be sufficiently strengthened by toiling against the wind. Yet He was also watching them—as He is us. Our trust in Him assures us He will not forsake us, nor will He stretch us beyond what we can bear. That sounds like severe mercy. And yet, in the words of Elder James E. Talmage:

> Into every adult human life come experiences like unto the battling of the storm-tossed voyagers with contrary winds and threatening seas; ofttimes the night of struggle and danger is far advanced before *succor* appears; and then, too frequently the saving aid is mistaken for a greater terror. [Yet] as came unto Peter and his terrified companions in the midst of the turbulent waters, so comes to all who toil in faith, the voice of the Deliverer—"It is I; be not afraid."[9]

CHAPTER 12

EXPECTATIONS

As we face the hard "when" questions, it helps to be schooled in what it means to wait upon the Lord. So what of "how" He should strengthen us—is that a question for us to answer, or for Him to answer?

Regardless of how much we desire the Redeemer's strengthening power, we really can't control—and if we are wise we probably shouldn't try to control—either *when* He will strengthen us or *how*. Even so, it is natural that we might want to give Him some advice about both questions. And we do that, consciously or not, when we set up expectations or make assumptions about what He will or should do for us. Those assumptions will influence our ability to find, recognize, and receive—or reject—the Lord's strengthening grace.

So what risks do we run when we let our expectations control the "how" question of what His blessings should look like? As we once heard Elder Jeffrey R. Holland say, "Just this once, could I possibly have a blessing that is not in disguise?" Let us then consider some strengthening blessings—and their possible disguises—under the heading of "expectations."

RISING EXPECTATIONS

As we saw in the previous chapter, many people in today's world get frustrated if they are kept waiting—and that makes it harder to understand a concept like "waiting upon the Lord." Much of our problem is that, in our consumer-driven, rights-oriented culture, we have been experiencing what some observers call "the problem of rising expectations." This is a "problem" because what people "expect" or feel "entitled" to can rise so fast that their expectations are often, almost by definition, impossible to achieve in reality. When expectations get too far ahead of reality, that gap can lead to chronic discontent.

A few years ago, Marjorie P. Hinckley, the wife of President Gordon B. Hinckley, shared an insight about expectations and reality. An interviewer asked her, "What is the secret of your happy marriage?" Sister Hinckley replied matter-of-factly, with a twinkle, "Oh, I just lowered my expectations!"

For the last half century or so, the commercial world, the media, and political advocates have worked to convince those at every socioeconomic level that they have a "right to expect better," economically, socially, legally, and in many other ways. We are also living through an astonishing electronic revolution that now offers marvels and comforts that kings and queens couldn't previously have dreamed possible—affordable, user-friendly devices and ideas that work wonders with virtually every dimension of the information age.

All of this has only heightened our take-it-for-granted assumption that we can now "expect" that whatever used to be hard, complicated, or expensive is now easier, within reach, accessible to everyone. The social media avalanche has added yet another component—even individual consumers are no longer isolated and powerless. Now we can decide on and advocate our own preferences, organize ourselves, talk to each other, and get our own message out to the masses without leaving our seats.

I thought of this cultural context recently when learning what had happened to the son of some longtime friends. I'll call him Rob. Rob's parents are deeply committed Latter-day Saints. They were blessed with a number of gifted and handsome children who excelled, it seemed, at whatever they pursued: the arts, sports, Church experience, social interaction, and education.

One day in St. George a family came to the temple to be sealed. As we got acquainted, I learned that Rob had been one of the missionaries who had taught them and helped them toward the high goal they were realizing that day with their temple sealing. They said they had invited him to join them for the sealing, but now, two or three years since his mission, Rob had just told them that he had essentially left the Church and was sorry he couldn't be with them in the temple.

Because I had known Rob and his family so well, this news came as a big surprise to me. Incredulous, I asked the family's father, who loved and admired Rob as "their" missionary, "What do you think happened with Rob?" He said he had asked Rob the same question, to which Rob had simply said, "Oh, the Church just didn't meet my expectations." Sharing their perplexed sadness, I wondered what that could mean.

One does hear occasionally about people who become disillusioned when they discover new information—even if it is new only to them—about some incident in Church history or some interpretation of Church doctrine or policy, and their discovery differs from what they had previously known or expected. But the issue of expectations can also take on larger proportions when it arises in our personal relationship with the Lord.

BUT IF NOT . . .

The book of Daniel offers one of the great scriptural stories about our expectations and the Lord's expectations for us. During the Babylonian captivity, King Nebuchadnezzar threatened to throw Shadrach, Meshach, and Abed-nego into a burning furnace unless they would bow down and worship the king's golden image. The three young men replied, "If it be so, our God whom we serve is able to deliver us from the burning fiery furnace, and he will deliver us out of thine hand, O king. *But if not,* . . . we will not serve thy gods, nor worship the golden image" (Daniel 3:17–18; emphasis added). So they said God *could* deliver them, and they believed He *would*—but *even if He didn't,* they would trust Him anyway.

Furious, the king cast them, tied and bound, into the blazing furnace. But then he was astonished when he peered into the fiery blast and saw not three men but "four men . . . walking in the midst of the fire, and they have no hurt; and the form of the fourth [man] is like the Son of God" (Daniel 3:25).

Elder Dennis E. Simmons once said that those three young men *knew* that God's only purpose was to help them—and all His children—return to Him and be with Him forever. For that simple reason, they exercised their faith that God would deliver them from danger, one way or another. *But if* their lives were *not* to be spared, their trust remained. And we will find that if we "respond in faith, the *Lord strengthens us.* The *but if nots* can become remarkable blessings."[1]

What motivated Shadrach, Meshach, and Abed-nego to endure the torturous heat of the furnace? If we were in their place, what would be our reason to be so unflinchingly submissive to God's will? In an abstract, idealistic sense it is easy enough to say that we want only to meet *His* expectations because, if we are His faithful followers, we really shouldn't have any expectations of our own; we should just accept His will, with no questions asked. That might be a stereotypical Sunday School answer, but it raises some important questions that deserve to be unpacked.

Should we, as true disciples, have no concern at all for our personal interests or desires—even our long-term interests? Are the righteous desires of our hearts, which we do believe He wants to grant, our desires—or His? Are His desires for us in *our* interest, or are they only in *His* interest? If they are mostly in His interest, does that mean He might occasionally toy with us? Might He playfully confront us with frightening "but if not" moments mostly to remind us that He, not we, has charge of the universe?

We don't think so. One clear element in the story of the fiery furnace assures us that He was not toying with the three Hebrews, and He won't toy with us. The "but if not" phrase is a key point of the story, but the Lord's presence in the furnace "with them" is equally compelling. It gives great meaning to the fearful "but if not," making clear that this story, and other trials like it, are never about His toying with us.

From baptism and the sacrament to the highest ordinances of the temple, the ordinances of symbolic sacrifice help us remember and even visualize the hour when Christ drank His bitter cup on our behalf. "As oft as ye do this ordinance," He said, "ye *will remember me* in this hour that I was with you" (JST, Mark 14:24; emphasis added). Those same ordinances should also remind us of what was going on in that fiery Babylonian furnace. For in that hour, He was *with them,* and strengthened them as they drank their own bitter cups. And so will He be with us.

The Savior took upon Himself "their infirmities," so "that he may know according to the flesh *how to succor his people* according to their infirmities" (Alma 7:12; emphasis added). This is His *strengthening* power, not His *redeeming* power. So He doesn't usually take away the heat of the fire as He does our sins, but He does succor and sustain us in the midst of the flame. And why let us remain in the flame? "The flame shall not hurt thee; I only design Thy dross to consume and thy gold to refine."[2]

This perspective may seem too easy, yet it assures us that the Lord is very aware—in His total empathy for us He is painfully aware—of the distress that must fill the hearts of His disciples who suspend their own mortal expectations and hopes. He is aware of those who yield with ultimate trust to their conviction that His expectations and hopes for them are, in the long run, better than anything they are capable of "expecting" for themselves. And His presence in that furnace sends the clear message that He understands, even "according to the flesh," how hard it is for us, especially in times of affliction, to accept His will when we really can't understand its implications. He wanted those three, and the rest of us, to know how fully He identifies with our fears and anxieties.

After all, no one else has experienced the dreaded "but if not" to the full extreme that He did—and apparently He too would have preferred to be spared: "Father, if thou be willing, remove this cup from me." Yet He too said "but if not"—"Nevertheless, not my will, but thine, be done." And in the moment of His greatest extremity, even the Giver of strength Himself received strengthening: "And there appeared an angel unto him from heaven, strengthening him" (Luke 22:42–43).

The Apostle Paul, a realist who knew whereof he spoke, described this dimension where our faith confronts our fears. He knew from his own experience that the "but if not" questions push us to decide if we will act on our faith even while facing anxious fears:

It is a fearful thing to fall into the hands of the living God. But call to remembrance the former days, . . . [when you] took joyfully the spoiling of your goods, knowing . . . that ye have in heaven a better and an enduring substance.

Cast not away therefore your confidence. . . . For ye have need of patience, that, after ye have done the will of God, ye might receive the promise. For yet a little while, and *he that shall come will come.* . . . Now the just shall live by faith: but if any man draw back, my soul shall have no pleasure in him. [For] *we are not of them who draw back.*" (Hebrews 10:31–39; emphasis added)

Paul knew what the three Hebrews knew: whatever happened in the furnace, they had in heaven waiting for them a more "enduring substance." Yet he honestly acknowledged what a "fearful thing" the "but if nots" can be. Paul's candor stirs up our courage to not "draw back."

IT WASN'T WHAT I EXPECTED

We have known some people who didn't draw back, and others who did. For instance, one young woman we know tried hard to live the gospel, even after the man she married made it clear that he didn't share her religious convictions. They had been unable to have any children. But after prayerful consideration, she felt that a child would help their marriage—and fulfill her lifelong desire for motherhood. They tried in vitro fertilization more than once, with no success. Then the marriage continued to fail, and within a few months they were divorced.

Her doctor told her that her difficulty in conceiving a child was probably due to a continuing medical condition that could still allow a pregnancy in the short run, but within about a year she would require a surgery that would end her ability to conceive. So she asked her honest question: should I find someone who would be willing to father my child, without marriage? Or what about artificial insemination? She knew that, for a single woman, Church teachings counseled against either option. But, she wondered, wasn't her motherhood important enough that, in her unusual circumstances, the Lord would understand her desire for an exception? She knew the Lord *could* help her somehow have a child—*but if not,* she wondered, "Does that mean I've done something wrong? Or is there some other reason why He isn't responding to my righteous desire?" As far as we know, she is still giving the Lord the benefit of her doubts.

Questions about childbearing are indeed filled with faith— and risk. Another friend finally married after she and her husband were in their thirties. With the news that they were expecting a child, her dream of home and family was about to be complete. Then her pregnancy became far more difficult than is normal, and the baby was born—beautiful but needing several future surgeries. The pregnancy and delivery also left our friend with serious physical impairments that affected her speech, her movement, and her balance. When we last saw her, she was functioning well below her normal capacity—but with hope that her condition would slowly improve. She said through her tears, "This was not quite what I was expecting." But those were also tears of joy. "I am so very happy," she said with an honest smile. "It is awful, but it is all so worth it."

Yet some do draw back. We're aware of two different men whose disappointed expectations have soured their attitude toward God. One of them lost a twenty-year-old son in an accident. That was years ago, and this father still says he can't believe in a God who would allow the death of a choice young man who had been the light of his father's life. The other man has almost identical feelings about the loss of his brother, a young father who died after a short and strange illness.

On the other hand, we know a single woman in her mid-forties who is discovering that Christ is with her in the heat of her questions. Her patriarchal blessing describes a beautiful life with a husband and children and says that together they will be of service in the kingdom of God on the earth. From the time she received her blessing as a teenager, it has represented everything she longs for. Although she finds faith-reinforcing solace in the gospel's "big-picture" perspective, she still has to face the lonely realities of each day and the disillusionment of treasured but yet unmet expectations.

In abject honesty she asks, "What happened? I'm doing everything I know to do, so what am I doing wrong? Are not my desires righteous? Why is He still holding back?" And then she asks the bedrock question that sounds so much like the one that came off the stone-cold floor of Liberty Jail: "Where did God go? If He is a loving Father, why would He bait me with such hopes for *this* life only to let them get dashed again and again with each passing year?"

Despite her frustration, she lives in "listening mode." Pieces of answers have come here and there that help make the still unexplained wait bearable. A few years ago, while sitting with her bishop during tithing settlement, he asked her if *she* had any questions for *him*. She lightheartedly blurted out, "You mean like, where is he?" gesturing toward her empty ring finger and the open seat next to her. Then with a fading smile she sincerely asked, "Did I miss a signal somewhere?" Before the bishop could speak, the Spirit entered the room, bringing them both to tears. "No," the bishop said quietly, "you haven't missed a signal. And the Spirit is telling me right now that when that signal comes, you *will* hear it. I know that because the Spirit has been giving you signals ever since you received the gift of the Holy Ghost as a child, and you have been following them. When the signal comes about this, you will know it."

Her gratitude for this profound reassurance was obvious as she shared the experience with us. Even so, the practical question for her still remains: "I am certain He will keep His promises somehow, but what do I do with today?" We know her well enough to know that she is not one who draws back. She is among those who, even in the heat of the furnace, step *into* the flames. Beneath the searing "but if nots," *she trusts Him.* For her, and others we know, the Abrahamic test is not a singular climb of Mount Moriah at the pinnacle of life or an untimely trek across the frozen plains, but rather a steady string of refining sacrifices in the tedium of every day.

And as is the case with many who walk that particularly lonely road, the temple has become her sanctuary, the place where she can consistently renew what it feels like to "know Him" as she does. She resonates with Paul's promise, "For yet a little while, and he that shall come will come" (Hebrews 10:37).

We know two other people, one a man and the other a woman, who have both confided in us about their longtime experiences with same-sex attraction. We became acquainted with the woman when she came to the St. George Temple to receive her temple endowment, the culmination of an odyssey of several years. During those years, she had separated herself from her partner and found her way back to the Church when she found a bishop who listened at length, understood with depth, and gave her his unqualified support.

She was eventually rebaptized and, supported by her family and by loving friends in her ward, became fully prepared for the temple. She has been learning the meaning of "but if not" in one of the most difficult of all places. And in many ways life is still a daily battle for her. But, she told us, "I can only do this because I love the Church and I have the faith that God has something better for me."

Our other friend tells us that many of his friends who have his same challenge have encouraged him to give up on the Church because they can't expect a change in Church doctrine that would approve of the relationships they desire to have. But, as he says, "God answers our prayers according to His timetable, His complete knowledge, and His perfect love. [And these outcomes in my life] have been so much better than what I would have chosen for myself. He has surprised me on the upside so many times, and I believe He will continue doing so. These include unique, personalized blessings that might not appear much to others, but they have deep meaning to me."

Not long ago, we attended the funeral for Bonnie Baker. When we first met Bonnie thirty years ago, she had been coping admirably with the lifelong limitations of moderate cerebral palsy. She was a bright, beautiful woman of deep, even fierce, faith. She fought hard for the college education she earned. She loved animals and children and missionary opportunities.

Bonnie wanted a normal life—marriage, children, the ability to run and dance and work. Talk about expectations. She had them. But instead—"but if not"—her circumstances only worsened. She developed multiple sclerosis, which gradually choked away her remaining physical strength. Then her doctor found that she had ovarian cancer and told her she would live only a few months.

However, the Bonnie we found in the hospital, then at her sister's home on hospice care, was wasting away only physically.

Buoyed up by constant care from her family, especially her mother, Bonnie's spirit seemed to grow stronger as her body became weaker. She was cheerful and good humored, observant and full of insights about this life and the next. We watched her becoming meek, full of love, and willing to submit to all that was being inflicted upon her.

As it turned out, Bonnie lived more than a year and a half longer than she or her doctor expected—one more way in which her life didn't unfold quite the way she had expected. In her final months she was bedridden, unable to do anything for herself. "This shell I'm living in is not me," she would say, glad that she could still smile and talk. But her sister told us that, like the handcart pioneers, Bonnie had chosen not to draw back, but to face what was ahead of her with faith and trust. When she could have lain there in bitterness over her frustrated expectations, she found peace instead. Paradoxically, when she knew she had no more physical control of her life and chose "to turn myself over to Him," then the peace came.

Bonnie had loved her Savior, and she came to know Him better in her extremities. She felt only gratitude for the way He had strengthened her spiritual well-being—the only form of being that mattered to her.

These stories prompt a natural question: What is the difference between the people whose unmet expectations lead them to "pull back" and those who, though equally disappointed, actually "pull forward"? We found one answer to that question a few years ago while attending a stake conference in Stockholm, Sweden.

TRUST OR BLESSINGS

Because the conference was in Swedish, a language translator named Jennifer Usterud was assigned to provide side-by-side translation to the congregation as we spoke to them in English.

She also sat behind us and whispered a translation as we listened to the other speakers. One of the congregational songs, a hymn we hadn't heard before, carried such an edifying spirit of serenity and reassurance that we asked Jennifer to translate it as they sang. Then we noticed it was from the Swedish LDS hymnbook, so we wondered why we had never heard it before.

After the meeting, Jennifer said the song is in the Swedish LDS hymnal because the Swedish Saints love it so much. It is a favorite old Swedish Christian song, with lyrics by Lina Sandell-Berg (1832–1903), who is still "Sweden's most celebrated author of gospel hymns."[3] Jennifer then said that a spontaneous translation couldn't possibly do justice to Sandell-Berg's writing because a hymn is a poem, and poetry must be translated into more poetry. So she offered to send us her translation when she could give it the time it deserved.

Several months later, the mail brought Jennifer's translation. She had needed to wait a long time for the inspiration she sought—but, as we soon saw and heard, the inspiration did come. She also told us why Lina Sandell-Berg's poetry is personally so dear to her: "I love her hymns because they are so genuinely from the heart. *Her faith was based in trust and not in blessings, and would therefore withstand any trial.*" By then we also knew that Jennifer was in her stake's Relief Society presidency, and that as a single mother raising three promising daughters, she knew firsthand about the difference between trust and blessings—and about dealing with disappointed expectations.

The two of us have come to appreciate this song (and Jennifer's translation of it) so much that we want to share it in a downloadable format at http://desbook.co/DayByDay. By having the music and lyrics before you, you can copy it, play it, and sing it. It conveys a memorable spirit of trust. Here is Jennifer's translation of the poetic text:

Day by Day

Let me live in moment after moment,
let me truly trust Thee day by day.
Let me not forget Thou art my Father.
Let me live by ev'ry word Thou sayest,
Every trial thou hast for me constructed,
and hast given me the strength I need.
Even when I cannot see tomorrow,
may I pay Thy counsel ev'ry heed.

I will walk the way Thou hast commanded,
even when the way is dark ahead.
When I fear, and when my spirit weakens,
I will trust in all that Thou hast said.
I will praise Thee for Thy loving kindness,
I will surely place my hand in Thine.
I will not be worried for tomorrow,
for I know that all Thou hast is mine.

Day by day I feel my spirit strengthen,
so that I can help my fellow man.
Let me see another's pain and sorrow,
so that I may help as best I can.
May I keep my hand in thine, my Father,
may I take each step with trust in Thee.
May I keep each one of Thy commandments,
that in heaven Thou canst welcome me.

We later learned about the tragedy that had given Lina Sandell-Berg the spiritual insight to compose these lines and her other faith-filled poetry. At the age of twenty-six she was on board a boat crossing a Swedish lake with her father, a Lutheran pastor, with whom she had enjoyed an unusually close relationship. (She had composed her first poems as a child at a desk he had set up for her in his own study.) Suddenly the boat lurched and, with Lina looking on, her father was thrown overboard and drowned.

In time, Lina found that God could consecrate her affliction to her gain, helping her find increased faith through her experience with sorrow and pain. As a result, "Lina had written hymns before, but now she poured out her broken heart in [many] beautiful songs" that influenced a Christian spiritual revival across Scandinavia after 1850. Some of her hymns, including the one we had heard in Stockholm, gained added appeal when her words were clothed in the simple beauty of Oscar Ahnfelt's (1813–1882) melodies. When he played his guitar and sang her hymns all over Scandinavia, Lina said he "sang her songs 'into the hearts of the people.'"[4]

There is much we could discuss from Lina's hymn. For example, thanks to Jennifer's unique LDS perspective, her translation of this line carries echoes from the individual promises of the temple sealing: "I will not be worried for tomorrow, for I know that all Thou hast is mine."

The core meaning of Lina's song can be distilled into Jennifer's one-line description of Lina's own contrite spirit: *"Her faith was based in trust and not in blessings, and would therefore withstand any trial."* When we assume that God should meet *our* "expectations," we are probably placing our faith in blessings and not in trust. Lina Sandell-Berg and those three Hebrew men in the furnace would tell us there is a better way: If we can just love God enough to trust Him, whatever the price, we are far better off to leave the rest to Him. Paul said it with such pure power: "All things work together for good to them that love God" (Romans 8:28).

If we do our part—the trust part—by living our love for Him, then He is able to cause all things to work for our good. If we can't even do that much, the problem isn't just that we're proud and stubborn. More seriously, the problem is that our failure even to turn our hearts to Him makes it impossible for Him to engage us enough in the growth process that He *can* make all things work for our good. Our insisting on our own expectations can prevent Him from fulfilling all that He desires to do for us.

Our willingness not to pull back can also lift and bless others—perhaps some of those dearest to us, who may watch us in our fiery trials. King Nebuchadnezzar did see with his own eyes "four men . . . walking in the midst of the fire, and they have no hurt; and the form of the fourth is like the Son of God" (Daniel 3:25). Something similar happened when Abinadi's fearless testimony before King Noah's court led him to a fiery death—and to the dramatic conversion of the watchful Alma (see Mosiah 17), thereby changing for the better the course of Nephite history—and the content of the Book of Mormon. Through our loving trust toward the Lord, He can cause "all things" to work not only for our good, but for the greater good.

CHAPTER 13

MARRIAGE,
AT-ONE-MENT,
AND THE TEMPLE

Because of the Atonement's blessings and the power of the temple's sealing ordinances, we can, if we are faithful, one day take the hands that have held ours and enter our Father's presence together. There we can embrace our loved ones and stay with them always, to "go no more out" (Revelation 3:12). The promise of eternal love is not just a high point along the pathway of a true follower—in some ways it is *the point* of the journey. But because of some recent developments within the modern society (including the national legalization of same-gender marriage), our desire and effort to fulfill this vision must now overcome formidable opposition. It might help to step back and look for some doctrinal and historical perspective on the current cultural chaos.

THE LONGING TO BELONG AND THE WANING OF BELONGING

Most people of all ages respond warmly and instinctively to the hope—the dream—of being together forever with those they love most. We each carry deep within ourselves an inborn *longing to belong* that naturally draws us first into our mother's arms, then to our father and to our siblings, then gradually extending to others. As we grow, this longing can mature and blossom into our own marriage. Then we may be blessed to learn for ourselves what it means to have joy in our posterity—an inkling of celestial joy.

Yet in today's culture, a provocative and unsettling idea runs directly counter to this instinctive desire. We could call it the *waning of belonging*—the growing assumption that in order to remain completely free and unshackled, no one should *belong* to anyone else. Children don't belong to parents; husbands don't belong to wives; nobody belongs to anybody. Thus many today honestly wonder whether the bonds of kinship and marriage are valuable ties that bind—or sheer bondage.

These opposing forces—the longing to belong versus the waning of belonging—are now locked in a kind of battle for, and within, our souls. And the current momentum is sliding toward the value of being more alone. Indeed, one of the "rights" most vocally demanded these days is the right to be left alone.

It is of course true that some people—sometimes tragically—have exploited and abused the trust placed in them by marriage partners or other family members. But those mistakes don't mean that the ideal itself is no longer worth striving for. Indeed, whether we *strive* to make a marriage work may be the most important ingredient in whether it does work.

Jesus did sacrifice Himself to offer us the great at-one-ment, not the great alone-ment. His matchless act of mercy makes possible the fulfillment of our deepest hunger to "be with" God and with each other, in an eternity of sharing and belonging together. That Jesus, the Holy One of Israel, would love *us* enough to want to be *with us* is a nearly unfathomable thought. He has also taught us from the beginning that it is not good for man—or woman—to be alone. We don't need to wonder which picture best captures the meaning of spiritual or psychological "freedom": being held in the arms of God and those we love most, or being separated—banished—permanently from their presence.

Still, the enemy of our souls, who seeks our eternal and lonely misery, tries to drive ever larger wedges between our relationships with one another and with God. That is why every sealing performed in our temples today is a victory in the battle for our eternal happiness.

That is also why the First Presidency and the Quorum of the Twelve in 1995 announced "The Family: A Proclamation to the World." By that time, our society was already in the eye of a great cultural storm that was battering as never before the centuries-old structures of marriage, family, parenthood, and childhood. I have tried to describe the historical context and some implications of that storm elsewhere.[1] Here we need only a brief summary, just enough to underscore why, as the storm swirls around us, each of us has a critical need to capture and take hold of the unique vision of marriage and family life taught in the temple. Only the Savior's Atonement and the temple's sealing authority make the fulfillment of that eternal vision of belonging possible.

HOW WE LOST THE PLOT

"What are your greatest concerns?" a newspaper reporter asked President Gordon B. Hinckley in June 1995 as he turned eighty-five. He replied, "I am concerned about family life in the Church. We have wonderful people, but we have too many whose families are falling apart. *I think [this] is my most serious concern.*"[2] Three months later, President Hinckley publicly gave us "The Family: A Proclamation to the World."

It was no coincidence that this solemn declaration was issued precisely when the Lord's prophet felt that, of all the subjects on his mind, unstable family life *in the Church* was his greatest concern. Later he added that the greatest challenge facing both America and the rest of world is "the problem of the family, brought on by misguided parents and resulting in misguided children."[3]

So this proclamation is not just a collection of pro-family platitudes. It is a serious prophetic warning about a major international problem. And now, two decades later, the problem is only getting worse, which shows just how prophetic the 1995 warning was. How is it that modern culture could have been lured away from widely shared, centuries-old moral norms about parents and children?

Humankind's oldest, most hoped-for story line has a familiar plot: boy meets girl, they fall in love, marry, have children, and—they hope—live happily ever after. That universal love story is so central to the great plan of happiness that it began with Adam and Eve, and for most Church members, it still guides our lives like the North Star.

The joys of human love and family belonging do give us hope, purpose, and a desire to live better. And for countless years, society generally supported this inborn longing to belong. Of course families had problems, but most people still believed that "tying the knot" of marriage created a relatively permanent family unit. And those knots held the fabric of society together, with "hearts knit together in unity and in love" (Mosiah 18:21).

In recent generations, however, the fabric has increasingly frayed, as we have experienced what some writers call "the collapse of marriage."[4] Many people outside the Church no longer see marriage as a source of long-term commitments. Rather, they now see marriage and even childbearing as temporary personal options. Yet permanent commitments to marriage and parenthood are like two anchor threads running through the design of our social tapestry. When those threads fray, the tapestry can unravel . . . and we can lose the plot, and the point, of the universal love story.

I have watched this unraveling from the perspectives of a father, a Church member, and a teacher of family law. Beginning in the 1960s, the civil rights movement spawned new legal theories about equality, individual rights, and liberation. These ideas helped the United States begin to overcome its embarrassing history of racial discrimination. They also helped the country reduce discrimination against women. These protections from discrimination are part of each citizen's *individual interests*.

Some forms of legal classification, however, are actually beneficial. For example, the law "discriminates" in favor of children on the basis of their age—they can't vote, drive a car, or sign a binding contract. And they receive years of free education. These laws protect children and society from the consequences of children's lack of capacity while also preparing them to become responsible adults and citizens.

Our laws have also given a privileged status to relationships based on marriage and kinship—not to discriminate against single and unrelated people but to encourage biological parents to marry each other and to raise their own stable children, who become the key to a stable continuing society. Such laws thus express society's *social interests* in the well-being of its children and—through those children—in society's own future strength and continuity.

A MASSIVE CULTURAL SHIFT

Historically, our laws maintained a workable balance between our "social interests" and our "individual interests" in family life, because each element plays an important role in a healthy society. However, in the 1960s and 1970s, U.S. courts began to interpret family laws in ways that gave individual interests a much higher priority than social interests, which knocked the legal and social system regarding families out of balance. This change was but one part of the transformation of American family law—the biggest cultural shift in attitudes about marriage and family life in 500 years. We can illustrate this transformation with some examples from U.S. law, although the laws of most developed countries have followed similar trends.

In a nutshell, advocates began using potent individual-liberation ideas to challenge laws that had long supported the interests of children and society in stable family structures. Courts and legislatures accepted many of these individualistic ideas, even when the ideas damaged larger social interests. For example, no-fault divorce was first adopted in California in 1968 and then spread across the United States. No-fault significantly changed the way people thought about marriage. Under the old divorce laws, married people couldn't just choose to end their marriage; rather, they had to prove spousal misconduct, like adultery or abuse. In those days, only a judge representing society's interests could determine when a divorce was justified enough to outweigh the social interest in marital continuity.

As originally conceived, no-fault divorce had worthy goals. It added irretrievable marriage breakdown, regardless of personal fault, as a basis for divorce, which simplified the divorce process. In theory, only a judge, who still represented society's interests, could decide whether a marriage was beyond repair. But in practice, family court judges deferred to the personal preference of the couple and eventually "liberated" whichever partner wanted to end the marriage.

These legal changes accelerated a larger cultural drift that no longer saw marriage as a relatively permanent social institution but rather as a temporary, private relationship, terminable at will—without seriously considering how divorce damaged children, let alone how it damaged society. Before long, judges' doubts about society's right to enforce wedding vows gave married couples the false impression that their personal promises held no great social or moral value. So now, when marriage commitments intrude on personal preferences, people are more likely to walk away. Many now see marriage as a "nonbinding commitment," whatever that contradiction means.

Reflecting these new attitudes, courts expanded the parental rights of unwed fathers and began to give child custody and adoption rights to unmarried individuals. This uprooted the long-established preference that family law had given, whenever possible, to the married, two-parent, biological family. Both experience and the social science research had clearly shown—and still show—that a family headed by married, biological parents almost always provides the best child-rearing environment.[5] But over time, the unwed-parent cases contributed to, and were influenced by, skyrocketing rates of unmarried cohabitation and births outside marriage.

Talking about no-fault divorce leads logically to a comment about same-sex marriage, especially in view of recent events. This has become a difficult and poignant topic, even though only seventeen years ago, no country in the world had ever legally recognized such marriages. However, "in the space of not many years" later (Helaman 4:26), the U.S. Supreme Court in 2015 gave nationwide constitutional protection to homosexual marriage.[6]

How could the very idea of same-gender marriage burst upon the international scene precisely when the historic concept of marriage had lost so much public value during the previous four decades?

One likely answer is that the "personal autonomy" theory of the first U.S. case to uphold same-sex marriage in 2001 simply extended the same individualistic legal concept that had created no-fault divorce. When a court upholds an individual's right to *end* a marriage, regardless of social consequences (as can happen with no-fault divorce), that principle may also seem to support an individual's right to *start* a marriage, regardless of social consequences (as can happen with same-sex marriage).

In other words, when people see man-woman marriage as just a matter of personal preference rather than as society's key social institution, it's little wonder that many would now say of same-gender marriage that individuals should be free to marry as they choose. That's what can happen when we lose track of society's interest in marriage and children. Clearly God loves all of His children and expects us to treat one another with compassion and tolerance—regardless of private conduct we may or may not understand. But it is a very different matter to endorse or promote that conduct by altering a legal concept—marriage—whose primary historic purpose was to promote society's interest in having biological parents rear their own children in stable homes.

The United States Supreme Court relied first on the personal autonomy theory, among other legal theories,[7] when it held in 2015 that same-gender couples have a constitutional right to marry. The Court's majority opinion also emphasized that "religions, and those who adhere to religious doctrines, may continue to advocate . . . that, by divine precepts, same-sex marriage should not be condoned." The Constitution's First Amendment protects the right of "religious organizations and persons" to teach "the principles that are so . . . central to their lives and faiths, and to their own deep aspirations to continue the family structure they have long revered."[8] It remains to be seen, however, to what extent the right to "advocate" religious beliefs will also protect *conduct* based on the "free *exercise*" of those beliefs against claims of discrimination based on opposition to same-gender marriage.

A few days after this decision was announced, the First Presidency and the Quorum of the Twelve Apostles publicly reaffirmed their previous counsel that "Marriage between a man and a woman" is "central to [God's] plan for His children and for the well-being of society" and that "sexual relations outside of such a marriage are contrary to the laws of God." At the same time, the Church leaders stressed that "The gospel of Jesus Christ teaches us to love and treat all people with kindness and civility— even when we disagree," and those who accept "same-sex marriage should not be treated disrespectfully."[9]

EFFECTS ON MARRIAGE AND CHILDREN

The cumulative effects of these changes on marriage and children came swiftly and ran deep. Since about 1965, the U.S. divorce rate has more than doubled, although it has dipped slightly in recent years—partly because the number of unmarried cohabiting couples has increased by an astonishing fifteen times, and their frequent breakups aren't included in the divorce rate. Today about half of all first marriages end in divorce; about 60 percent of second marriages do. The United States is the world's most divorce-prone country.[10]

Today over 40 percent of U.S. births are to unmarried parents. In 1960 that number was 5 percent.[11] About 50 percent of today's teens now consider out-of-wedlock childbearing a "worthwhile lifestyle."[12] The fraction of children being raised in single-parent families since 1960 has increased fourfold, from 8 percent of all children to 31 percent;[13] and among parents who have only a high-school education, that number is now 70 percent.[14] Over half of today's U.S. marriages are preceded by unmarried cohabitation.[15] What was highly abnormal until the 1960s is the new normal.

In Europe, 80 percent of the population now approves of unmarried cohabitation. In Scandinavia, 82 percent of firstborn children are born outside marriage.[16] When we lived in Germany recently, we sensed among Europeans that, in many ways, marriage is no more; marriage has gone away. As a French writer put it, marriage has "lost its magic for young people," who increasingly feel that "love is essentially a private matter which leaves no room" for society to say anything about their marriage or their children.[17] In the U.S., a recent story on CNN reported that, in the minds of many "millennials" (those age eighteen to twenty-nine), the very idea of marriage is becoming antiquated and irrelevant.[18]

Taken together, these statistics send an ominous message because the children of divorced or unwed parents have about *three times* as many *serious* behavioral, emotional, and developmental problems as children living with their married mother and father. By every measure of child well-being, these children are far worse off. And when children are dysfunctional, society becomes dysfunctional.

In giving some examples of that dysfunction, we acknowledge that some elements in such general trends may have multiple causes. In the past five decades, juvenile crime has increased sixfold. Child neglect and all forms of child abuse have quintupled. Psychological disorders among children have all worsened, from drug abuse to eating disorders; depression among children has increased 1,000 percent. Domestic violence against women has increased. And poverty has shifted increasingly to children.[19]

HOW SERIOUS ARE THESE PROBLEMS?

The Lord's prophet, President Hinckley, did say in 1995 that these issues were his "most serious concern." And the trends that troubled him then are now considerably worse. As a *Time* magazine writer put it: "There is no other single force causing as much measurable hardship and human misery in this country as the collapse of marriage. It hurts children, it reduces mothers' financial security, and it has landed with particular devastation on those who can bear it least: the nation's underclass. . . . The poor [have uncoupled] parenthood from marriage, and the financially secure [blast] apart their [own] unions if [they] aren't having fun anymore."[20]

Recent research by Harvard political scientist Robert Putnam shows the effects of the marriage collapse on the many children in single-parent homes where the parent has only a high-school education. Putnam's tragically typical but horrific case studies based on personal interviews put some compelling faces on the overall statistics.

For example, David grew up mostly with his dad, but he had nine half-siblings and no fixed address. "Adults moved in and out of his life without worrying what happened to the kids." He went to "seven different elementary schools," and school was "a problem," but he still wants "a higher education" so he can get a job. He got his girlfriend pregnant, then she took up with a drug addict guy, but David still loves "being a dad." He posted on Facebook, "I always end up at the losing end. I just want to feel whole again."[21]

Kayla's mom left her abusive first husband, lived with her boss for a while, and they had Kayla. Her mom then lived with several other men who drank a lot, but she never had a regular job. Kayla's dad got an eighteen-year-old girl pregnant, then left her when he found she was in an abusive relationship with her stepfather. Kayla grew up with five step-siblings, saying her mom wasn't "there for her." She hated school and felt abandoned.[22]

When Elijah was a child he often saw "people being kidnapped and raped and killed." He saw a child killed in a drive-by shooting when he was four. He didn't see much of his mom but he visited his dad in jail. Once his dad beat him for burning down a lady's house. Later his mom kicked him out of the house for getting "high and drunk every night." He dreams of being a preacher, but he still "just love beating up somebody." He's got "a lot of personal issues."[23]

From such stories and the extensive data behind them, *New York Times* columnist David Brooks draws the conclusion, "We now have multiple generations of people caught in recurring feedback loops of economic stress and family breakdown, often leading to something approaching *an anarchy of the intimate life.*" In looking for basic causes, Brooks believes that the vital missing ingredient in these millions of families is not money or social policy; rather, *the problem is the absence of "norms,"*—the "habits and virtues" that determine a society's health. For example, he writes, "In many parts of America there are no minimally agreed upon standards for what it means to be a father. There are no basic codes and rules woven into daily life." And these norms *"weren't destroyed because of people with bad values. They were destroyed by a plague of nonjudgmentalism, which refused to assert that one way of behaving was better than another."*[24]

Why include these unsettling insights about the destruction of our social norms regarding marriage and parenting in a book about the temple and the Atonement? Because this chaotic shift in the prevailing cultural paradigms is already contaminating and disorienting us, our children, and our children's children. The pollution is almost unavoidable. We see it all around us, in our neighborhoods and in our own extended families. Even below the conscious levels of our thoughts and attitudes, this pervasive absence of norms, of expectations, and of common-sense judgment can affect and alter our assumptions and behavior about the most critical personal and spiritual relationships in our lives.

TURNING OUR HEARTS

One golden but tattered thread in this unraveling social tapestry symbolizes the heart of the problem: the children—bone of our bones, flesh of our flesh. Something true, even temple-like, about the very word *posterity* resonates deeply within our collective memory. It's about children, procreation, eternal bonds of affection, the priesthood's sealing power, descendants, and ancestors.

The child-parent tie matters so much that the Lord sent Elijah in 1836 to "turn the hearts" of the fathers and the children toward each other. If those hearts do not so turn, He said, "the whole earth [will] be smitten with a curse" and "utterly wasted" at Christ's coming (D&C 110:15; Joseph Smith—History 1:39; see also Malachi 4:6). In today's world, those hearts do appear to be turning—but too many are turning away from rather than toward each other, thereby rejecting Elijah's promise.

Are we already living in the time of the curse? Perhaps. Many of today's children (and therefore society—the whole earth) are indeed being "wasted" (devalued, made useless, rendered desolate) by the current confounding attitudes.

The doctrine about the value of stable families is clear—and is substantiated by years of research. We don't need to return to all of the rigid family laws of fifty years ago, but today's children desperately want and need a father and a mother and a permanent sense of *home* to give them safety and encouragement to grow in every good way. If we could care more about our children and their future, people would marry before becoming parents. They would sacrifice more, much more, to stay married. Children would be raised, whenever possible, by their biological parents. Ideally, there would be no elective abortions or unwed births.

Of course, some exceptions are needed—some divorces are justified, and adoption can be heaven-sent. Yet in principle the family proclamation says it perfectly: "Children are entitled to birth within the bonds of matrimony, and to be reared by a father and a mother who honor marital vows with complete fidelity."[25]

But we are suffering from collective amnesia. We are not hearing the mystic chords of our eternal, or even recent, memories. The enemy of our happiness wants to convince us that the sacred, long-term bonds of family affection are confining, when in fact no relationships are more liberating and fulfilling.

Building a good marriage is not easy. It isn't supposed to be easy. *But when a confused culture confuses us about what marriage means, we may give up on each other and ourselves much too soon.* Yet with the gospel's eternal perspective, as taught in the scriptures and the temple, we can transcend the modern marital chaos and make our marriages the most satisfying and sanctifying— even if also the most demanding—experiences of our lives.

CHAPTER 14

The Temple and the Natural Order of Marriage

Like the ancient mariner, most of us look to the heavens to get our bearings—and we do that through the temple. Every time we go to the temple, the ordinances reorient us to the godly natural order of the universe. And the North Star in that heavenly order is eternal marriage. It is at the very core of God's plan for us.

It is true that many devoted men and women do not now live in the kind of marriage they desire. Church doctrine of course encourages marriage and discourages divorce. But marrying is not always under our control. And there are some times when divorce is the better choice.[1] Whatever else happens, whether we are married or not, whether we have children or not, the promises of our doctrine are sure and clear: no eternal blessing—no blessing of the temple—will be denied those who are truly faithful.

LDS scholar Hugh Nibley wrote: "The temple is built so as to represent the organizing principles of the universe. It is the school where mortals learn about these things. . . . The earth temple [is] in the middle of everything, . . . around which all heavenly motions revolve, the knot that ties earth and heaven together."[2] The most important knot is tied when a husband and a wife are sealed. When this knot is secure, it holds our social tapestry together, and not just for this life. And the power of the temple etches God's natural order about marriage and family life into our hearts.

THE MARRIAGE OF ADAM AND EVE

We first learn the temple's teachings about marriage from the story of Adam and Eve—the primal story of the temple. Adam and Eve were the first people on earth to receive the Atonement. They were also the first parents to know the love a newborn child brings, the soul-stretching sacrifices of raising a child, and the agony of watching children use their agency unwisely.

When Father Lehi taught his family about Adam and Eve's experience, one of his first statements was about children. If Adam and Eve had stayed in the Garden of Eden, he said, "they would have had no children; wherefore, they would have remained in a state of innocence, having no joy, for they knew no misery" (2 Nephi 2:23). Further, they would have tasted neither sorrow nor sin because "man could not act for himself save it should be that he" is enticed by (and experiences) both the bitterness of evil and the sweetness of good (2 Nephi 2:15–16).

In other words, had they remained in Eden, they could never have had the experiences that made it possible for them to know the meaning of their very existence, to fathom the satisfactions of actual joy. We grasp meaning only in the midst of contraries. Thus only those who have lived in the depths carved out of their hearts by tribulation can have room enough for their hearts to contain and truly comprehend the fulness of joy that awaits them.

When Adam and Eve learned from the angel how Christ's Redemption would bring these very principles together to make their growth possible, they rejoiced: "Eve . . . heard all these things and was glad, saying: Were it not for our transgression we never should have had seed, and never should have known good and evil, and the joy of our redemption, and the eternal life which God giveth unto all the obedient" (Moses 5:11).

So the temple's foundation story is the story of a married couple who, through their shared earthly experience, were schooled by the confluence of the sweet and the bitter. At the beginning of their relationship, Adam and Eve both acted separately from one another. When the Lord asked Adam about his choice to eat the forbidden fruit, Adam answered, "The *woman* thou gavest me, and commandest that she should remain with me, she gave me of the fruit . . . and I did eat" (Moses 4:18; emphasis added). But later, after they had lost both Abel *and* Cain, the scriptures let us see a picture of Adam and Eve being brought to their knees together: "Adam and *his wife* mourned before the Lord, because of Cain and his brethren" (Moses 5:27; emphasis added). Together they were coming to understand more about the bitterness that life can inflict—and about the sanctuary they had in each other.

The Adam and Eve story offers us layers of learning about marriage. Their story shows us, for example, the Restoration's positive view about the Fall. We know that Eve and then Adam chose wisely in the garden because only the natural, mortal consequences of eating the fruit could provide the experience—including the children—needed to fulfill God's plan for them, and for us. In contrast, traditional Christianity incorrectly teaches that Eve's choice was a terrible mistake, bringing down the wrath of God on all mankind. Some Christian churches still teach that because women are the daughters of foolish Eve, wives should be dependent on their husbands.

Reacting strongly against this idea, most people today would say that a wife should be independent of her husband. And, in fairness, they would add, a husband should also be independent of his wife. But when both spouses are independent of each other, they usually accept only today's "nonbinding commitments," so they are likely to leave their marriage when the fun stops—or when the trouble starts.

Which is correct: *dependence* or *independence*? Neither one. The restored gospel—unlike the rest of Christianity—teaches that Eve and Adam's choice in the garden wasn't a mistake or an accident; rather, their action was a deliberate, even glorious, part of the plan of salvation. Thus the Restoration sees Eve—and all women—as noble beings who are the complete equals of men.

So Eve is not dependent on Adam, nor is she independent from him. Rather, Eve and Adam are *interdependent* with each other. They are "equal partners" who "help one another" in everything they do.[3]

BRINGING TO THE ALTAR A BROKEN HEART AND CONTRITE SPIRIT

The Adam and Eve story also teaches us about sacrifice—both in general and as a sanctifying dimension of marriage. When Adam and Eve left the garden, the Lord asked them to build an altar and offer sacrifices. They didn't understand the purpose of sacrificing an animal in this solemn, ceremonial way until the angel explained, "This thing is a similitude of the sacrifice of the Only Begotten." Therefore, the angel continued, "thou shalt do all that thou doest in the name of the Son. . . . And in that day the Holy Ghost fell upon Adam, . . . saying, . . . as thou hast fallen thou mayest be *redeemed, and all mankind, even as many as will*" (Moses 5:6–8; emphasis added).

The sacrifices that Adam and Eve placed on that ancient altar therefore anticipated, symbolized, and prepared them to accept Christ's own redemptive sacrifice in their behalf. This ordinance played a key role in helping them understand what it would mean for them to be "redeemed": to have life after death, to be forgiven, and to receive and engage the Savior's Atonement in ways that would advance their growth toward a fulness of both comprehension and joy.

From that time until the coming of Christ, the Lord's people practiced the same sacrificial ordinance whenever the priesthood was available to them. During the time of Moses, for instance, the ordinances of the tabernacle in the wilderness (the outdoor temple) focused on specific details that pointed unmistakably toward Christ. Their sacrifice was not just any animal—it was typically a lamb, a firstborn and unblemished lamb, with each clue pointing toward the coming of the Lamb of God.

The ordinances of our own day also point us unmistakably toward Christ. We look back in time to His sacrifice through the bread and water that are prepared on the altar we call the sacrament table. And we look timelessly both forward and backward through the temple ordinances, which are administered on altars of covenant, prayer, and sacrifice. All of the ordinances point us toward Christ's sacrifice, and when we personally extend that symbolic pattern we can learn what it can mean for us to live *"in similitude" of that sacrifice* in our daily walk.

As Elder Bruce R. McConkie wrote: "If we had sufficient insight, we would see in every . . . rite that is part of revealed religion, in every performance commanded by God, in all things Deity gives his people, something that typifies the eternal ministry of the Eternal Christ. . . . It is wholesome and proper to look for similitudes of Christ everywhere and to use them repeatedly in keeping him and his laws uppermost in our minds."[4]

After completing His earthly mission, the Savior Himself taught that rather than continuing to offer animal sacrifices, "Ye shall offer for a sacrifice unto me a broken heart and a contrite spirit" (3 Nephi 9:20; see also 2 Nephi 2:7). And as we saw earlier, the sealing of a temple marriage gives us the opportunity, the invitation, and the aspiration to offer to one another and to the Lord, by covenant, the sacrifice of our own broken heart and contrite spirit.

A marriage relationship based on this sacred pattern could be described as a triangle. The husband and wife stand at the base of the triangle, one at each corner. Each one looks toward the other in his or her covenant of sacrifice. At the same time, each one also looks upward toward, and offers sacrificial covenants to, God, who stands at the apex of the triangle.

In the unfolding days and details of their lives, both husband and wife try to live the pattern of their covenants by treating one another as the Savior Himself would. As they also continually nourish their personal relationship with the Lord, each one ascends along his or her side of the triangle, drawing ever closer to God. As that occurs, the triangle helps us visualize what happens in their husband/wife relationship—the closer each one comes to God, the closer they come to one another. And finally, when they reach the apex, each is "at one" with God—and they have also now become "at one" with each other.

This covenantal, sacrifice-based understanding of marriage differs starkly and powerfully from the prevailing cultural view of marriage today. In His parable of the good shepherd, Jesus described a hireling—someone who is paid to care for the sheep. When the wolf comes, He said, the hireling "leaveth the sheep, and fleeth." Why does the hireling run away? Because his "own the sheep are not." By contrast, Jesus said of Himself, "I am the good shepherd. . . . I lay down my life for the sheep" (John 10:11–15).

Many people today treat their marriage—or their unmarried relationship—as an informal arrangement between two hirelings. When a hireling feels threatened by some wolf of trouble, he or she simply flees. Why should hirelings risk their comfort or convenience, let alone their lives?

But when we offer in our marriage a broken heart and a contrite spirit in similitude of the Good Shepherd, we give our lives for the sheep of our covenant, a day, an hour, or even a minute at a time. This process invites us to take upon ourselves both the afflictions and the joys of our companion and children, choosing to emulate in our own limited way how the Savior takes upon Himself our afflictions.

"Be you afflicted in all his afflictions" (D&C 30:6), said the Lord to Peter Whitmer about his missionary companion, Oliver Cowdery. Isaiah echoed that phrase in describing Christ and those He redeems: "In all their affliction he was afflicted" (Isaiah 63:9; D&C 133:53).

We once asked some temple workers what they thought it would mean to live the life of a broken heart and a contrite spirit in marriage, to treat one's spouse as Christ Himself would treat us. One of them said, "It means choosing to be kind—all the time." Another said, "Trying to care more about your spouse's needs than you do your own." One more said, "I will offer not only my heart, but also my arms and my hands." And, "It's the sacrifice of learning to give up the natural man within me." And finally, "It takes a broken heart and contrite spirit for me to overcome my pride and be forgiving the way Christ forgives me."

Another temple worker lost his wife after she had suffered a debilitating illness for several years. He told us, "I thought I knew what love was—we'd had over fifty blessed years together.

But only in caring for her in these last few years have I discovered what love really is."

By tirelessly giving of himself to her in her afflictions, this man discovered a hidden reservoir of compassion in his heart that a hireling will never know. The accumulation of such discoveries produces a sanctifying effect—one gesture of kindness or forgiveness or forbearance at a time.

PERFECTION AND RECONCILIATION

A friend asked recently, "How close to perfection must we live in order to receive the exalted promises of a temple sealing?" Husbands and wives know each other so well, especially those who seek for eternal blessings, that on some days they can honestly wonder if they are living close enough to perfection—or if their spouse is.

Moroni gives us the answer: If you "deny yourselves of all ungodliness" and "love God with all your . . . strength," then "by his grace ye may be perfect[ed] in Christ" (Moroni 10:32). One way to rid ourselves of *ungodliness* is to stay close to the temple, where "the power of *godliness* is manifest" (D&C 84:20; emphasis added). Further, loving "God with all *your* might" includes loving your husband or your wife as completely as *you* are capable of loving.

As we deny ourselves of ungodliness and honestly love God as fully as we know how, Christ's perfecting grace will bless us enough to complete the process of making us holy. A First Presidency letter written in 1902 suggests what Christ's total sacrifice combined with our own total sacrifice will look like:

> After reaching the perfected state of life people will have
> no other desire than to live in harmony with [righteousness],
> including that which united them as husband and wife. . . .
> Those who attain to the first or celestial resurrection must

necessarily be pure and holy, and they will be perfect in body as well. . . . Every man and woman that reaches this unspeakable condition of life will be as beautiful as the angels that surround the throne of God; . . . for the weaknesses of the flesh will then have been overcome and forgotten; and both [will] be in harmony with the law that united them.[5]

I know a woman who came to understand the hope this statement can give. She was married about fifty years ago in the temple. After she and her husband had had several children, his turbulent life led to their divorce and to his excommunication from the Church. Then she gave up her own Church membership and chose some thorny paths. Later her former husband passed away.

Years later I met her when she and her daughter came to my office to explore whether she could ever return to the temple. After a peaceful conversation about how we can learn from experience without being condemned by it, we discussed the processes of repentance, rebaptism, and the eventual restoration of the temple blessings she had lost along with her Church membership. I explained that the restoration ordinance would also restore her temple sealing. "Would you be ready for that?" I asked.

The daughter spoke first. "I have bipolar disorder. My son is bipolar. We know far more about that disorder now than we used to, and we take medications that help. Looking back, I believe my father was bipolar, and that probably influenced many of the hard things in our family's life. Knowing what I do now, I don't judge him anymore."

After a pause the mother answered softly with evident contrition, "If I really can return to the temple someday, I will be ready for my sealing to be restored."

As they left my office and I watched them walk down the hall,

I realized that the temple and Elijah's sealing power are sources of *reconciliation*, not only turning the hearts of children and parents toward one another, but also turning the hearts of wives and husbands toward one another. Some weeks later I received a message that the mother was being rebaptized.

The natural order of marriage that God gave to Adam and Eve is worth whatever it takes—to find it, to build it, and to keep it in our lives. And husbands and wives who try to live like the Good Shepherd will discover, and they will give to each other, a more abundant life.

CHAPTER 15

MISSIONARY WORK, THE TEMPLE, AND REAL GROWTH

When Nephi first became the prophet-leader of his people, he was spiritually mature and felt unwavering trust in the Lord. Yet he was also acutely conscious of his own shortcomings, feeling a continuing need for faith and repentance. Those first principles clearly are "first," and our need for them never really diminishes as we learn and grow:

"Notwithstanding the great goodness of the Lord . . . my heart exclaimeth: O wretched man that I am! Yea, . . . my heart groaneth because of my sins; nevertheless, I know in whom I have trusted. . . . O Lord, wilt thou redeem my soul? . . . May the gates of hell be shut continually before me, *because that my heart is broken and my spirit is contrite!*" (2 Nephi 4:17, 19, 31–32; emphasis added).

At the same time, it was also Nephi, only a few chapters later, who explained that faith, repentance, and baptism are but the entryway to the "path which leads to eternal life." And once on that pathway, we must "press forward with a steadfastness in Christ," cultivating the higher principles of hope, charity, and "feasting upon the word of Christ" to keep moving, enduring, and growing (2 Nephi 31:18, 20; 32:3).

Nephi was talking here about the complete pattern of spiritual growth that is familiar to us by now. We could profit from his example by looking more often and more deeply at the entire series of ordinances and principles of the two priesthoods—from baptism all the way to the temple sealing. Thus can we grow, as Nephi did, to our full spiritual stature "of the knowledge of the Son of God, unto a perfect man, unto the measure of the stature of the fulness of Christ" (Ephesians 4:13).

NEW CONVERTS: GROUNDED, ROOTED, AND ESTABLISHED

One practical way of demonstrating this pattern is to look at the natural sequence of a new Church member's experience. This sequence is intended to help new members become "grounded," "rooted," and "established" in both the gospel and the Church. It also helps them envision and experience conversion as an actual process of learning to live the Savior's way of life, not merely as joining the Church.

The Lord spoke often in the Book of Mormon about the need to "establish my Church" (see, for example, Mosiah 27:13; Alma 4:4; 3 Nephi 21:22)—not only to establish the institutional Church, but to establish each member, the way a healthy, living tree establishes itself with deep roots: "And blessed art thou [Alma] because thou hast established a church among this people; *and they shall be established,* and *they shall be my people*" (Mosiah 26:17; emphasis added).

When a tree sets its roots, it relies on a dominant taproot, which grows down vertically and is the main root from which other roots sprout horizontally. When the taproot is strong, it is the heart of the root system, supplying nourishment and steady strength to establish the plant even when some lateral parts of the root system may be disturbed or weakened.

The Apostle Paul, whose ministry was often devoted to helping new converts and new Church units, knew all about the taproot of a personal relationship with Christ. He spoke of new members' need to be "*rooted* and built up in [Christ], and *stablished* in the faith" (Colossians 2:7; emphasis added) and to "continue in the faith *grounded and settled,* and be not moved away from the hope of the gospel" (Colossians 1:23; emphasis added).

We can apply this sequential perspective to the way missionaries and Church members look at the process of finding, teaching, baptizing, and retaining new converts. As we do, consider whether and how our approach helps new members become truly "established," like a tree with a strong root system. "But if ye will . . . nourish the tree as it beginneth to grow, . . . it shall take root; and behold it shall be a tree springing up unto everlasting life" (Alma 32:41). Sustaining that "springing up" process will nurture the new convert through every ordinance, every covenant, and every principle of the ascending Aaronic and Melchizedek levels of growth.

Alma said this nourishing process requires "faith with great diligence, and with patience, looking forward to the fruit thereof" (Alma 32:41). In order to help missionaries and ward members encourage each step in that patient, long-term nurturing, the Church's handbook for ward leaders instructs the ward council to regularly "discuss the progress of each new member and identify areas where he or she may need more support," and to "use the New and Returning Member Progress form as a guide for this discussion."[1]

This progress form is only a tool, a set of symbols for what should be a very real process of spiritual development through the sequential ordinances and principles of the two priesthoods. The form does show visually what that sequential growth process looks like—at least on paper. Its purpose is not merely to have local leaders check boxes mechanically, but to give them concrete steps and cues so they can teach new converts the more fundamental process of personal change and growth in their faith and testimony—just as Jesus taught in the parable of the sower: "He that received seed into the good ground is he that heareth the word, and understandeth it; which also beareth fruit, . . . some an hundredfold" (Matthew 13:23).

A Utah bishop I know recently shared with me an email written by a sister missionary from his home ward who had been serving in a Latin American country for several months. She described her participation in a recent missionary training meeting in which she had learned for the first time how ward leaders and missionaries can use the Member Progress form. The form lists a number of steps that ward leaders and full-time missionaries should follow to help new converts during their first year of membership or others during their return to Church activity. Notice when and how often the form points toward the temple:

- **Within One Month after Baptism or Return to Activity**
  - The bishop has interviewed the member and reviewed the principle of tithing and other worthiness matters to assist in preparation for temple worship
  - Eligible males have been interviewed for and received the Aaronic Priesthood
  - The member is enrolled in the Gospel Principles course
  - Ward and full-time missionaries are reteaching the missionary lessons (as outlined in *Preach My Gospel*)

- **Within Six Months after Baptism or Return to Activity**
  - The member has been interviewed for and received a responsibility or calling in the Church
  - The member is regularly attending sacrament meeting
  - The member has started a family group sheet

- **As Soon as Appropriate during the First Year**
  - Eligible and worthy males have been prepared for and received the Melchizedek Priesthood
  - Members ages twelve and older have participated in proxy baptisms in the temple (where feasible)
  - Eligible members have completed the temple preparation seminar

- **When Prepared, but Not Before One Year Following Baptism**
  - Eligible and worthy adults have been endowed
  - The family has been sealed in the temple (if applicable)[2]

OUR ULTIMATE GOAL

Because this sister missionary was quite excited to discover the key concepts and purpose of the form in helping new members get "established," she told her family about it in her next email home. She had learned that the form

has the goals [needed] to make sure people who are recently baptized make it to the temple. I had the opportunity [in a role play] to be a "Recent Convert" named Maria. [The discussion leaders] taught with such love and such power that I really felt the Spirit, and I wanted [even in the role play] to go talk to the bishop to get [a temple recommend] interview!

The thing that hit me the most is that our ultimate goal is to get to the temple! They had me read the very last goal first, and then [they] testified with power, that if I followed the steps in the form, and if I was faithful, I could be sealed with my family forever. . . . The Spirit hit me really strongly, and I realized that

I need to increase my faith to be able to tell people that, and I need to work with recent converts to [help them prepare to receive their temple endowment and sealing], because the gospel is for families! One of the ways to do this is by helping the investigator feel loved and important and help them to realize the light they have that they can help share with their family! We also . . . teach the lessons again after baptism—what better time to have them invite their family and friends to listen! Ah, I love the gospel!![3]

My bishop friend was so inspired by this missionary's discovery that he asked two other recently returned missionaries, "What was your main goal as missionaries?" Both of them said something like, "To help people get baptized." To which he said, "What about the temple—wasn't that your ultimate goal for your investigators?" The two missionaries looked a little surprised; then they looked at each other, nodded, and said, "Of course! Why didn't we think of that?" So he shared what the other sister missionary had written, and they all agreed—baptism is only the first major step toward the larger goal of being endowed and sealed in the temple.

In addition to following the steps on the progress form, it is crucial to help new members build the personal relationships with other members that will give them the support system they need to stabilize their newly planted tree of faith as its root system becomes "established." As President Gordon B. Hinckley often said, each new member needs (1) a friend, (2) an assignment, and (3) nourishment from "the good word of God" (Moroni 6:4).[4] And even those steps are but a *means* to the larger *end* of helping the new convert taste and internalize the spiritual experiences that are the lifeblood of nourishing the roots of their growth.

Sometimes we focus too exclusively on the "preparatory priesthood" portion of our missionary purpose—which can appear to conclude with the convert's baptism. Of course we should "invite others to come unto Christ" through repentance, baptism, and confirmation.[5] But that is only the beginning of receiving the fulness of the gospel and the Savior's Atonement.

Going through the temple—or, much better, letting the temple go through us—is not only desirable, it is essential if we are to receive all of the Atonement's redeeming, strengthening, and perfecting blessings. The lesser priesthood's elements in that sequence are fundamental, yet they are only the first steps. And "endure to the end" is a call to summon the energy needed to move on to the next steps. It is not a signal to take a seat and put our feet up.

President Hinckley emphasized the retention of new converts as one of the major themes of his presidency. In a missionary conference in Bolivia, for example, he asked the missionaries to focus directly on the temple: "Will you please see that every convert who comes into the Church while you are here on this mission is so taught that he or she will grow in faith and the year after baptism he or she will be ready to get a temple recommend . . . [and] will be ready to go to the house of the Lord?"[6]

During the years when President Hinckley was emphasizing this need for retention, in stake priesthood leadership meetings I would sometimes involve the leaders in a little demonstration of his message. I would ask the mission president to come forward and stand on the far left side of the room; then I'd ask the temple president to stand on the far right side. I would have the mission president give a baton-like object (such as a pencil) to one of his missionaries and ask the missionary to carry the baton toward the temple president. The baton represented a new convert.

Halfway across the room, I would ask the ward mission leader to stand ready to receive the baton as if he were in a relay race. As the missionary approached him, he would begin to move toward the temple president with his hand outstretched behind him until the missionary put the baton in his hand. The missionary and ward mission leader would each keep a hand on the baton until the ward mission leader held it securely—so they could keep up their momentum without dropping the baton. (Sometimes I would ask the mission president, "President—does the ward mission leader start running when he sees your missionaries coming?") The ward mission leader would then carry the precious baton safely to the temple president, representing the convert's receiving his or her temple endowment.

Current Church leaders of course still stress retention, as they always will. While training local leaders in recent years, visiting Church authorities have often called for "real growth" in missionary work. That is, when convert baptisms have been increasing rapidly in a given location, leaders should compare other statistics over several years to see if the number of people attending sacrament meeting or paying tithing is growing at the same rate as the number of convert baptisms. If not, perhaps "real growth" of the personal, spiritual kind is actually declining, despite the appearance of statistical growth through baptisms.

During his years as a member of the Quorum of the Twelve, Elder Neal A. Maxwell became a serious student of "real growth" issues. Based on some multiyear studies that focused on Great Britain, for example, Elder Maxwell concluded:

> The "key to having a multigenerational church" is to have "LDS marriages at the beginning." Converts who don't marry Latter-day Saints are far more likely to "drop off the radar scope" of Church activity. *And when the marriage is in the temple,* the likelihood of ensuring the continued Church activity of an entire family over the generations is extremely high. [From other research done at Church headquarters, Elder

Maxwell knew that] LDS children in international areas whose parents are married in the temple are *nine times* more likely to serve missions and marry in the temple than are LDS children whose parents were not married in the temple. In the United States and Canada, the rate is now four times higher when parents marry in the temple.[7]

Drawing on this background, Elder Maxwell once taught all of the General and Area Authorities that family sealings in the temple are the long-range key to really "establishing the Church." Drawing his theme from Isaiah 58:12, "Raise up the foundations of many generations," he said, "We seek successive generations of grandparents, parents, and children who are 'grounded, rooted, settled,' (Eph. 3:17; Col. 1:23) and sealed in the holy temple."[8]

More recently, President Russell M. Nelson reiterated this message in counseling new mission presidents: "Missionary labors should begin with this glorious end in mind [the temple endowment and sealing]. . . . Most of all, we want the grandchildren of your missionaries and the grandchildren of those whom your missionaries baptize to be endowed and sealed in the temple. We want multigenerational families of faith. God wants His children to return to Him, converted, endowed, and sealed as families."[9]

As we think more deeply about real growth, there is indeed something crucial about being both endowed and sealed in the temple—steps that make all the difference in whether a new member puts down the spiritual roots needed to nourish lasting spiritual growth. For that reason, the most significant indicator of "real growth" is probably to ask what percentage of recent converts in a given location have been both endowed and sealed in the temple after they are older than the natural age by which most marriages have occurred, say age thirty or thirty-five.

That is a very idealistic standard, of course, but it does

represent the best possible environment for establishing the Church and raising children in Zion—that is, in a Christ-centered home led by temple-married parents. I have been sobered to learn that in a few areas of the Church, that percentage is painfully low. That isn't a surprising outcome when one considers the many barriers that stand in the way of new converts whose spouses are not Church members, or who are still single (perhaps single parents), or who encounter the multiple sources of personal opposition that make it hard to sink permanent spiritual roots even in an intact marriage.

Talking about new converts who fall away from Church activity, one former mission president said he believes that the worldly local culture just reclaims those people too easily. The Master Teacher said the same thing in the parable of the sower: "He also that received seed among the thorns is he that heareth the word; and the cares of this world . . . choke the word, and he becometh unfruitful" (Matthew 13:22).

This parable also tells us, as Elder Dallin H. Oaks said, that "We have the seed of the gospel word. It is up to each of us to set the priorities and to do the things that make our soil good and our harvest plentiful. We must seek to be firmly rooted and converted."[10] One of the best ways to "make [their] soil good" is for new converts to transplant their root system from the sandy soil of their local culture to the spiritually fertile ground of a Zion culture. This cultural shift can begin for them within their own ward or branch and their own family.

That requires more than a temporary willingness to change lifestyles and give up local cultural habits that conflict with Church standards. The "real growth" question is both very personal and long-term, concerned with whether the convert has moved, step-by-step, through the entire process of internalizing not only the temporal culture of the Aaronic Priesthood but also the spiritual culture of the Melchizedek Priesthood—the temple. This transformation is suggested symbolically in the temple by moving from a room representing "the world" to a room filled with enough additional light to prepare us one day to move into the celestial realm. Then, although we still live *in* the world, we are not *of* the world (see John 17:14–16).

This kind of "real growth" is individual, not just institutional. It happens one person and one family at a time. And it is most likely to happen when there is a temple nearby. That's a key reason why we now have so many temples across the globe. When this kind of growth takes root, it also tends to impart a repeatable vision to children raised by "fully grown"—spiritually mature—parents; and those children will pass it on to their children.

A STORY FROM EUROPE ABOUT REAL GROWTH

I have gratefully seen some of this transforming growth in my own children and grandchildren. And I have seen it in the lives of converts in many countries and cultures—as illustrated in a multigenerational family from Europe whom I have known well for half a century.

In 1962, I met a young married couple, Friedrich and Renate Wolfart, in Ludwigshafen, Germany, in a miraculous way. My companion, Elder Robert Keeler, had been in the mission field only a few days when he and another new missionary met Renate while tracting. Neither missionary could speak much German yet, so their conversation at her front door was very brief. Much later I learned that Renate somehow thought they were Americans who were in Germany for some kind of Catholic youth gathering.

The next day Elder Keeler and I set out to find her. When I asked for the family's name and address, he was crestfallen. "I'm sorry," he said. "I was so excited about her that I forgot to write down the family name or the street name. But they are out there in our tracting area someplace . . . on the top floor of an apartment house. I'm sure I'll recognize the name when I see it on that little name sign they have by their doorbells! And we really need to find her. Elder Hafen, I felt a very clear spiritual witness that she would someday join the Church."

We picked a street and began climbing to the fifth floor of one building after another. After running up and down those polished wooden staircases for a couple of hours, I tried to call off what seemed to me a useless quest. But Elder Keeler had felt such a spiritual conviction about her that he was unyielding. I took a deep breath and decided I should teach him a lesson about writing down names and addresses, so I sped up our pace, assuming that my seasoned tracting legs would soon wear him down.

After a few more frustrating hours, he recognized the name: Wolfart. When she began to open the door, he whispered, "That's the lady! Talk to her, talk to her!" Renate didn't want to talk much at the door, so we made an appointment to come back when Friedrich would be home. In a few weeks and after hearing the missionary lessons, he was ready for baptism, but she wasn't—and she didn't want him to be baptized, either. Friedrich had a testimony, but he knew he could damage their close relationship by being too hasty. He was eventually baptized, with her support. A few months later, I returned to Ludwigshafen for her baptism on the last day of my mission.

The Wolfarts attended Church in the Ludwigshafen branch, gradually developing good relationships with the other members. They sensed how a branch could be a little Zion community. They also learned not to get too ruffled by the occasional imperfections they encountered. Within a few years Renate was called as the branch Relief Society president. Then, after they became part of the Mannheim stake, Friedrich was called as the ward bishop. By then they had been blessed with four children.

Years later, after their oldest child, Volker, had served a mission on Temple Square in Salt Lake City, his parents made their first trip to the United States to pick him up and see Utah. Friedrich said to me then, "Well, you brought the gospel to us in Germany, so we sent Volker to bring it back to you."

The Wolfarts had "overcome" the same kinds of opposition that all new members face. And over time, they patiently nourished the seeds of faith, took the Book of Mormon and other scriptures seriously, grew to love the temple, and could see that living the gospel blessed their marriage and each of their children. They embraced the Aaronic Priesthood dimensions of their Church membership; then they stepped up to the Melchizedek Priesthood dimensions by continually renewing the covenants and principles of the temple ordinances.

When Marie and I were living in Germany in 2003 on a Church assignment, Friedrich and Renate sent us an invitation to the temple sealing for their youngest daughter, Irina. All of their other children would be with them in the Frankfurt Germany Temple that day with their eternal companions. Because I thought the Wolfarts may not know that I was authorized to perform sealings, I called them to ask, "Who will be performing the sealing?"

Friedrich replied, "I will."

Surprised, I asked, "How can you do that?"

"Oh," he said, "I've been a sealer in the Frankfurt Temple for several years."

So we had the sweet privilege of watching Friedrich perform the temple sealing for his own daughter. As we listened, I offered a silent prayer of gratitude for the blessing of having watched the spiritual development of the Wolfart family for forty years. I was tasting the sweet fruit of their having chosen to internalize and live the gospel.

Friedrich and Renate Wolfart had long ago made the full transition to living in the world without being of the world. The worldly German culture couldn't reclaim them because they, spiritually speaking, had gone to Zion. They didn't need to move to Utah to find Zion. They found it by building it with the Lord's help in their own family, in their own ward and stake, and in their own temple district. Of course, like all the rest of us, they aren't perfect. Yet watching them this long has let me see personal "real growth" in its fully flowered form.

And incidentally, speaking of young German converts, after Friedrich had served as bishop, he was called as the executive secretary to his stake president in Germany. That leader's life also illustrates real growth of the personal kind. His name is Dieter F. Uchtdorf.

More recently, the Wolfarts' son Volker served as a bishop in Switzerland. For Volker and his faithful, equally yoked wife, Petra, the gospel is at the center of their lives every day. In 2015, Friedrich sealed his returned-missionary grandson Philipp and his bride, Natasha Reading, in the Swiss Temple. The children of their marriage will be Friedrich and Renate's great-grandchildren— which reminds me that my own great-grandfather John G. Hafen joined the Church in Switzerland as a young man, just before coming to Utah in 1861. So there's some kind of full circle there about taking the gospel back and forth between Europe and Utah for 150 years—with the bedrock, temple-based principles of obedience, sacrifice, and consecration bearing the same "real growth" fruit in each family, regardless of the surrounding environment.

When the Wolfart family's ward leaders and missionaries

encouraged them through those steps from baptism to their temple endowment, that was still just the beginning of their journey as Christ's followers. And on the day when Friedrich and Renate were sealed to each other and to their children, that was surely a *once-in-a-lifetime experience* in the temple. But from then on, as a Christ-centered family in a Zion community (their ward and stake), they have been blessed by a *lifetime of experience* in the temple. Their devotion has prompted them to support other converts in becoming grounded, rooted, and established in the restored gospel. And the Wolfarts' tree of faith will keep bearing fruit, season after season, if they continue to nourish it with the same diligence and patience that has brought them thus far.

Such trees as the Wolfarts' are being planted and nourished by individuals and families all across the globe, for the world is now dotted with temples. As each tree takes root and grows, "behold, it [will become] a tree springing up unto everlasting life," bearing sweet and precious fruit from which all may "feast . . . until [they] are filled, that [they] hunger not, neither shall [they] thirst" (Alma 32:41–42).

CHAPTER 16

Keep the Covenants and the Covenants Will Keep You

The followers of Jesus who journey toward His presence are *His covenant people.* He keeps His covenant to strengthen and succor us as we keep our covenants to cleave unto Him. Sometimes that cleaving asks us to trust Him beyond our ability to understand what He is asking of us. But when our faith is based on trust and not on blessings, He can lead us where we need to go—to places we are not wise enough to ask about. And thus can He help us grow, strengthening our personal development as far as we will allow Him. When we keep our covenants with Christ, He will keep us.

During Elijah's ministry, when Israel was suffering through a crippling drought and famine, God "commanded a widow woman . . . to sustain" Elijah, of whom she knew nothing. As he approached her, Elijah asked for food. She, the widow of Zarephath, had only a "handful of meal . . . and a little oil in a cruse," which she had planned to share with her child, "that we may eat it, and die." But Elijah asked again for the food, saying "fear not," for "the barrel of meal shall not waste, neither shall the cruse of oil fail."

The widow then "did according to the saying of Elijah."

Elder Jeffrey R. Holland called her act an expression of faith "as great . . . as any I know in the scriptures."[1] And they "did eat many days," for, miraculously, the meal and oil did not fail. But then the widow's child fell sick and died. Elijah took the child and "cried unto the Lord, . . . let this child's soul come into him again." The Lord "heard the voice of Elijah," and the child "revived." (1 Kings 17:9–24).

Overcome with gratitude, the widow cried, "What shall I render to the Lord for all His benefits to me?" And Elijah answered, "Thou shalt love the Lord thy God, love him with all thine heart, and with all thy soul, and with all thy might. O blessed are they who fear Him!"[2]

The widow woman was a true follower. Faced with starvation, she still trusted Elijah's promise of divine care—and the barrel and the cruse failed not. Then, after the shock of her child's death, she witnessed the restoration of his life. Immediately came her instinctive exchange with Elijah, which captures the reciprocal nature of grace in clear simplicity: How could she possibly render her boundless thanks to God? By living her gratitude. By loving the Lord with her whole soul. This wasn't bargaining or a fifty-fifty contract, but an open-ended covenant in both directions. For her part with her widow's mite—total consecration with no expectation, only trust. For His part—all that the Father hath. And for both, their bedrock motivation was simply to love, with all their souls.

What would it look like to see someone live her whole life as that widow lived? We believe it might look like the life story of Lydia Goldthwaite Knight. Young Lydia began sustaining Joseph Smith's prophetic calling almost as soon as her foot touched the ground in Kirtland in 1835. She was a twenty-two-year-old new convert who desired to gather with the Saints. When Vincent

Knight approached her, he said, "'Sister, the Prophet is in bondage, . . . and if you have any means to give, it will be a benefit to him."

Vincent probably didn't know that Lydia had first heard the gospel from Joseph Smith personally a year earlier in Canada. Joseph had taught her and another family for several days before baptizing them. He came to know Lydia's story, how she had been married at sixteen, then abandoned by a deceitful husband, and how her two small children had died.

As he left her in Canada, Joseph had pondered her discouraging circumstances and said, "Sister Lydia, the Lord, your Savior, loves you and will overrule all your past sorrows and afflictions for good. . . . Be comforted and let your heart rejoice, for the Lord has a great work for you to do. Be faithful and endure unto the end and all will be well."[3]

So Lydia instinctively replied to Vincent's appeal on the Prophet's behalf, "Here is all I have. I only wish it was more." She emptied her purse, "containing perhaps fifty dollars, [into] his hand as she spoke."[4] This was *all* the money her parents had given her to travel and to begin her life in Kirtland; she was left unable to buy even her own supper and night's lodging. Vincent used the money to free Joseph, then offered Lydia a place to stay with his family.

This intuitive act of consecration found an echo two years later in Kirtland, when a similarly devoted young convert named Eliza R. Snow arrived from her home in Mantua, Ohio. Her parents had also given Eliza her inheritance as she left home—and she promptly donated all of it for the building of the Kirtland Temple.[5]

As Lydia's and Eliza's life stories unfolded, both stories illustrated the Lord's promise: "[Those whose] hearts are honest, and are broken, and their spirits contrite, and are willing to observe their covenants by sacrifice . . . are accepted of me. For I . . . will cause them to bring forth as a very fruitful tree which is planted in a goodly land, by a pure stream, that yieldeth much precious fruit" (D&C 97:8–9). The Lord's grace interacts with the sacrifices of a contrite spirit to bear fruit.

It is no coincidence that the next verses after this passage connect directly to the temple—a potent symbol of the fruitful tree: "It is my will that a house should be built unto me in the land of Zion . . . that [the Saints] may be perfected . . . in all things pertaining to the kingdom of God. . . . [And if] it be not defiled . . . my presence shall be there" (D&C 97:10–16).

Temple covenants are always two-way. As we make promises to the Lord, He makes promises to us: "With the taking of each covenant and the assuming of each obligation a promised blessing is pronounced, contingent upon the faithful observance of the conditions."[6]

How does this work in practice? Elder Neal A. Maxwell said, "*If we will keep our covenants, the covenants will keep us* spiritually safe."[7] President Boyd K. Packer added:

> When you come to the temple and receive your endowment, and kneel at the altar and be sealed, you can live an ordinary life and be an ordinary soul—struggling against temptation, failing and repenting, and failing again and repenting, but always determined to keep your covenants. . . . Then the day will come when you will receive the benediction: "Well done, thou good and faithful servant: thou hast been faithful over a few things, I will make thee ruler over many things: enter thou into the joy of thy lord" (Matthew 25:21).[8]

"THEY ARE MY FRIENDS"—THE KNIGHT FAMILY AND JOSEPH SMITH

Lydia Goldthwaite's story blends with the family story of Joseph and Polly Knight to illustrate how temple covenants and the grace of Christ's Atonement can come together over the generations. These stories also interest us because we discovered only after we were married that both of us are the Knights' direct descendants. In the next chapter, this family story also explores the question of how much the temple's sealing power can reach out to rescue posterity who stray.

Joseph and Polly Knight befriended Joseph Smith in 1825, when nineteen-year-old Joseph was still being tutored by Moroni. Working for the Knights, Joseph formed lifelong friendships with their sons, including Newel, who was close to Joseph Smith's age. In 1826, Joseph Smith told the Knights about Moroni and "a gold book of ancient date"[9] that he would soon receive. Some of the family didn't believe him, but Joseph Knight always did.

On September 21, 1827, after four years of preparation, Joseph was ready to receive the plates from Moroni. Joseph Knight was at the Smith home that night. Joseph Smith and Emma left for Cumorah at midnight, borrowing Joseph Knight's horse and wagon to carry the plates. The next morning, Joseph and Emma returned about breakfast time.

In Richard Bushman's narrative, "After breakfast, Joseph called Joseph Knight into another room and, with the happy enthusiasm of a young man, told him that everything was 'ten times better than I expected.' He described the plates and the Urim and Thummim, saying 'I can see anything; they are marvelous.' And the plates 'are written in characters, and I want them translated.'"[10] Joseph Knight supplied some of the paper for the translation, and he often made sure Joseph had enough to eat while translating. He "was always giving [to Joseph Smith] and expecting nothing in return."[11]

By 1830, Joseph Smith had found "little support [for his prophetic claims] from anyone outside his family." As the first converts joined the Church, they usually came one or two from a family and three or four from a city. But, contrary to this pattern, "twenty-one people came into the Church through the Knight-Peck connection in the first few months, forming the core of the Colesville [New York] branch."[12]

Years later in Nauvoo, when Joseph Smith was feeling overwhelmed by harassment from his enemies, he recorded the names of those who had stood by him "in every hour of peril." One of those names was "my aged and beloved brother Joseph Knight, Sr., who was among the first to administer to my necessities" in the work of the Restoration. "He has [ever] been faithful and true. . . . Behold he is a righteous man [and] his name shall never be forgotten. There is his son Newel Knight, [and his other son] Joseph Knight Jr., whose names I record in the Book of the Law of the Lord, with unspeakable delight, for they are my friends."[13]

In the School of the Prophets in Kirtland, Joseph Smith introduced a covenant of affectionate brotherhood, in the context of covenants with God: "Art thou a brother or brethren? I salute you in the name of the Lord Jesus Christ, in token or remembrance of the everlasting covenant, in which *covenant* I receive you to fellowship, in a determination that is fixed, immovable, and unchangeable, to be your friend and brother *through the grace of God* in the bonds of love, to walk in all the commandments of God blameless, in thanksgiving, forever and ever" (D&C 88:133; emphasis added).

This tender language, reflected in the feelings between Joseph and the Knights, suggests that sometimes other people can be instruments in the Lord's hands to convey His grace—as Elijah did for the widow. Grace conveyed to us by the Lord's representatives is also reciprocal—keep your covenants, and your covenants will keep you. Said another way, sustain the priesthood, and the priesthood will sustain you. That was the relationship between the Knight family and Joseph Smith—a relationship that continually showed how mutual sacrifice is necessary for covenants to be reciprocally effective.

NEWEL AND LYDIA

Lydia Goldthwaite came to Kirtland in 1835 to be with the Saints. A few months later, Lydia met Newel Knight, who had been called back from Missouri to help build the Kirtland Temple. They were both boarding with Hyrum and Jerusha Smith.

At first Lydia felt she couldn't marry Newel because her missing first husband, Calvin Bailey, might be alive somewhere. After three days of fasting and prayer, Newel asked Joseph Smith to seek the Lord's direction for them. Joseph prayed, then told them the Lord approved of the marriage. Theirs was the first marriage Joseph performed. Within a short time, Lydia learned that Calvin had died.

In April 1836, after the temple's dedication, Newel prepared to take his new bride to rejoin the extended Knight clan in the turmoil of Missouri. "Are you not in rather straitened circumstances?" Joseph Smith asked about their pending thousand-mile journey to Clay County. Having received no pay for his work on the temple for more than a year, Newel replied with understatement, "We are rather cramped."

Sister Lydia, Joseph continued, "I have not forgotten how generously you helped me when I was in trouble." The Prophet then handed the couple almost twice as much money as Lydia had given him.[14] Both Lydia's gift and Joseph's gift came not from a contract but from two-way feelings of generous consecration.

After surviving the abysmal persecutions of Missouri, Lydia and Newel retreated with the Saints to Nauvoo, where again Newel was called to help build the temple. Once when Newel fell ill for two weeks, Lydia sent a message to their priesthood leaders, first to apologize for his absence and second to request "on behalf of my husband . . . whom I love and reverence, even as Sarah did Abraham" that they pray for him and that they consecrate a bottle of oil for him (which she sent with the letter).[15] They did as she asked, and he was healed.

Also in Nauvoo, Lydia was sick with malaria when many other Saints were also stricken. She asked Newel to take a white handkerchief to Joseph Smith, having faith that if he could bless it and return it to her, she would be well. But she only grew worse. Fearing death, she asked Newel to go see Joseph again. Newel confessed that he hadn't dared bother Joseph the first time because other Saints' needs overwhelmed him. This time Joseph blessed the handkerchief and assured him that Lydia would recover— which she did. Newel and Lydia's continued trust in the Lord, in each other, and in Joseph kept them close to the sources of grace.

THE RAVENS WILL FEED YOU

In the spring of 1846, three months after being sealed in the Nauvoo Temple, Lydia and Newel fled Illinois with their seven children. Brigham Young sent the Knights with two companies of Saints north up the Missouri River in search of an alternate route west. These Saints accepted the invitation of the Ponca Indians to camp with them for the winter there, hoping to continue west in the spring. One cold January night, Newel felt an acute pain in his side. No tried remedy brought relief. Through seven days and nights of excruciating anxiety, Lydia watched "the breath of the being she loved better than life itself slowly cease."[16]

"'Lydia,' the dying voice faintly whispered, 'it is necessary for me to go. Joseph wants me [on the other side]. . . . Don't grieve too much, for you will be protected.' [17]

"'Oh, Newel, . . . don't give up; oh I could not bear it. Think of me, Newel, here . . . with seven little children. . . . I cannot let you go.'"[18] He tried to hang on, and Lydia writhed in pain with him. Finally Lydia prayed for forgiveness if she had asked amiss that Newel might remain, and she released him to God's will. Within moments his pain ceased, and he was gone.[19]

A month later, after a meeting about the trek west, Lydia wondered how she could possibly prepare her fatherless family for the journey—especially since she was expecting another baby. "Oh, Newel," she cried out, "why hast thou left me?!"

> As she spoke, he [came to] her, a lovely smile on his face, and said, "Be calm, let not sorrow overcome you. . . . I was needed behind the vail. . . . You cannot fully comprehend it now; but the time will come when you shall know why I left you and our little ones. Therefore, dry up your tears. Be patient, I will go before you and protect you in your journeyings. . . . Although the ravens of the valley should feed you and your little ones you shall not perish for the want of bread."[20]

The ravens will feed you—a symbol of grace, with another echo from the prophet Elijah (see 1 Kings 17:6).

Newel's visit fulfilled promises in the patriarchal blessing Lydia had received from Joseph Smith Sr. just after their marriage in Kirtland. That blessing had affirmed that "the Lord has given thee a kind and loving companion for thy comfort. . . . Your souls shall be knit together and nothing shall be able to dissolve them: Neither distresses nor death shall separate you. . . . Angels shall minister unto thee; thy heart shall be comforted."[21] Death would not sever their bonds of marriage—even before they received the ordinance of eternal marriage.

Still, Lydia's "heart cried out in sorrow many times, for her burden seemed more than she could bear."[22] A week after their baby was born, Lydia called to Newel again as rain poured through her rough cabin's roof, soaking the bedclothes. He came to her once more, repeating his promise of protection. Even in the drenched linens, "a pleasant warmth crept over her."[23]

In addition to the strength Newel brought Lydia from beyond the veil, Lydia was continually assisted through her years of single motherhood by both physical and spiritual service from priesthood brethren. Once they built a small house for her. Another time a man she didn't know told a miller to put up twenty pounds of flour for her. Later on, the brethren harvested her crop of wheat for her family—small samples of how other people can be instruments of the Lord's grace.

In another echo of Elijah and the widow, when Lydia's youngest son, Hyrum, was snatched from drowning in a creek, she called for the elders to act upon their "commission" in the Lord's name. But it appeared to be too late: "there was no breath in him." She clutched the child to her chest and recalled the promise in her patriarchal blessing that her "heart [would] not be pained because of the loss of [her] children." The brethren felt the child was too far gone, but Lydia was unyielding. "I could not be denied. They finally laid their hands on the lifeless child and prayed for him. Life returned and he began to breathe."[24] The Lord continually extended His grace to Lydia Knight because she continually sustained the building of His kingdom—and His kingdom was built to sustain His covenant people.

"MY WAGONS ARE AT YOUR DISPOSAL"

When Lydia felt ready to begin her trek to Zion in 1848, she counseled with Brigham Young, who had returned to Winter Quarters for his family. In addition to provisions required to travel, she would need another year's worth of supplies in Utah to get established. He counseled her to stay in Winter Quarters until she could "find something to come to."

Then he said, "If you feel so disposed, you can let your three

yoke of oxen and two wagons go towards helping to fit out someone who can go and take care of themselves when there."[25] His
words reminded Lydia of a covenant Newel and other elders had
made to each other in Nauvoo to give all they possessed to assist
the Saints who went west, a covenant "never to cease their exer-
tions" until they had helped all safely get to Zion.[26]

Because she regarded Newel's covenant as her own, she responded to Brigham as she had when Joseph needed help: My
oxen and wagons are "at your disposal." Lydia was never compen-
sated for her animals and wagons—but she hadn't offered them
because she expected compensation. She trusted that the Lord
would provide.

Lydia lived near Winter Quarters with her seven children in
"a half-cave, half-hut on the bank of the creek"[27] that "flooded
when it rained," was cold in the winter and stiflingly hot in the
summer, and remained "impossible to make, or keep clean."[28]
Susa Young Gates said this was one of the most miserable places
where anybody could have lived.[29] But for Lydia, "enough grief
had already touched her life" that "she knew how to fit joy into
the corners."[30]

When they finally headed west in 1850, Lydia had to borrow sixty dollars to rent the oxen she needed for the journey, a
debt she later worked two years to repay.[31] Soon after she reached
Zion, the cow they had brought across the plains gave her family the first milk they could churn into butter. After counseling
together, they gave their first pound of butter to the bishop for
tithing. They weren't sure how much more butter the cow would
give them, but ever "willing to observe their covenants by sacrifice," they wanted to pay the first tenth rather than the last tenth.
They always had butter after that.

Lydia became the plural wife of John Dalton in the Salt Lake

Valley for five years. She later married James McClellen, a widower, feeling concern for his two motherless daughters. She went with him to live near St. George, where her stepson Samuel Knight served with Jacob Hamblin as a missionary to the Indians. After twenty years of marriage, James passed away.

"ETERNITY . . . A FOOTSTEP AWAY"

When the St. George Temple was dedicated in 1877, Brigham Young called Lydia as an ordinance worker, and she served there for seven years. At times the early-morning "temple carriage" picked her up from her home for her day's work in the temple. To her, temple work was "so constant and pleasant that she could not feel lonely,"[32] and "eternity seem[ed] only a footstep away."[33]

She did the ordinance work for more than seven hundred of her deceased family members and friends. Then one day in 1884, Lydia had breakfast, completed the temple work for the last family name in her possession, and came home not feeling well. That night she took her own footstep into eternity.[34]

Vilate Raile's poem "Pioneers" describes the energy Lydia Knight allowed the Lord to set in motion through her and Newel to their descendants.

> *They cut desire into short lengths*
> *And fed it to the hungry fires of courage.*
> *Long after, when the flames died,*
> *Molten gold gleamed in the ashes;*
> *They gathered it into bruised palms*
> *And handed it to their children*
> *And their children's children.*[35]

What is the "it" they gathered? "Molten gold," which comes after the dross is removed through covenant-keeping, backbreaking, and yet spirit-refining fire. "Grace shall be as [our] day,"[36] even though, as one soul-stretched friend once put it, "grace is really hard work."

As we understand the poem, God's desires for them became their desires—and their courage. As the darkness of dross was removed from their desires, they had within them ever more gleaming light. As the Lord has said, "If your eye be single to my glory, your whole bodies shall be filled with light" (D&C 88:67–68). And the gleam of this gold is the doctrine that if we keep our covenants with Him, He will keep us spiritually safe.

Marie's father, Ray Kartchner, is a great-great-grandson of Newel and Lydia Knight. Through his ancestral stories, we have seen that no matter when a lineage joins the Church, the blessings of the temple and its covenants flow through the generations to lift, comfort, strengthen, and sustain their posterity.

Ray was raised by a mother whose hands were bruised somewhat as Lydia's had been. With those hands, she led her family of five children after her husband died when Ray was two years old. By her pioneer-like example she continued to teach the pattern of covenant keeping to her children and her children's children. Ray learned that pattern well, and he handed it to Marie with a gentle reverence that has made it easy for her to envision God as both the source of law and the source of love.

The Lord's covenants with us, and ours with Him, feed the "hungry fires of courage," burning our desires into ashes *and* gold. And so we trust that our children, and their children's children, will stay close enough to that fire to see the gleaming in the ashes.

Grace is reciprocal. Lydia and Newel Knight had kept their covenants, and their covenants had kept them safe. But there is more to the Knight family story. . . .

CHAPTER 17

The Reach of the Sealing Power

The life story of Newel and Lydia's son Jesse Knight raises a familiar but provocative question: How far will the temple's sealing power reach out to rescue the wandering children and grandchildren of faithful, temple-married parents? Some Church members believe that eventually, regardless of when or how far some of their posterity may stray, the sealing power will bring them back. The answer to their question rests on the central issue of agency. It may help to ask it this way: If God extends redeeming grace and exalting power through the full blessings of Christ's Atonement and the priesthood ordinances, why must each of us still engage the process so willingly?

Jesse Knight was born in Nauvoo and was only a toddler on that cold Nebraska night in early 1847 when his father, Newel, died. He came west with the wagon-train Saints and grew up under the watchful care of his faithful mother. But in his adult years, he became inactive, even hostile toward the Church. Among other things, Jesse objected to the way he thought Church leaders and members treated Gentiles (nonmembers of the Church) in Utah.

Lydia wondered and worried and prayed for years about Jesse. During what turned out to be Lydia's last visit to Jesse's home in Payson, Utah, from her home in St. George, Jesse asked her, "Mother, how is it you are not preaching to me as you usually do?" She answered, "Jesse, I have prayed in the Temple for my children many times and on one occasion the Lord made known to me that I was not to worry about you any more, that you would one day understand for yourself. . . . I never intend to argue again with you about religion."[1]

A few years after Lydia's death in 1884, Jesse had an experience that awakened his spiritual senses. His children all became terribly sick from poisoned well water. His two-year-old child, Jennie—"the idol of the whole family"—was afflicted first, and the doctor expected she would not live. Lydia-like, Jesse's wife Amanda called for the elders. Jesse protested that inviting them would make him feel like a hypocrite because he "had no faith in the Church." But Amanda insisted, and the elders blessed Jennie as the family all knelt around her. Immediately Jennie regained consciousness and noticed the flowers in her window. "From that very moment," wrote Jesse's son William, "my father's life was changed. He had seen the power of the Lord made manifest and remembered the words of his mother."[2]

Even as Jesse's heart was turning toward the Lord, many of his family remained deathly ill. Then, despite his prayerful pleading, eighteen-year-old Minnie died—but not before explaining that when Jennie had been so sick, Minnie had privately offered the Lord her own life as a sacrifice so that her two-year-old sister might live. As Minnie's breath left her, she prayed, "Oh God, bless our household." Jesse then remembered that years earlier, when Minnie was a baby, she had had diphtheria, and he had "promised the Lord that if he would spare her life I would not forget Him. I had not kept that promise. . . . I prayed for forgiveness and help. My prayer was answered and I received a testimony."[3]

In the years that followed, Jesse became a mining prospector in the Tintic Mountains near his home in Payson. One day in 1896 while he was prospecting, Jesse "heard a voice distinctly say to him, 'This country is here for the Mormons.'"[4] Urged on by this prompting, Jesse located what he considered a promising site. He then invited an experienced miner named Jared Roundy to evaluate it and perhaps join Jesse in staking a claim to it. Roundy said he wanted no interest in an "old humbug like this." BYU Geology Professor Jeffrey Keith, who has seen this property with his trained eyes, agrees that there was "no reason to anticipate finding anything of worth in [that] vicinity."[5]

But Jesse confidently named it the "Humbug" claim, picked a likely spot there, and began the arduous task of driving a tunnel through layers of mountainous rock with a single jackhammer. His other equipment consisted of a wheelbarrow. One day as they walked together up the steep mountainside, before they had found any promising ore, Jesse's son William heard his father say, "We are going to have all the money that we want as soon as we are in a position to handle it properly. We will someday save the credit of the Church."

William was astonished at his father. But Jesse "had a strong feeling that he was going to have a great responsibility" to help the Church, and he wanted his children to understand that "any money we should get [would be] for the purpose of doing good and building up the Church."[6]

After two months of hard-rock digging on their primitive tunnel, they found a rich enough deposit of silver and gold that they sold the ore in two shipments for about $20,000. That same year,

President Wilford Woodruff confided in the local bishops that the Church was in financial difficulty and needed to find members who could make loans available. While on his way home one Sunday afternoon, Jesse Knight's bishop Joseph Keeler said he heard "a voice as audible as that of a person" say "Jesse Knight will lend the Church $10,000."[7] Bishop Keeler went directly to Jesse's home. Jesse said he would have a check for $10,000 ready the next morning, which Bishop Keeler then hand carried to the First Presidency. That was only the beginning of Jesse's generosity to the Church.

Despite his earlier premonitions, Jesse really didn't know on that day whether his mining venture would produce more ore. But perhaps he wanted to do what his mother had done in Kirtland, when she emptied her purse for the Prophet; and what she had done at Winter Quarters, when she gave her oxen and wagons to Brigham Young to help another family. By that time, Jesse had come to know that sacrifices of the heart mean more to the Lord than monetary sacrifices.

Jesse's Utah mines eventually netted more than $10 million in 1900 dollars. In today's terms, that is the equivalent of about $800 million.[8] Thus Jesse Knight became "the willing conduit through which the Lord poured out a needed blessing" on the Church.[9] Among other things he donated much of the land on which the present BYU campus is located, along with most of the cost for four of the first eight campus buildings. The current Jesse Knight Building at BYU is a memorial to his place in the university's history.

In one illustration typical of Jesse's willingness to keep his covenantal promises, President Heber J. Grant once asked him for $5,000 for a purpose Jesse didn't fully understand. President Grant suggested that he go home and pray about it. Jesse did so and returned with a check for $10,000, saying to President Grant, "Next time I'll just pay what you ask without praying about it."[10]

What does the intergenerational Knight family story teach us? The story gives rise to some good questions. What caused Jesse to receive a new spiritual heart? What role did his parents' temple sealing and his mother's unusual faithfulness play in his return? What about the sacrifices of his father, Newel, and of his grandparents Joseph and Polly Knight?

The entire story does suggest that the principle of "keep your covenants and your covenants will keep you" applies up and down the generational ladder. After reflecting on this story, Jeffrey Keith asked, "Do blessings carry forward that far?" He then answered his own question with Moses's stirring words: "Know therefore that the Lord thy God, he is God, the faithful God, *which keepeth covenant and mercy with them that love him and keep his commandments to a thousand generations*" (Deuteronomy 7:9; emphasis added).

To what extent, then, will the temple's sealing power ensure the return of posterity who stray? Will it be enough to bring all of them back, if the sealed parents are faithful, no matter where or why or when the children wander?

In a widely quoted statement, Elder Orson F. Whitney once said that Joseph Smith "never taught more comforting doctrine" than the promise that the eternal sealings of faithful parents would save not only themselves but their posterity:

> Though some of the sheep may wander, the eye of the Shepherd is upon them, and sooner or later they will feel the tentacles of Divine Providence reaching out after them and drawing them back to the fold. Either in this life or the life to come, they will return. They will have to pay their debt to justice; they will suffer for their sins; and may tread a thorny path; but if it leads them at last, like the penitent Prodigal, to a

loving and forgiving father's heart and home, the painful experience will not have been in vain.[11]

Some parents have taken this statement to mean that the temple's sealing power will unconditionally assure the eternal return of all their posterity. However, in a 2003 general conference message, President James E. Faust said that some people have misunderstood Elder Whitney's statement:

> A principle in this statement that is often overlooked is that they must fully repent and "suffer for their sins" and "pay their debt to justice" [in this life or beyond the veil]. . . . Mercy will not rob justice, and the sealing power of faithful parents will only claim wayward children upon the condition of their repentance and Christ's Atonement. . . . Perhaps in this life we are not given to fully understand how enduring the sealing cords of righteous parents are to their children. It may very well be that there are more helpful sources at work than we know. I believe there is a strong familial pull as the influence of beloved ancestors continues with us from the other side of the veil.[12]

Newel and Lydia Knight were sealed in the Nauvoo Temple. They were covenant keepers, and they were blessed for their devotion. For years Lydia had exhorted Jesse to follow her example, with what Lehi called "all the feeling of a tender parent" (1 Nephi 8:37). But when Jesse kept pushing her away, Lydia took her desires to the Lord in His temple. She later told Jesse what the Lord had whispered to her about him, and she didn't worry about him anymore. Like Alma the Elder, perhaps she asked the Lord for *His* intervention of grace in her gifted son's life, knowing that her lifetime of consecration was all she could do. Lydia didn't bargain with the Lord—she just continually gave Him all she had, holding nothing back, and He kept His promises in His own way and in His own time.

The Lord did come to Jesse, answering not only Lydia's prayers but those of Jesse's wife and family. But He didn't compel Jesse to submit. It's not that He *won't* help faithful parents, but that He *can't* override the agency of His children—because they *cannot* grow spiritually unless they are willing to participate in the process. Even the grace of God can't make us grow unless we reach out, as Agnes Caldwell did, to take hold of it.

Jesse finally got the message, but only after paying the high price of losing his child, then enduring his own self-chastening repentance. He was so unhappy about his past life that he later calculated every dollar he should have paid as tithing during his years of inactivity—and he repaid it, with interest. No Church leader would have expected him to do that. That same attitude motivated Jesse to consecrate his means to the Lord's work long before he had ever earned a penny. He wouldn't have been that devoted if he had just been trying to please his mother. His own heart had to be in it.

Had two generations of Knight ancestors not been so faithful, would the Lord have intervened so directly in Jesse's life? Perhaps not. His father's sacrifices and his mother's prayers do seem to have had what President Faust called a "strong familial pull," perhaps like Alma's prayers for his son. The angel said the Lord had sent him to young Alma in direct answer to his father's pleading (see Mosiah 27:14).

At the same time, as we learn from Lehi's family, even when an angel comes to the wayward children of faithful parents, that doesn't ensure lasting conversion. The sealing blessings given to his consecrated parents might have increased the likelihood that Jesse would choose the path of faith, but the outcome still hinged on whether Jesse would *want* to accept what the Lord and his parents offered him.

Not long ago I found a new understanding about all of this while attending a funeral. A young man was killed in a freakish incident. I will call him Will Jackson—not his real name. I hadn't met Will, but I had known his brother for years, and I knew that the Jackson family were faithful members of the Church. For several years Will had wrestled with addictions and mental health concerns. He had struggled to keep a job and had no real relationship with the Church. At the funeral, his parents, his family members, and other friends were all stunned with bewildering grief.

During the funeral, I saw why the obituary had said that Will loved his family and friends with unusual tenderness. I was moved by the gentle, unfeigned affection his family showed toward him and his memory. The funeral program showed a picture of Will, who was single, with admiring, affectionate nieces and nephews hanging on to him. Then, as they sang during the service, I saw those same children weeping in disbelief that he was gone. His parents sat in utter but somehow serene sadness on the front row—genuine, salt-of-the-earth, peaceable followers of Christ whose unaffected manner conveyed how fully they had always loved and accepted Will, each other, and the Lord.

The talks from his siblings had a meek, nonjudgmental tone. Their affection for him was obviously greater than whatever they hadn't understood about his choice to dance to a different drummer—and apparently because of that affection, he had periodically returned to them like a homing pigeon. His sister said Will had a natural gift for music. Her children had loved hearing him sing his song about the moon—"I like to go there," he sang, "but I wouldn't want to live there."

I began my part on the program with D&C 42:45, which describes both sides of what we had been hearing and feeling that day: "Thou shalt live together in love, insomuch that thou shalt weep for the loss of them that die." If his family and friends hadn't loved him so fully, it wouldn't have hurt so much to see him go.

I told them about my experience in my late teens—the four a.m. phone call all those years ago telling me that my older brother Mike had just been killed at midnight when a speeding fire engine ran a red light and smashed into his car. I was home alone in the morning darkness, and I felt the same shock, confusion, and sudden loneliness the Jacksons were feeling. There was so much I didn't, couldn't, understand. For several years Mike had not been close to the Church, but he had been close to me and to our family. That closeness returned strongly a few years later when I was able to act as his proxy for his temple ordinances.

All the things I didn't understand about the brother I love remind me of the family in *A River Runs Through It*. Paul, the younger of two sons of a Presbyterian minister, had gifts and questions and attitudes much like Will's, and like Mike's. The others in the family all loved Paul, but he chose to live in ways that didn't make much sense to them. Paul was "the only man in the world who had held his mother in his arms and leaned back and laughed." Yet to his mother, Paul was the man she "loved most and understood least."[13]

He remained something of a mystery to his family, in spite of the affection and good times they shared when Paul went fishing with his father and brother. Then his young life ended in a tragedy that was never fully explained, and more than one mystery died with him. Toward the end of the story, Paul's brother,

Norman, remembered these lines from one of the last sermons he had heard his father give:

> Each one of us here today will at one time in our lives look upon a loved one who is in need and ask the same question: We are willing to help, Lord, but what, if anything, is needed? . . . Either we don't know what part of ourselves to give or . . . the part we have to give is not wanted. And so it is those we live with and should know who elude us. But we can still love them—we can love completely without complete understanding.[14]

Will's life, like Paul's life and Mike's life, was a work in process, and their families did love them completely without complete understanding. They were still figuring out who they were and who God is; but each in his own way was taking steps. I remembered what Nephi said when the angel asked him, "Knowest thou the condescension of God?" Nephi didn't know the answer. So he just honestly said, no, he didn't understand, but one thing he did know: "I know that [God] loveth his children; nevertheless, I do not know the meaning of all things" (1 Nephi 11:16–17).

I wanted Will's non-LDS friends at the funeral to know how Nephi, and we, could know that God loves His children, even when our understanding is limited. In a book called *Heaven: A History,* two non-LDS scholars reviewed what people in Western society have believed about heaven over the centuries.[15] When their historical survey reached the modern age, they reported two main findings about how people think of heaven today.

First, they found that many people want to believe that heaven is a place where we will be with those we knew and loved on earth. Many also want to believe that God will be someone we can relate to, even someone we can "hug."

Second, they found that today's Christian churches have little to say about this hunger to understand heaven—with one exception: The Church of Jesus Christ of Latter-day Saints, which has Christianity's most fully developed theology about heaven and the afterlife. This theology teaches us that life goes on beyond the veil, and that with temple ordinances and faithfulness, even marriage and family relationships can continue. And missionary work continues there for those who didn't hear the gospel in this life—or who heard it but are still figuring things out.

As for the nature of God, LDS doctrine teaches that when Joseph Smith came out of the Sacred Grove in 1820, he emerged with a totally new understanding about God: He not only has a body, He has a heart. For example, Joseph Smith's translation of the Bible gives us the story (in the book of Moses) of the prophet Enoch, whose city of Zion was taken into heaven. Enoch drew close enough to see God weeping over the sorrows of His wayward children who were yet on the earth.

Terryl Givens has said that this scriptural story of "the God who weeps" is, by itself, among the most remarkable religious documents to come from the nineteenth century because it verifies with such clear power that we are God's offspring and that His love for us is intimately, intensely personal.[16] He is not an incomprehensible essence. The God who weeps is indeed a God we can embrace—and He waits to embrace us. That is why Brigham Young said that God "is the Father of our spirits; and if we could know, understand, and do His will, every soul would be prepared to return back into His presence. And when they get there, they would see that they had formerly lived there for ages; that they had previously been acquainted with every nook and corner, with the palaces, walks, and gardens; and they would embrace their Father, and He would embrace them and say, 'My son, my daughter, I have you again;' and the child would say, 'O my Father, my Father, I am here again.'"[17]

Will Jackson was a perpetual explorer. He took months and more to travel the globe in a quest for knowledge and meaning—his "mystic journey," as some people call their trip to Machu Picchu in Peru. When I think of Will, I remember J. R. R. Tolkien's line that "Not all those who wander are lost." And when I imagine Will walking toward the waiting embrace of his Heavenly Father, I'm thinking of his earthly parents, whose marriage was sealed in the holy temple. Will was born in the covenant of that sealing, but he has his agency. He will come back only if he wants to—enough to repent fully and accept Christ's Atonement. Would Will want to, that much? On the day of that funeral I believed that he would, because of the home and family in which he grew up. We had all sensed the unconditional and affectionate love within the Jackson family. Theirs is a home where, as our Primary children sing, "love is spoken here."

So when Will draws close to the loving pull of his eternal, celestial home, it will feel very familiar to him. The felt and spoken language of loving and being loved will be sweet to him. Being welcomed into the arms of that love will almost surely be the desire of his heart. And he won't rather live on the moon. The homing pigeon will prefer to be Home.

As I returned home from the funeral I asked myself again, will the natural gravity of the sealing power really bring back, without compulsory means, the children who wander? Yes, *if* we have loved them so much and so well that their own desire to return is strong enough to sustain their complete repentance.

This realization helps me in my own marriage and my own family, because I once heard President Howard W. Hunter answer a question about child-to-parent sealings by saying that in the eternities, nobody will be sealed to someone they don't want to be sealed to. That knowledge motivates me to live in such a way that my wife and our children and their children will *want* our family sealings to continue.

I could also see more clearly that as we try to love our posterity as authentically as Brother and Sister Jackson do, the motives behind our love—the why and the how of our affections—will be purified.

And since those who die are given some season for repentance (see D&C 138:32–34), our descendants will yet have further opportunities to learn—both from their own experiences and from those of others—what matters most in the eternities. We each learn in our own way and in our own time, but we can and do learn. And even though the wandering ones still need to "come to themselves" (see Luke 15:17), the Knight and Jackson family stories show us that the sons and daughters of faithful, sealed, loving parents have the best of reasons to come home.

CHAPTER 18

SAVIORS ON MOUNT ZION: RESTORING THE GENERATIONS

When Moroni first visited Joseph Smith in 1823, four years before Joseph received the plates, the angel told him that God would "reveal unto you the Priesthood, by the hand of Elijah" (D&C 2:1). Thirteen years later, Elijah fulfilled this promise in the Kirtland Temple, where he committed to Joseph and Oliver Cowdery the keys of the priesthood's sealing power.[1] He told them that he had come to "turn the hearts of the fathers to the children, and the children to the fathers, lest the whole earth be smitten with a curse" (D&C 110:15).

This mutual turning of hearts, both up and down the ancestral chain, is among the most striking examples in which the doctrines and blessings of temple work directly coincide with the doctrines and blessings of the Savior's Atonement. Only He makes it possible for us to live beyond the grave, and only through the temple's sealing ordinances can our most prized personal relationships continue after death, allowing us to be eternally "at one" with each other—and with Him.

SAVIORS ON MOUNT ZION

When we perform proxy ordinances, we are *vicariously* helping to make salvation and exaltation possible for others—which is what Christ's Atonement does for us. Thus we sometimes say that doing temple work allows us to be "saviors on Mount Zion" for others—it is a Christlike work, performing ordinances for those who cannot do it for themselves.

Joseph Smith said that the word *turn* in the phrase "turn the hearts of the fathers to the children" is more accurately translated as "bind, or seal" the hearts. Then he said that the object of Elijah's mission is for the Saints to be saviors on Mount Zion: "But how are they to become saviors on Mount Zion? By building their temples . . . and receiving all of the ordinances . . . in behalf of all their . . . dead, and redeem them that they come forth in the first resurrection and be exalted to thrones of glory with them: and herein is the chain that binds the hearts of the fathers to the children . . . which fulfills the mission of Elijah."[2]

Family history work, the temple, and the Savior's Atonement also bless our relationships up and down the generational chain in ways that extend beyond the specific performance of ordinances. For example, current Church teachings about family history emphasize that in addition to doing historical research and performing vicarious ordinances, we should also "turn our hearts" toward past generations by recording and remembering personal stories about specific ancestors—and then turn their hearts, and ours, toward our posterity by sharing with our children and grandchildren those same stories.

WHY FAMILY STORIES MATTER

No wonder Lehi rejoiced with what he "found upon the plates of brass" obtained from Laban. When he first saw those plates, he was at the edge of his knowledge, and perhaps at times at the edge of his faith, leading his family into a wilderness where he had never traveled before. He learned from those plates *who he was*—his identity—that he was a descendant of Joseph who was sold into Egypt.

When he saw what his ancestor Joseph had experienced ("Joseph . . . was preserved by the hand of the Lord, that he might preserve . . . all his household from perishing"), Lehi could immediately have more confidence that he might receive a similar blessing. "If they can do it, we can do it," we so naturally say of our ancestral stories. Therefore, when he "saw all these things, he was filled with the Spirit," because he could foresee the same divine protection for *his* posterity. No wonder he instantly wanted to preserve those records and teach their stories and commandments to his posterity (see 1 Nephi 5:14–22).

The value of preserving and sharing ancestral stories was recently verified by researchers who were trying to understand why some people, including children, are better able than others to cope with serious, even disabling stress and trauma. One study found that "the more children knew about their family's history, the stronger their sense of control over their lives, [and] the higher their self-esteem." This factor was indeed "the best single predictor of children's emotional health and happiness." Those with "the most self-confidence" had what one researcher called "a strong 'intergenerational self.' They know they belong to something bigger than themselves."[3] A related study found that even among those affected by the tragedy of September 11, 2001, the people who "knew more about their families proved to be more resilient, meaning they could moderate the effects of stress." And the most helpful family stories are those that speak candidly and fairly about weathering life's natural "ups and downs," rather than exaggerating positive or negative attitudes or events in an unrealistic way. Thus, concludes writer Bruce Feiler, "If you want a happier family, create, refine and retell the story of your family's positive moments and your ability to bounce back from the difficult ones. That act alone may increase the odds that your family will thrive for many generations to come."[4]

Here is one of our own family stories about the turning of hearts between the fathers and the children. Our oldest son, Jon, was born shortly after my father's unexpected death at age sixty. We gave him my dad's name—Orval—as his middle name, but the name didn't mean much to him in his early years. When he took up debate in high school and learned that his grandfather had been a debater for BYU in the 1920s, he became more interested. Because my dad had kept a priceless personal journal during much of his adult life, I was able to show Jon his entry about debating in front of the BYU student body against a team from an eastern university. I left that journal volume with him, hoping he would want to read more of it.

Jon was good to his core, and he had a mind of his own. Occasionally he would ask a question that told me he was reading at least some of the journal, but I had learned by then that he thrived best without pressure. So we just waited and listened.

Several weeks later, Jon came to our room to talk late one night. At one point he asked me to tell him more about my dad, whom he had never known. But by reading the journal, Jon had been coming to know his grandfather and how he approached his problems. When I wondered why he had asked, he said that in the midst of some of his typical-teenager questions, he'd felt his grandfather's influence close by. So I shared a few personal stories about my father, and Jon took it all in.

Some months later, our family traveled to St. George during a time when Jon was trying to decide about serving a mission. One

Sunday afternoon, with no explanation, he drove alone to the then-isolated little canyon where his grandfather had loved to ride his horse and think about his life and life in general—the place, in fact, where he had passed away. Jon had read of this canyon toward the end of the journal and had seen it from a distance, but he'd not been in it. So he went there to walk around and sort out some of his own questions about his faith, his mission, and his future. A few months later, at his missionary farewell, Jon mentioned the sacredness of that day and described the sense of direction he carried home from his grandfather's canyon.

Years later, Jon was invited to assist the people at Tuacahn when they built their outdoor theatre and later their charter high school in that same canyon. Because the place was still such a tangible link to his grandfather, he accepted their invitation despite living some distance away, and that association continues still. Now with grown children of his own, Jon tries to reflect many of the values his grandfather worked to live by.

Having watched this kind of relationship develop between my father and my son, all because of an honest personal journal, I have no doubt that Elijah planted in Jon's heart the same promises the Lord had planted in my father's heart—and in my own. There really is a bond and a sense of belonging across the generations on both sides of the veil. This bond has helped shape my own identity and values. It makes our ties with the eternal world more real, sharpening our spiritual focus and lifting our confidence in the future—here and hereafter.

This family story is but one example of how I know for myself what Nephi knew: "Having been born of goodly parents, therefore I was taught somewhat in all the learning of my father" (1 Nephi 1:1). I have also learned over the years, however, that not everyone has had the blessing of being "born of goodly parents."

Parents tend to pass along their own life patterns to their children, which is one reason why growing up in the home of "goodly parents" can be a far more valuable and enduring blessing than some of us who had such parents can appreciate—until we see the alternatives.

WHEN FAMILY STORIES ARE DIFFICULT

The reality is, of course, that because parents unavoidably pass along their own values, habits, and attitudes to their children, that value transmission process can include negative influences as well as positive ones. What happens when the landscape for the family narrative is marked with ancestors who made poor choices that damaged other people? Some of those stories do show us how "the iniquity of the fathers" can be visited "upon the children unto the third and fourth generations" (Numbers 14:18). And the consequences of that process can be both disturbing and severe for the children on whose heads the ancestral iniquities are visited.

There are many variations on this theme. For example, as we have already seen, children raised in dysfunctional family circumstances are themselves more likely to create their own dysfunctional families—and sadly, the number of such families has been increasing in recent years. More specifically, the research on victims of childhood sexual abuse shows that, although there are many exceptions, a high percentage of the adult perpetrators of abuse were themselves abused as children, especially among women.[5]

I also learned recently from people who provide spiritual support for the inmates of Utah prisons and jails that a large fraction of the inmates suffer from drug and alcohol addictions—and that many of them were raised by parents who had similar addictions. In addition, sometimes people who have serious anger-management problems grew up in a home where at least one of the parents was unable to control his or her temper. To the children in such homes, outrage could seem to be a normal way of dealing with opposition or uncertainty.

All of us stand as links in a great family chain, holding the hands of ancestors on one side and descendants on the other. Within this chain, most people naturally pass along to the next generation both the strengths and weaknesses of the pattern from their own childhood homes—like passing along an electrical current. For that reason, a parent who was damaged in childhood will often pass that trauma on by inflicting it onto his or her own children, whether consciously or not. And that natural tendency can be magnified by parents who act out negative behavior in confused attempts to break free of their own distress.

We have already seen that people who perform temple ordinances for their progenitors can be "saviors on Mount Zion" for those who preceded them. Does that happen only when we do ordinances? Or are the ordinances but portions of a larger pattern by which individuals in a family chain can bless both their ancestors and their descendants by how they respond to life's adversities? Is it possible to absorb or alchemize the effects of painful experiences rather than passing on the pain? If it is, perhaps the process of doing that is part of being a savior on Mount Zion. That is a clear echo of what Christ did—He absorbed darkness and alchemized (meaning transformed) it into light and now passes the light to us.

TRANSITIONAL FIGURES AS CHRIST FIGURES

We once heard BYU Religion Professor Catherine Thomas tell about growing up in circumstances of emotional abuse, the child of an alcoholic father. After joining the Church, marrying, and having children of her own, she was plagued with recurrent feelings of fear, guilt, and anger that seriously impaired her relationships at home. Late one night, she reached a crisis point while waiting for an absent teenage child. She cried out in anguish to the Lord "for deliverance from my indefinable distress." The words "go home" came to her clearly, but without explanation.

She acted on this impression by flying immediately to her parents' home, where she found her father just concluding a rehabilitation program that invited her participation as his adult child. This experience opened a new world of understanding for her, identifying previously hidden connections between the emotional deprivations of her own childhood and her adult confusion. She saw that her preoccupation with her own troubles had caused her to pass some of that distress on to her own family. Through great effort over much time, she then learned to "repent of bad mental habits: fear, self-pity, self-condemnation, [and] unforgiveness." Yet, significantly, she "found I did not have this power fully in myself to reshape and heal my mind, but Christ did."[6]

This story is echoed in research done a few years ago by BYU psychologist Allen Bergin on the place of religious values in psychotherapy. Bergin developed the concept of the "transitional figure" to describe someone recovering from childhood trauma who is able to change the pattern in his or her family history. Such persons use their personal link in the family's intergenerational chain to *transform,* rather than to pass along, the current of harm. "Instead of seeking retribution, one learns to absorb the pain, to be forgiving, to try to reconcile with forebears, and then become a generator of positive change in the next generation."

Bergin recounts the story of a young woman whose therapist encouraged her to place herself in such a transitional role, temporarily setting aside years of bitter feelings toward the father who had abused her. Like Catherine Thomas, she also went "home."

But rather than confronting her father again over the pain he had caused her as a child, she simply spent time with him, learning about his identity and experiences, including tape recording and transcribing her interviews. Her therapist reported that this became "a gentle experience occurring in a forgiving atmosphere," and it "caused a dramatic reconciliation between the woman and her father," helping *him* "to face certain realities he had never faced."[7]

Those who develop the needed capacity and strength—aided by the Lord's strengthening blessings—can halt the intergenerational flow of affliction. They would then fit Isaiah's imagery: repairing the family "breach" in ways that "raise up the foundations of many generations":

> And if thou draw out thy soul to the hungry, and satisfy the afflicted soul; then shall thy light rise in obscurity. . . . And the Lord shall . . . satisfy thy soul in drought, and . . . thou shalt be like a watered garden, and like a spring of water, whose waters fail not. And they that shall be of thee shall build the old waste places: thou shalt *raise up the foundations of many generations;* and thou shalt be called, The *repairer of the breach.* The *restorer of paths to dwell in.*" (Isaiah 58:10–12; emphasis added)

These words sound very familiar because they describe what Christ Himself did. He took upon Himself undeserved affliction, heaped upon Him by people who might have said they loved Him. And in the ultimate exchange of sweet for bitter, He assumed the bitter, then offered healing even to those who had unleashed the pain He absorbed.

He repaired the breach that separates us from Him and from His Father, not just by stopping the onrolling forces of darkness but by exchanging darkness for light, good for evil—and passing onward a repeatable pattern of goodness. For us to act in some similar way, to the extent of our limited capacity, is to be a Christ figure in our own family chain. We become a transitional point in the war between good and evil, stopping the current of evil by absorbing and even transforming it, thereby protecting the innocence and emotional and spiritual health of the next generation. Thus we become "the foundations of many generations"—with a sacrifice that can also help make possible the healing and change of those whose past failures sent the jolts into our own systems.

THE TEMPLE CAN HELP US REPAIR THE BREACH

The two of us learned more about the reality of these concepts in our associations with temple workers and patrons. We learned that the "savior on Mount Zion" pattern represented in the ordinances can also play a role in the turning of children's hearts to their fathers in more personal ways. By teaching us, over and over, the value and the patterns for turning our hearts toward both our ancestors and our posterity, the temple can help us make transitions and other contributions that bless the generations upstream and downstream.

For example, a woman in her forties brought her mother to the temple in a desire to help her mother heal old wounds within their family—as part of repairing her relationship with the Lord. The younger woman explained in her mother's presence how and why she had forgiven her father after much earlier bitterness. Her attitude helped thaw her mother's frozen heart, and we watched how a transitional figure can help repair a generational breach.

An ordinance worker told us that after years of strain, she had privately reached the stage in her own healing process where she was able to forgive her father for serious past wrongs. She prayerfully wrote down her statement of forgiveness, not to give to him, but to help herself say what she wanted to say—and mean it.

After a few days of feeling at peace, she called her father. Just as she began expressing her feelings, his heart already seemed to melt—because, he said, only a few days before her call, he had felt a desire to forgive his deceased grandmother for some wound in his relationship with her. He had sensed that desire on the same day when his daughter was crossing her own bridge of forgiveness by putting her feelings into writing. It was as if, she said, some cleansing process were taking place in her entire ancestral line—and she could also already sense a cleansing in the line to her descendants.

Another woman told us that her father, not a member of the Church, had for years been hostile toward her because she had joined the Church. Then, within hours after his death, she had a sacred experience that made it clear to her that he now desired her help to receive all of the temple ordinances.

During our years in the temple, several people shared personal experiences that all led to a similar conclusion: When they had made needed changes in their own lives, including repenting, working to repair relationships, and finding ways with the Lord's help to extend forgiveness—often toward people who had passed away—they clearly felt that their own reconciliation with the Lord and with their family members had somehow helped make it possible for others to change, on both sides of the veil. A typical example was the woman who said, "When I was finally able to forgive my deceased father for childhood abuse, I sensed that my change of heart had in some way also encouraged him to change."

Such experiences add another layer of meaning to the phrase "redeeming our dead."

CHAPTER 19

CONSECRATION

Consecration is the result of our contrite, self-willed choice. *We decide* how dedicated we will be *to* God, how much of our hearts we will give to Him. *Sanctification*, on the other hand—becoming saintly, like Christ—is ultimately a gift of grace *from* God.

As our consecration deepens—as our hearts become more open, more yielding to Him—He sanctifies our souls in fulfillment of His covenant with us: as we "deny [ourselves] of all ungodliness, and love God with all [our] might, mind, and strength, *then* . . . by his grace [we] may be . . . sanctified in Christ." In response to our honest efforts toward consecration, then, He will complete us, making us "holy," a condition we cannot develop solely by ourselves (Moroni 10:32–33; emphasis added). But if we hold back, He *cannot* sanctify us. "Those who will not endure chastening . . . cannot be sanctified" (D&C 101:5).

Thus those who inherit the perfecting sanctification of celestial life are they who "offered *sacrifice in the similitude of the great sacrifice* of the Son of God, and . . . suffered tribulation in their Redeemer's name" (D&C 138:12–13; emphasis added). And through fasting, increased humility, and increasingly firm faith in Christ, the Saints of Helaman's time experienced "the purifying and the sanctification of their hearts, which *sanctification cometh because of their yielding [consecrating] their hearts unto God*" (Helaman 3:35; emphasis added).

It is no accident, then, that the temple teaches us so much—and its covenants ask so much of us—regarding obedience, sacrifice, and consecration. In opening the doors to the Atonement's perfecting, sanctifying blessings, no doctrines and no covenants play more important roles than these three.

SACRIFICE OR CONSECRATION?

Sacrifice is what we *give up,* while consecration is what we *give.* For example, the Word of Wisdom asks us to sacrifice (give up) such habits as using alcohol or harmful drugs. King Lamoni was ready to give up his sins: "I will give away all my sins to know thee" (Alma 22:18). Consecration, on the other hand, asks us to give *ourselves* to the Lord, such as when we are asked to devote precious time and energy to a Church calling—sometimes for a few hours, sometimes for years.

At times sacrifice and consecration overlap, such as when we pay our tithing. We "give up" (sacrifice) whatever else we might have done with the money. But we are also "giving" (consecrating) our means to help build the Lord's kingdom. One of the enduring images of both sacrifice and consecration is the Savior's story of the poor widow's mite. He said she gave "more . . . than all they" who gave "of their abundance"—because from "her want," she gave the Lord "all that she had" (Mark 12:43–44). As someone once said, this story is not about what we give; rather, it's about what part we decide to keep for ourselves. President Gordon B. Hinckley once linked the widow's mite to tithing and consecration:

I hold in my hand a widow's mite. It was given me in Jerusalem many years ago and I was told that it is genuine. . . . I keep it in my office as a constant reminder of the fearsome responsibility of spending that which comes of the consecration of the members of the Church. . . .

Some time back a small, bent, elderly woman came to my office. . . . She said she had just come over from the temple. She took from her purse her checkbook. She said that she had been a widow for many years, that life had not been easy for her. . . . She had faithfully paid her tithing all her life. She felt she would not live much longer. Now, she said, she felt she ought to be doing more to help than she had done. In a hand shaky with age, she wrote a check for $5,000. She handed it to me. I noted the address where she lived. It was a poor neighborhood. I confess that as I looked at that check tears came into my eyes. I have held many larger checks than that in my hands. But as I held the check of this widow woman, I was almost overcome by her faith and the seriousness of the trust that was mine in the expenditure of her *consecrated* contribution."[1]

Many of our other offerings carry dimensions of both sacrifice and consecration. As explained in the Church booklet *Preparing to Enter the Holy Temple,* through the covenants of the temple, "We covenant to give of our resources in time and money and talent—all we are and all we possess—to the interest of the kingdom of God upon the earth."[2] President Hinckley said that the covenant of sacrifice includes

the willingness to sacrifice for this the Lord's work—and inherent in that law of sacrifice is the very essence of the Atonement, the ultimate sacrifice made by the Son of God in behalf of each of us. Consecration, which is associated with it, a willingness to give everything, if need be, to help in the on-rolling of this great work. And a covenant of love and loyalty to one another in the bonds of marriage, fidelity, chastity, morality.

If our people could only learn to live by these covenants, everything else would take care of itself, I am satisfied. We would not have to worry about sacrament meeting attendance . . . willingness to serve missions . . . divorce and the many requests for cancellation of temple sealings. We would not have to worry about any of those things.[3]

Such tangible consecration makes concrete our offering of a broken heart and a contrite spirit—because "a willingness to give everything" means that we consecrate with the conscious choice that, when necessary, we, like the widow in her want, will hold nothing back.

THE UNITED ORDER, THE TEMPLE, AND CONSECRATION

In order to understand better what consecration means, let us review the historical context in which that term and its associated principles came into both the temple and the understanding of the Latter-day Saints. We can then consider its more contemporary meaning.

The Lord first revealed the temple ordinances to Joseph Smith, who gave the first endowments to several Church leaders in the upper room of his store on May 4, 1842.[4] A few years later Brigham Young oversaw the administration of endowments for the living to about 5,600 Latter-day Saints in the Nauvoo Temple.[5] However, endowments for the dead were first administered in the St. George Temple in early 1877—the first temple dedicated after the Nauvoo Temple. At that same time, under the direction of Brigham Young and St. George Temple President Wilford Woodruff, the temple ordinances were first put into written form.[6]

During the years of construction for the St. George Temple (1871–1877), perhaps in preparation for the Saints to receive the blessings of that temple, Brigham Young also instituted the united order in several communities, especially in southern Utah. Members of the order would consecrate all of their property to the bishop, who in turn gave them an assigned stewardship for some portion of the order's property and activity. The most successful example of how the united order could function as a community economic system was probably in Orderville, Utah, near St. George.

For various reasons, the united order did not succeed for very long. Yet today key elements of its doctrinal foundation are still very much alive. As LDS historian Richard Bennett wrote, "The united order failed [in the mid-1870s] as an economic system. However, the adoption of the endowment for the dead [in 1877 in the St. George Temple] with its emphasis on *obedience, sacrifice, and consecration* fulfilled [Brigham Young's desire] to rebuild a Zion community and re-establish a consecrated people."[7] The united order's key principles of sacrifice and consecration are still embedded in the temple's teachings—and we renew our commitment to them each time we perform proxy endowments.

Because of this historical context, personal stories from the pioneer Saints of southern Utah provide memorable examples of what temple-based consecration looks like—and what it can mean, with or without the united order. That is perhaps a central reason why our Church leaders have worked so hard—through visitors' centers, historic sites, museums, and stories over the general conference pulpit—to keep the spirit and stories of the early pioneers alive. The pioneers' attitudes and actions personify and teach consecration—and we can apply their lessons to our own lives.

A WRETCHED, BARREN COUNTRY

The very creation of St. George was an exercise in both sacrifice and consecration. The town was first settled in December of 1861 by 309 families, mostly from northern Utah, whose names were simply announced over the pulpit in Salt Lake City at October general conference just two months earlier. That announcement was the first time any of those people knew they were being called on a potentially lifelong mission. The new settlement was to be a major Church hub in southwestern Utah. But the public announcement must have stunned them because, as all those called families knew, that forlorn corner of Utah was a formidable place to live.

Robert Gardner, for example, wasn't at the conference but heard of his family's call from a neighbor. In shock, he said, "I looked and spit, took off my hat and scratched my head and thought and said 'all right.'" He went to see President George A. Smith, a counselor in the First Presidency, who said if Robert didn't want to go, he could see President Young about taking his name off the list. Robert replied, "I expect he would, but I shan't try him." George A. responded, Robert, you are "the kind of [man] we want."[8]

Elisha Averett came home weary from a long day at work to hear the news that his family had been called to go. Elisha dropped into his chair and lamented, "I'll be damned if I'll go." But then he stood and said, "Well, if we are going to go to Dixie, we had better start to get ready."[9]

Joseph Allen Stout wrote that he was glad to go, but his wife "felt bad, for she thought she could not live in a hot climate. . . . I began to try to sell out, but there was so many called at the same time that I could only get one yoke of oxen and a one year old heifer . . . the whole . . . which I left . . . was worth 1200 dollars."[10]

Summarizing multiple reactions, William Fawcett said, "Some made excuses, some backed out. . . . Some would not sell without sacrifice, others clung to their property or deserted their missions. Some thought they were called for a punishment."[11]

Yet for the most part, they felt as did John Pulsipher, who at first really did not want to go either, because he "had a good home, was well satisfied, and had plenty to do." But, "then the Spirit came upon me so that I felt to thank the Lord that I was worthy to go."[12]

Living now amid the climate-controlled comforts of the twenty-first century, when St. George is often billed nationally as an ideal retirement destination, we might find their reluctance hard to understand. But First Presidency member George A. Smith once referred to the St. George region as the "most wretched, barren, God-forsaken country in the world."[13] (Yet President Young still named the town after George A. Smith!)

Then in 1871, only ten years after launching the settlement, Brigham Young made another stunning announcement: They were to build a temple in St. George—the first temple to be completed since the Saints had left their beloved Nauvoo. Construction on the Salt Lake Temple had started nearly twenty years earlier, but it would take twenty more years to finish it—and Brother Brigham could see that he would never live that long. Yet he felt a keen sense of urgency because of a special charge he had received from Joseph Smith.

During his final meetings with the Twelve in the months before his death in June 1844, with the Nauvoo Temple still under construction, Joseph said he had given them "every key, *every ordinance*, every principle, and every Priesthood . . . that belong to the last dispensation."[14] "The Lord is about to . . . let me rest awhile."[15] Speaking specifically about temple ordinances, the Prophet said that the endowment for the dead was to be administered only in dedicated temples. And to Brigham Young he said:

"Brother Brigham, this [the temple ordinance work] is not arranged perfectly; however we have done the best we could under the circumstances in which we are placed. I wish you to take this matter in hand: organize and systematize all these ceremonies."[16]

President Young would ultimately carry out this charge to establish the temple work—and yet his actual time administering ordinances *in a temple*[17] would be limited to forty-six days in Nauvoo and four months in St. George. In those compressed circumstances, he directed the restoration of the doctrine, ordinances, and policies for temple work for the living and the dead. It took three temples to complete that part of the Restoration: Kirtland, Nauvoo, and St. George.

ONE SINGLE THING

David H. Cannon was an assistant to Wilford Woodruff in the first St. George Temple presidency and was later the temple president himself for thirty-one years. An early experience in his marriage illustrates how he and the other settlers developed attitudes of contrite submission to God during the harsh settlement years. David and his wife Wilhelmina were called to leave their home in Salt Lake City with the original settlers in 1861. But, according to Lyman Hafen's account of their family story,

> Wilhelmina was hardly cut out to be a pioneer woman. She grew up in the genteel society of Back Bay, Boston, where water and greenery were as common as air. She was little more than five feet tall and tipped the scales at around 100 pounds. She had fine, sensitive features, loved books, poetry and fine music, and always endeavored to make her home a place of beauty. But here in St. George her first home was nothing more than the wagon box she had arrived in, then a dugout with a dirt floor in the side of a hill surrounded by red sand,

greasewood, mesquite and creosote. It would be years before she had a shingled roof and plastered walls around her again.

Wilhelmina tried bravely to stand against the constant struggle of wind, sand, rain, and mud. She felt swallowed up and defeated among the barren hills and emptiness of the landscape. Her husband David spent the long days working in the fields. She washed and cooked and labored with only her small son for company, and sometimes when her husband returned home he found her weeping.

And then one day, as the legend goes, she became so despondent she cried to David: "If you could only show me one thing about this country that was lovely or beautiful—one single thing."

"And if I could?" David responded.

"Then I would feel it was worthwhile staying here and working for the future."

As April melted into May, David searched for something beautiful, some spot of loveliness on the lonely, parched landscape. Willie continued to battle the dirt, the insects, the heat. She carried water, stoked the fire, scrubbed the clothes and did all the household chores until her petite body ached with fatigue. But her heart was not in it.

Then one day, as he returned from the fields, David looked down at his feet and saw something that stopped him short. It was a sego lily, its lavender cup delicately shaped and shaded, its golden brown eye marked as by an artist's brush. He found several blossoms nearby and carefully picked the exquisite flowers from the red sand and even more carefully carried them home.

When Wilhelmina held the flowers in her hand she was overcome by their beauty. To her they were like fairy bells, something out of this world. And, as the legend goes, she said, "Any valley that can produce so much beauty is worth every effort on the part of men, and the wholehearted cooperation of every woman."

It is said that after that day Wilhelmina Cannon had only praise for this place where she lived until she was nearly ninety years old.[18]

HOW WOULD YOU LIKE SUCH A HOUSE NOW?

One other story from those who settled this same region captures a key insight about the effects of consecration. In 1867 Brigham Young called William and Elizabeth Wood to help settle an extension of the Dixie Cotton Mission ninety miles southwest from St. George along the Muddy River in Moapa Valley, Nevada. One historian wrote that no other colonization in North America presented greater difficulties than those faced by the settlers on the Muddy.[19] To accept this mission call, the Woods sold their profitable butcher shop and their comfortable home in Salt Lake City.

Conditions in the Muddy settlement were even more harsh than in St. George. As one descendant of that group said, "Those people were so poor, they couldn't even pay attention."[20] After five years of frustrating effort, William's family lost everything, and the settlement failed in 1872. Many of these settlers moved 150 miles northeast to Orderville, just in time to join the united order there—for which the humility they felt from experiencing the Muddy was severe but ideal preparation.

The Woods returned penniless and exhausted to Salt Lake City, where they began living in a dugout with a sod roof and a dirt floor. One day William and Elizabeth stood looking at the beautiful home they had sold to accept their mission call. William asked, "How would you like such a house now as our old home?" Elizabeth replied, "I would rather [live in a] dug-out with [our] mission filled, than [live] in that fine house with [our] mission unfulfilled."[21]

Why would Elizabeth feel that way? Her answer implies not

simply that she was glad she survived the hardships, but that she believed they had learned and grown by facing their hardships—in ways she couldn't have done otherwise. Like the handcart survivors, they came to know God in their extremities.

The sego lily is the official state flower of Utah—not just because it was a bloom of beauty in the desert, but because eating the bulb of its roots gave the early Saints critically needed nourishment. So, speaking symbolically, perhaps the Woods and the Cannons also discovered how consecration begets the personal nourishment of both cooperation and spiritual growth: "And in the barren deserts there shall come forth pools of living water; and the parched ground shall no longer be a thirsty land. And they shall bring forth their rich treasures . . . and they shall be filled with songs of everlasting joy" (D&C 133:29–33).

GRUMBLING AND MT. TRUMBULL

My father, Orval Hafen, was born near St. George, a grandson of those original settlers sent by Brigham Young. In 1936, he was serving in the presidency of the St. George Utah Stake. One day he wrote in his journal that some members of their high council would grumble and make excuses when they were assigned to drive sixty miles on a Sunday to visit the Saints in Mt. Trumbull, Arizona, on monthly speaking assignments. Mt. Trumbull was where the builders of the St. George Temple had found, milled, and hauled the huge pine trees used for the temple's rough lumber only a few decades earlier.

Nobody liked to go to Mt. Trumbull because the primitive gravel road was too rough on their cars. When one high councilor complained that he always got assigned to go, the stake presidency checked and found that he had been to Mt. Trumbull only once in the past three years. Another high councilor had to be assigned four months in a row before, as my father wrote, "Mt. Trumbull was finally honored with his presence."

My father contrasted these men with one of their youngest high councilors, who was always "willing to perform faithfully every call we have made on him, including buying his own gas." Then he wrote, "I'm just wondering, is a man really converted if he isn't willing to sacrifice for his religion. . . . Can there be degrees of conversion?"

What is the difference between people like the Woods, the Cannons, the young high councilor—and those other brethren who wouldn't make the rugged drive to Mt. Trumbull? There are indeed "degrees of conversion," and like other matters of degree, over the long term the differences can become magnified into shallow complacency—or sanctifying consecration.

As the southern Utah stories suggest, the tough demands of pioneer times nourished a rich religious culture that produced thrift and character and stable families. But now one wonders if the comforts and the modern evils that accompany luxury and urban living are descending upon the posterity of the first settlers enough to put those pioneer values at risk. Perhaps that is why, when she was in her eighties, my mother would often ask our children at the dinner table, "Well, what did you do today that was hard for you?"

The pioneers blessed their posterity by conquering the very oppositions that had so profoundly shaped their character. The irony of that statement is echoed in Winston Churchill's introduction to the last volume of his World War II memoirs: "How the great democracies won the war and thus were able to resume the follies which had so nearly cost them their lives."[22] Is it possible, then, during a time of prosperity to develop the spirit of consecration and character that was so clearly formed by a time of poverty and sacrifice? That's a provocative question for us today, no matter where we live.

ACTIVE OR CONSECRATED

I once heard Elder Neal A. Maxwell say that it would change the entire Church if in every ward we could have just three or four more families who were truly consecrated disciples of Jesus Christ instead of just being "active" in the Church.

We talk often about the difference between being "active" and "less active" in the Church. Perhaps we should talk more about the additional distinction between being active in the Church and being a truly consecrated disciple. Being active is of course a significant indicator of progress. Yet it is only the emerging stage of our discipleship, the Aaronic Priesthood level, not yet the more mature Melchizedek Priesthood level of spiritual development. A life of consecration will naturally take us out of our comfort zone—just as it did the Cannons and the Woods. But, as a friend once said, "If we don't get out of our comfort zone, we won't learn; and if we don't learn, we won't grow; and if we don't grow, we won't find joy."

And consecration is not just about offering material possessions. Echoing his previous comment about the difference between sacrificing an animal and sacrificing ourselves, Elder Maxwell said, "Ultimate consecration is the yielding up of oneself to God. Heart, soul, and mind. . . . If we desire [to receive the Father's] fullness, we cannot hold back part! . . . How could we be entrusted with His 'all' until our wills are much more like His? Nor could His 'all' be fully appreciated by the partially committed."[23]

For sound reasons stemming from our human nature and the natural process of growth, the Lord cannot give us everything He has until we have consecrated all that we have on the altar of sacrifice. "Where your treasure is, there will your heart be also" (Matthew 6:21). Our hearts will thus follow what we most want and value—our "treasure," and that may require that we learn how to discipline our desires. Eventually, if we haven't really given our whole hearts to the stretching, expanding process of our own spiritual growth, we won't—can't—grow. Growth is inherently a step-by-step process, line upon line. Gradually we gain strength and wisdom until we are ready to step higher.

And the temple, with its metaphors and symbols that carry us upward a step at a time through the progression of the two priesthoods, is designed to teach, symbolize, and embody that very process—both His consecration to us and ours to Him. "And also all they who receive this [Aaronic and Melchizedek] priesthood receive me. . . . And . . . all that my Father hath shall be given unto him" (D&C 84:35–38).

When we answer the Savior's entreating command and come to Him in our brokenheartedness and our contrition of spirit, He can then make something of our lives that we never could alone. If we clasp His hand and run, He can make molten gold from the fires of our afflictions. He can make beauty from our ashes.

The two qualities, a broken heart and a contrite spirit, are companions that give meaning to each other and mark our progress in the disciple's journey.

In the moments when we are jolted by heartbreaking experience, we have a choice. In the face of the pain, we can either close our hearts to God in bitterness or open our hearts to Him in contrition. It is in choosing to be contrite that we bring our whole selves to God and give Him something to work with.

In another sense, the two terms suggest a sequential process. In the early stages of our discipleship, many of us are like the active but not yet consecrated Church members in Zarahemla, who Alma said "persist in . . . setting [their] hearts upon the vain things of the world" (Alma 5:53). And hearts "set so much upon the things of this world" (D&C 121:35) are "hearts *so set* they must first be broken."[24] In Brigham Young's down-to-earth language, "Many of the Saints are still glued to this earth and lusting and longing after the things of this world. . . . Where are the eyes and the hearts of this people?"[25] So the law of sacrifice first asks that we *give up* whatever vain things our hearts are set on or glued to.

Once our hearts are "broken" enough to be softened, we are freed up to make our consecrated offering to God. If we *give* our hearts to Him with a contrite spirit, *then* He can mold, shape, and develop our hearts, ultimately to become like His heart. But unless we fully offer Him our hearts and our will, holding nothing back, He cannot do all He desires to do with us—and for us. *His* heart is also set—not upon the things of this world, but upon doing all we will allow Him to do for our growth and benefit: "What is man . . . that thou shouldest set thine heart upon him?" (Job 7:17).

In this sequence, the principles and ordinances of the Aaronic Priesthood help us break the hold of the world on our hearts, helping us to let go of it and to be cleansed from worldly stains. The *redeeming blessings* of Christ's Atonement help make this stage possible.

Then the principles and ordinances of the Melchizedek Priesthood help us to lay hold on—even to seal our hearts to—the Lord, thereby offering our *wholehearted* participation in the lifelong process of our becoming sanctified, holy, and like Him. Through the relationship He creates with those who accept His Atonement, the Savior extends to them His *strengthening* and *perfecting blessings*, often through the ministry of the Holy Ghost. Those blessings help us to fulfill the potential of this mature stage of our growth. While repentance and baptism focus fundamentally on "the *cleansing* of the soul, the temple focuses [primarily] on the *development* of the soul."[26] Taken as a whole, then, the complete process shows that real consecration requires both a broken heart *and* a contrite spirit.

Some specific, practical examples of the difference between being merely "active," in contrast to being "fully consecrated" Church members, might make these ideas more concrete.

Some years ago, for instance, I was struck by the contrast between two people I interviewed on the same afternoon for possible faculty positions at BYU. Both of them were active in the Church, both were professionally qualified to join the faculty, but their *attitudes* differed significantly. In both interviews, I said, "As you know, BYU is sponsored and actively supported by the Church, so the campus has a more religious environment than most other universities. How would you feel about working in this environment?" One of the applicants said, "Oh, the Church isn't a big problem for me. I can live with it. So I think I could put up with the campus environment." The other one said, "The Church and the gospel mean absolutely everything to me. I would give anything to work and live in this environment."

Second, I heard two active Church members speak in the same sacrament meeting. One speaker said that he had found a good article in a Church magazine, which he then read aloud—and that was his talk. The other speaker had prayed for inspiration and studied to decide what scriptures, ideas, and illustrations would be of greatest help to her and her fellow Saints. Even with that much preparation, she spoke from her heart and included her own experience and testimony.

Third, two young men returned at about the same time from having served full-time missions. Soon after removing his missionary name tag and dark missionary suits, one of them also removed what he considered a kind of spiritual façade that he had in effect painted on himself like a veneer to seem "churchy," taking on the appearance of a missionary. He soon reverted to most of his pre-mission language, habits, and lifestyle. The other person also removed his name tag and well-worn dark suits, but he said that on his mission he had seen the gospel change people's lives—and it had also changed his life, permanently. He wanted to, and did, live in ways that cultivated the spiritual missionary climate he had come to associate with his growing relationship with the Lord.

And finally, two people were called to new positions in their ward. One of them said the calling was not something she was interested in, but she accepted it and gave it no more of her precious time than necessary. She felt like she was just "going through the motions," but she didn't mind doing it. The other person, after serving for a few months, said, "I mostly just 'accepted' the calling before—I didn't know much about it. But now I have a kind of passionate commitment to it—to the Lord and to the girls I've been called to know and serve."

CONSECRATION BUILDS CONFIDENCE IN GOD

The sixth Lecture on Faith, originally approved by Joseph Smith to be taught in the School of the Prophets in the winter of 1834–1835, teaches us that "a religion that does not require the sacrifice of all things never has power sufficient to produce the faith necessary unto life and salvation." This is true because "through the medium of the sacrifice of all earthly things" we come to know that we "are doing the things that are well pleasing in the sight of God":

> When a man has offered in sacrifice all that he has for the truth's sake, not even withholding his life, and believing before God that he has been called to make this sacrifice because he seeks to do his will, he does know, most assuredly, that God does and will accept his sacrifice and offering and that he [does] not seek his face in vain. Under these circumstances, then, he can obtain the faith necessary for him to lay hold on eternal life.[27]

In contrast, "those who have not made this sacrifice to God do *not* know" that the course of their life is pleasing to God. Rather, "it is a matter of doubt and uncertainty in their mind." And those "whose minds are under doubts and fears cannot have unshaken confidence" in God, which leaves them with weak faith. When that happens, they "will not be able to contend against all the opposition, tribulations, and afflictions which they will have to encounter in order to be . . . joint heirs with Christ Jesus; and they will grow weary in their minds, and the adversary will have power over them."[28]

The temple ordinances offer a needed opportunity for the Saints to make these sacrificial covenants. As Brother Brigham said to the early Utah settlers, "Should we live in peace year after year, how long would it be before we were glued to the world? Our affections would be so fastened to the things of the world that it would be . . . contrary to our feelings to attend to anything but our own individual concerns to make ourselves rich."[29]

His concern about being "glued to the world" was also a major theme of his talk at the dedication of the St. George Temple in 1877. He knew how the covenants of the temple could help us remove that worldly glue and shift our sense of attachment to a higher purpose—to "let the affections of thy heart be placed upon the Lord forever" (Alma 37:36). So in bringing us to the altars of sacrifice, those covenants teach us about consecration. The purpose of the temple covenants is not just to remind us of pioneer sacrifices, but to evoke *our* sacrifices, because the Lord still designs to build Zion by establishing "a consecrated people."[30] Zion is not only a geographic place, it is the gathering of people who have come together because their hearts are being purified: "for this is Zion—the pure in heart" (D&C 97:21).

CHAPTER 20

SANCTIFICATION

The scriptures sometimes speak of "justification" and "sanctification" together (see, e.g., D&C 20:30–31; Moses 6:59–60) because, as Elder D. Todd Christofferson said, "they are elements of a single divine process that qualifies us to live in the presence of God." At the same time, he said, the two elements "may be viewed as distinct topics,"[1] another instance of a prism letting us see two different colors within the same beam of light. The separate colors help us visualize each part of the process more clearly, even when both parts are in motion simultaneously.

Justification is the ongoing process by which the Savior's grace satisfies the law of justice on condition of our repentance. As we are thus "justified," we are forgiven or pardoned of our sins, relieving us of "the punishment that justice would otherwise exact for disobedience."[2] In the metaphor of the weeds and the flowers, justification removes the unsightly weeds from our lives. As they are cleared from our heart-land, we can till the ground, then plant and cultivate the flowers of sanctification.

The flowers are symbols of the further process by which, following baptism and forgiveness, we can eventually become

222

complete and holy, as He is holy. The Savior makes both justification and sanctification possible, as we meet the conditions for each one. Then have we become "just [justified] men made perfect [sanctified] through Jesus . . . who wrought out this perfect atonement" (D&C 76:69).

Sanctification, the "flowers of grace,"[3] is thus the process of our being made "pure and holy"[4] to the point that we become "a saint through the atonement of Christ" (Mosiah 3:19),[5] "purified even as he is pure" (Moroni 7:48). This perfecting blessing is the culmination of a maturing, refining process that is blessed by His grace and facilitated by "the Holy Ghost, which Comforter filleth with hope and perfect love" (Moroni 8:26). Then are we "*sanctified* in Christ" (Moroni 10:33; emphasis added), thereby receiving God's quality of life: eternal life, "the greatest of all the gifts of God" (D&C 14:7). And "the names of the sanctified" are recorded among "them of the celestial world" (D&C 88:2)—suggesting that this process may not be completed until we are beyond the veil.

These sanctifying endowments include above all the gift of *charity,* the capacity to love other people as Christ Himself loves them (see Moroni 7:44–48). Another gift is *hope*—the sure promise of being "raised unto life eternal" (Moroni 7:41). Still another is the *peace of God*—the gift that "passeth all understanding" (Philippians 4:7), a peace not of this world but of Him: "Peace I leave with you, *my peace I give unto you.*" As He promised, "I will not leave you comfortless: I will come to you" (John 14:27; 14:18). So endowed with His capacities, our overall character will reflect a divine nature—not only because we desire to be that way, but because that is how we have become.

SANCTIFICATION—ON WHAT CONDITIONS?

As with most other blessings of grace, the perfecting blessings are conditional ones—they are not ours simply for the asking.

And sometimes, as we saw earlier in the story from the life of Elder Neal A. Maxwell, meeting these conditions can be very demanding because the hard way may be the only way to learn some of what we don't yet understand—or can't yet live. Moreover, as the Lord said of the Saints in Missouri who had been subjected to severe persecutions, "They must needs be chastened and tried, even as Abraham, who was commanded to offer up his only son," because if they will not *"endure chastening"* they *"cannot be sanctified"* (D&C 101:4–5; emphasis added).

Still, our part of this interactive process is—if we are willing to stretch ourselves enough—within our reach. The conditions that give us access to the perfecting blessings deal mostly with the spirit of the law, our core internal attitudes, our sacrifices, and our consecration.

The scriptures are filled with references that describe, simply and eloquently, the essential qualities of this internal kind. They tell us how we must live, what we must do and be, so that we are prepared fully to receive and assimilate the gifts of the divine nature when they might be bestowed upon us. We have already seen a few of these phrases, but as we consider a more complete scriptural inventory, it helps to ask how these qualities—which are *within* our reach—are different from the perfecting gifts, which we cannot reach on our own.

Mormon tells us, for example, that in order to qualify to receive such gifts as charity and hope, we must first become "meek, and lowly of heart." Indeed, "none is acceptable before God save the meek and lowly in heart" (Moroni 7:43–44). By our own disciplined desires and choices, and with time and practice, we can develop meekness and humility. When we have become meekly "acceptable before God," living actively as Christ's "true followers" (Moroni 7:44, 48) we will be eligible for Him to "bestow" upon us the gift of charity. Notice that this same "if-then" pattern for receiving divine qualities is repeated in numerous other passages:

- "*Bridle all your passions,* that ye may be filled with love" (Alma 38:12; emphasis added here and in all scriptures below).
- "Pray . . . with *all the energy of heart,* that ye may be filled with this love" (Moroni 7:48).
- "He hath bestowed [charity] upon all who *are true followers of his Son*" (Moroni 7:48).
- "Sanctification through the grace of . . . Jesus Christ [comes] to all those *who love and serve God with all their mights, minds, and strength*" (D&C 20:31).
- "[Because they chose] *to repent and work righteousness . . .* therefore they were . . . *sanctified . . . by the Holy Ghost*" (Alma 13:10–12).
- "*Submissive, meek, humble, patient, full of love, willing to submit* to . . . the Lord . . . as a child doth submit to his father" (Mosiah 3:19).
- "They did *fast and pray oft,* and did wax stronger and *stronger in their humility,* and firmer and *firmer in the faith of Christ,* unto . . . the sanctification of their hearts, *which . . .* cometh because of their *yielding their hearts unto God*" (Helaman 3:35).
- "*Deny yourselves of all ungodliness,* and love God with *all your might, mind, and strength,* then . . . by his grace ye may be . . . sanctified in Christ" (Moroni 10:32–33).
- "Because of *meekness and lowliness of heart . . .* the Holy Ghost . . . filleth with hope and perfect love, which love *endureth by diligence* unto prayer" (Moroni 8:26).
- "For whoso is *faithful unto . . . the magnifying their calling,* are sanctified by the Spirit" (D&C 84:33).
- "All among them who know their *hearts are honest, and are broken, and their spirits contrite, and are willing to observe*

their covenants by sacrifice . . . are accepted of me . . . [and I] will cause them to bring forth as a very fruitful tree" (D&C 97:8–9).

- "[Those who are] *meek and lowly in heart* . . . shall find rest to their souls" (Alma 37:34).
- "You that are . . . the *peaceable followers of Christ* . . . have obtained a sufficient hope by which ye can enter into the rest of the Lord . . . because of *your peaceable walk with the children of men*" (Moroni 7:3–4).

Taken together, the italicized phrases describe the condition of *a contrite spirit*—the overall *attitude* we must cultivate to receive the exalting powers of saintliness. And there is a crucial distinction between this attitude—our willful contrition—and the gifts of sanctification. It isn't possible for us simply to choose to love other people, always, with the same divine love that Christ has for us. But it *is possible* for us to choose to become meek, or choose to become a "true follower of Christ." Following Him is within our reach. So is the life of a "peaceable walk," or fasting and praying "oft," or "waxing stronger in our humility," or loving God "with all *our* might"—loving others as fully as we can, regardless of how limited, even inept, we feel or are.

The italicized phrases in these scriptures do not describe achieved perfection, but they do describe attitudes we can develop on the way to that perfection. Some other scriptural passages, such as the Sermon on the Mount, do describe achieved perfection. In that sermon of sermons, the Savior set the bar very high: no anger, no impure thoughts, love your enemies, . . . and be ye therefore perfect (see Matthew 5–7).

Although we can't reach these lofty aspirations only on our own power, we can sometimes, even if fleetingly, come close enough to touch and sense them. It's not that we must reach the top of that mountain on *our* own, but that, as we climb, He will at times lift us and carry us as *His* own. The Beatitudes and the sermon that follow them are a description of what gifts, what character, will ultimately be "*added upon*" (Abraham 3:26; emphasis added) those who choose to follow Him. These are the characteristics of becoming as He is—a picture of what true followers will become through the combination of their exertion and His endowment of grace. The great sermon is, then, a set of aspirations and blessings one day given to those "who come unto me" (3 Nephi 12:3) as fully as they are able; it is not just a statement of impossible demands.

ATTITUDES AND ATTRIBUTES

The italicized phrases in that list of scriptures, then, refer to in-process *attitudes,* while the sanctified characteristics of the divine nature refer to completed *attributes.* Attitudes reflect our self-chosen direction, our orientation, even our frame of mind. Attributes are more about outcomes and the completed results of usually long-term processes, even though attributes are in a sense the by-products of the attitudes we persistently cultivate.

Receiving the attributes of Divinity is not something we can confine to a routine list of "things to do today." But we *can* choose the daily attitudes of being more humble, meek, selfless, and peaceable in our walk with our fellow men. And if we give these steps our honest effort over time, we can keep up with Him enough to hold on to His hand and run with Him until, Agneslike, we are prepared for His strong arms to lift us to safety.

We welcome the encouragement of the Lord's tender entreaty, referring to His own sacrifice as He reaches for us when we are stretching to be faithful. Here He speaks about attitudes and next-step actions more than about accomplished attributes:

"Fear not, little flock; do good. . . . Behold, I do not condemn you; go your ways and sin no more. . . . Look unto me in every thought; doubt not, fear not. Behold the wounds which pierced my side, and also the prints of the nails in my hands and feet; be faithful, keep my commandments, and ye shall inherit the kingdom of heaven" (D&C 6:34–37).

The tone and language of this passage raise an important question. Does Christ sanctify us, or is there some sense in which we sanctify ourselves? The answer is yes—the scriptures speak of both, because the process is interactive. For example, "Therefore, *sanctify yourselves* that your minds become single to God, and the days will come that you shall see him; for he will *unveil* his face unto you . . . in his own time, and in his own way, and according to his own will" (D&C 88:68; emphasis added; see also D&C 43:11).

Temple overtones rustle in the word *unveil.* Moreover, "that your minds become single to God" sounds like those earlier italicized phrases we saw—a process that asks for our discipline, our energy, toward a specific focus that is under our control. So perhaps "sanctify yourself" is one more way of encouraging us to work on those attitudes that bring us close enough to receive His sanctifying power. A similar verse makes explicit reference to the temple: "And ye are to be taught from on high. *Sanctify yourselves and ye shall be endowed with power*" (D&C 43:16; emphasis added; see also Luke 24:49).

HOW THE TEMPLE HELPS

How, then, might the temple help us to develop the "attitudes" that lead to the long-term "attributes" of sanctified godliness? Since the temple with its higher ordinances is explicitly concerned with making "the power of godliness" manifest to us in the flesh, perhaps it could play a key role in helping us to develop the attitudes that will qualify us to be endowed with the qualities of His very nature.

Elder Marion D. Hanks said something about the temple and sanctification shortly after he had completed his service as president of the Salt Lake Temple some years ago. This is a paraphrase based on my notes from his talk: "The temple can bring to us a sanctifying growth—but only as we move from being *acquainted* with the temple, to having *experience* with the temple, to knowing true *worship* in the temple, not as spectators, but as *participants in the process of giving our hearts to God, which is how sanctification comes.*"

During our years in the St. George Temple, we met many people whose experience demonstrated what it means to be a full participant rather than mostly a spectator in true temple worship. People who are intimately familiar with the temple, those who go simply because they love being there, have found that something about being in and around the temple somehow lifts them to live with an increased measure of "gentleness and meekness, and . . . love unfeigned" (D&C 121:41).

The temple, through its ordinances and covenants, is all about clarifying our sense of direction—aligning us to the natural order of the timeless universe. It is like a natural spiritual magnet that always points true north. Whenever we are close enough to the temple in the right spirit, its magnetic force will help align our own internal senses to point north spiritually—just as the scrambled particles of an element will line up to point north when brought next to a natural magnet. And that alignment can help us feel and live the daily walk of the Savior's peaceable followers.

We saw this orienting effect over and over. One evening, for example, I needed to conduct an exit interview with one of our ordinance workers because he had been called as a bishop, and Church policy asks that bishops not carry a temple calling in addition. As we began to talk, he said he didn't want to be released—his temple service had been the most powerful spiritual experience of his life, even though he and his wife had served less than a year. When I asked why it had meant so much, he replied that somehow, for reasons he couldn't quite pinpoint, their two weekly temple shifts had changed the "culture" in their home.

"So many things changed for the better," he said, "our family conversations, the music, the tone of voice, the gospel discussions, and our attitudes toward one another." Members of their family had noticed the difference and had figured out that it was because of the temple calling—so they hoped he wouldn't be released. I said, "Don't be concerned. You'll be a fine bishop. And you will teach your ward members to love the temple the way you do. Then someday you'll be back."

A sister ordinance worker said that the work she and her husband did in the temple together each week had given them a renewed and closer unity in their marriage, filling a need that they had long been puzzling and praying about. Another temple worker couple echoed that "in some fashion the sacred union between Adam and Eve distilled upon our souls and upon our marriage" in a way that blessed them with love for others in the temple and "radiated with us far beyond" their assigned temple time.

One other temple worker confided in me that he had struggled for years with controlling his temper, a problem he had worked hard to overcome, but not with the success he desired. But somehow—again in ways he couldn't quite identify—his calling to serve in the temple had specifically helped him keep control when he needed to, inside or outside of the temple.

I also came to know an intelligent, jack-of-all-trades kind of man who found more than an ordinary number of reasons to spend time in and around the temple. When I commented to his close friend about his unusual affection for everything about the temple, I learned that this man had years earlier suffered through some horribly traumatic experiences in the Vietnam War. After years of searching for more serenity in his life, he had found that being inside or even close to the temple unfailingly brought him the peace he hungered to find.

In conversation after conversation, we learned from people who had discovered that the temple is a place of healing, peace, reconciliation, and even of rejoicing. It is also a place of mourning and seeking—a place for people who are trying to rebuild crumbled lives, who carry daunting burdens, or who search for answers to seemingly impossible questions. They all go into the temple, and for many of them, the temple helps, sometimes profoundly.

Sometimes they come back, and back again, until the peace comes, and they keep coming. People often want to talk to the temple president or the matron, whether they know them or not, because they just want to express gratitude for what the temple means in their lives. It is a tangible symbol of their relationship with the Lord, often giving concrete meaning to the sense of at-one-ment they seek and feel increasingly with Him. And they feel it enough to pay their own constant price: they make their covenants inside the temple; then they find ways to live those covenants with more conviction inside their homes and their hearts.

One temple patron said that years earlier, a teenager suffering from some combination of a drug and alcohol addiction ran over this patron's mother in a pedestrian crosswalk. She died from the accident. Her family members were heartsick and furious at this reckless boy whose carelessness had taken their mother's life. I don't know all that happened in the months and years after the accident. But during those following difficult years, the young man found a way to grow out of his problems enough to change his life's direction.

Members of the patron's family also found enough charity

to play a role in helping him find his way back to the Church. Eventually this patron and others from his family were present in the temple sealing room when this young man was sealed to his wife and children. As the patron watched the sacred ceremony, he felt a totally unexpected power come over him that caused him to feel more complete forgiveness and charity than he would ever have thought possible. He was healed when he extended healing to someone who had caused him great sorrow.

One of our most gifted and devoted ordinance workers told us about her life. Beth (not her real name) was raised by a single mother in what was then the outskirts of St. George. Her mother led a deeply troubled life, troubles that too often spilled over into Beth's life. Beth didn't know who her father was, and even in her youngest years, she longed to know her father and feel some connection to him.

One day, when Beth was about four, two men from the ward near their small trailer home came by for a home teaching visit—the only such visit she can recall from her childhood years. Beth remembers only that they shared some kind of little story, and she doesn't remember seeing them again. But something about their demeanor, their kindness, set her to thinking that perhaps their gentleness was how it would feel to have a father of her own.

A few years later, when she was just old enough to ride a bicycle, Beth happened to ride past the temple—and she felt a desire to stop and walk around on the grounds. After that, she would often ride her bike to the temple grounds, lean it against a tree, and then sit on the shady grass and look at the temple, letting it carry her thoughts. Someone had told her that the temple was Heavenly Father's house, and the idea made perfect sense to her. Being there let her feel that she did have a Father, and this was His house. From then on, the temple was the safest, most peaceful place she knew.

After her temple marriage, Beth and her husband found ways to stay close to the temple during the years when they were raising their children. The refuge of the temple continued to shelter them. Later they became ordinance workers, and they continued in that role even after receiving the shocking news that she had an incurable illness that would (and did) take her life within a short time. Our temple presidency gladly granted her request to remain an ordinance worker indefinitely.

On one occasion, Beth gave us soft white cloth temple envelopes she had made—just the right size to hold ceremonial temple clothing. On the outside she had embroidered the outline of the St. George Temple, and just below that, the words from Luke 2:46, "They found Him in the temple." That's where Beth had found Him—not by occasionally dropping in, but by continually finding Him inside and then following Him outside the temple.

One of the most telling of the "attitudes" that help us climb toward sanctification is meekness—as in, "meekness and lowliness of heart" (Moroni 8:26). Elder Neal A. Maxwell talked and wrote often about meekness, especially in his later years, because his sure spiritual instincts told him this was a key quality in his own quest for true, sanctifying discipleship. I thought of Elder Maxwell, and meekness, when I met a man, about age seventy, who was in the temple to receive his own endowment and to be sealed to his wife. I'll call him Larry.

As we got acquainted, Larry told me he had joined the Church only one year earlier. Many years before that, as a young college freshman, he said he had attended the University of Utah. He was having a miserable experience on the campus until he met "a guy in the Student Affairs office" named Neal Maxwell, who simply became Larry's "friend, Neal." This "Neal guy" helped him during several visits to navigate a range of complexities that transformed his freshman experience into a stable foundation for his other student years.

Larry said he left college and served in the Vietnam War—an experience that, he said, devastated his entire life. Without sharing any details, he just said his war years were so ugly that, no matter what other things he did, he had spent the next several decades in complete bitterness, "and it's been a long, very hard journey—until now."

"So how did you come to join the Church only a year ago?" I asked. "You must have known something about Mormons from your early years at the U of U." He paused for a thoughtful moment, then said, "Well, it took me a long time. But I finally figured out that instead of my telling God what to do, maybe I needed to let God tell me what to do."

I leaned forward as the tears rose. "Larry, I knew your old friend Neal Maxwell, actually quite well. You may not know that he passed away a few years ago." I paused. "I have a hunch that he is aware that you have chosen to be here today and he's very happy for you. It wouldn't surprise me to know that he found some way to help you get here—because today, as his former student, you will complete your real 'freshman orientation.'" I also thought, but didn't say, that Elder Maxwell would have given Larry an "A" for meekness because of what Larry had "figured out." Getting beyond his preoccupation with his own trauma enough to be more submissive to God's will was a major paradigm shift for Larry, and that shift brought him along the path that led to the temple.

Thinking now about Elder Maxwell, and about Larry's discovery of meekness, brings to mind a poem by Mary Karr that Elder Maxwell came to appreciate enough to quote in one of his last public talks in 2004. It suggests how Elder Maxwell's own meekness, which he had deliberately cultivated for years, helped him view his own terminal illness. The poem's understanding of meekness also explains how preparing for the temple ordinances helped Larry in ways that would greatly accelerate his sanctifying process. This is also the poem Marie mentioned in this book's Prologue, which brings us full circle.

Who the Meek Are Not

Not the bristle-bearded Igors bent
under burlap sacks, not peasants knee-deep
in the rice-paddy muck,
nor the serfs whose quarter-moon sickles
make the wheat fall in waves
they don't get to eat. My friend the Franciscan
nun says we misread
that word meek *in the Bible verse that blesses them.*
To understand the meek
(she says) picture a great stallion at full gallop
in a meadow, who—
at his master's voice—seizes up to a stunned
but instant halt.
So with the strain of holding that great power
in check, the muscles
along the arched neck keep eddying,
and only the velvet ears
prick forward, awaiting the next order.[6]

No wonder Elder Maxwell liked this imagery. He had been at such a full gallop before his stunned, almost instant halt. And then, holding the power in check, he had also pricked his ears forward, awaiting the next order.

Elder Hanks said that the temple can help us discover and develop attitudes like meekness, humility, and unfeigned love not merely by our being spectators—even frequent spectators—but by our being *participants* in the process of giving our hearts to God. What is the difference between being a temple spectator and a temple participant in this sense? I once asked that question of an ordinance worker who understood the difference herself because she had found it and lived it. She said, "It's all about desire. If you want to get below the surface in the temple, you begin with desire—and the Lord will respond."

DISCOVERIES BELOW THE SURFACE

The temple's ordinances and covenants are intentionally not static—they are dynamic and interactive. They respond to us as we respond to them. And that layered, symbolic interaction gives us access, time by time and visit by visit, to the temple's sanctifying power. As one friend put it, "I can choose the experience I have in the temple [as I] focus on fundamental gospel-centered truths regarding the nature of God, the purpose of life, our divine potential, and the gift of Christ's Atonement." This includes her pondering "about Eve's role in implementing God's plan." She has also begun thinking more about *receiving* "Jesus's Atonement individually as a result of a very personal direct relationship with God, independent of marital status." She has thus discovered "what it means to me to consider Adam and Eve as the story of receiving the Atonement. This approach unlocks one's ability to commune more effectively with God during the endowment."[7]

One of the newer temples in the Salt Lake Valley, the Oquirrh Mountain Temple, offers a vivid image of what lies in layers below the surface of the temple. During the first fifteen years after the Saints entered that valley in 1847, some of them grazed cattle and cut timber in the Oquirrh Mountains. Then in 1863 someone discovered gold and silver ore in the Oquirrhs. Later on, others found there the massive copper deposits that became the world-famous Bingham Copper Mine. Historians tell us that "so much wealth has been taken from the Oquirrhs . . . that the value of minerals taken from Bingham Canyon alone exceeds by eight times all of the finds of the California and Klondike gold rushes plus the yields of Nevada's Comstock Lode." One historian has called this "the richest hole on earth."[8]

Some good people go to the Oquirrh Mountain Temple today and, like the livestock men on the Oquirrh Mountains before the ore was discovered, walk around on the surface of the mountain without realizing what abundant spiritual treasures lie buried beneath their feet. Other people will pay the price, climb the temple mountain, and dig deep enough to unearth the treasures the Creator has deposited there as they reflect on, live, and internalize their temple covenants.

Marie especially likes this poem by Elizabeth Barrett Browning, which for us captures an attitude that digs symbolically deeper:

> Earth's crammed with heaven,
> And every common bush afire with God;
> But only he who sees, takes off his shoes.
> The rest sit round it and pluck blackberries.[9]

The bushes on the Oquirrh Mountains are now afire with God, just like the burning bush Moses saw. But only those who desire enough to see with their spiritual eyes will take off their shoes, sensing that they are on holy ground, with eternal riches under their feet. And as they become more meek, some will also take the shoes off their hearts.

Finally, we have the assurance of knowing that sanctification is not some kind of secret privilege reserved only for the elite few or for those who survive impossibly traumatic experiences. This blessing is not for the few but for the many—"even as many as will" (Moses 5:9).

Hear how widespread the blessings of sanctification were in

Alma's day—and note the likely connection of the sanctifying experiences to ordinances, perhaps temple ordinances:

"Now they, after *being sanctified by the Holy Ghost,* having their garments made white, being pure and spotless before God, could not look upon sin save it were with abhorrence; and there were *many, exceedingly great many,* who were made pure and entered into the rest of the Lord their God. . . . Now *these ordinances* were given after this manner, that thereby the people might look forward on the Son of God, it being a type of his order [or priesthood]" (Alma 13:12, 16; emphasis added).

Our temples are often placed in very visible, attracting locations—like a city on a hill—for the very purpose of making the invitation of their sanctifying power very broad, even universal, as opposed to a hidden or secret location that would imply blessings for only a very select few.

Our temples also possess a kind of spiritual gravitational pull that makes their invitation feel stronger as we come closer.

I felt that invitation very early. When I was a teenager in the then-small town of St. George, Utah, my friends and I somehow inherited the custom of frequently walking or driving our cars around the city block where our pure white temple stood. At the end of almost any school activity or party or date, we would always take our cars for "a spin around the temple" before driving home. No one had asked us to do this, and none of us ever analyzed the practice—we just did it.

Looking back now, I can see that this familiar pattern invited our lives to revolve in the temple's orbit, as the earth revolves around the sun. In that pattern, the temple holds us close with its pull of spiritual gravity—with enough power to offset the dark force whose strong contrary gravity tries to pull us away and into a downward spiral. And being in the temple's orbit holds us in the orbit of Him whose house the temple is.

CHAPTER 21

When "Almost"
Is Enough

It is difficult to write anything at all about either the Savior's Atonement or the temple—let alone both sacred topics in the same book. Each topic asks us to bend every effort to begin comprehending even the smallest part of what the Father and His Son have provided for us. The trail that They have cut for us and that we have set our feet upon is utterly demanding and yet utterly liberating. In inviting our response to both the Atonement and the temple, the Lord asks us to give all we have. Yet through both together, we can receive "all that my Father hath" (D&C 84:38). Nevertheless, our feet will move only as far as our answers to two questions will carry us: What do we most desire, and how far are we willing to be stretched?

It's not that the Lord *won't* give us salvation and exaltation without our wholehearted engagement; it's that He *can't*. All of our experience teaches us that if our heart isn't fully engaged in the process, we won't grow. If we don't freely give our will—and everything else we have—to the Lord, we cannot become capable of benefiting from all of His grace. After all, our will is the only unique possession we have to give Him. He already gave us every-thing else.[1]

So we must acknowledge again what Nephi stated: "It is by grace that we are saved, *after all we can do*" (2 Nephi 25:23; emphasis added). The sometimes haunting question is, how much *is* "all we can do"? In an important sense, doing or giving "almost" everything is not enough. If we almost keep the commandments, we almost receive the blessings.

King Agrippa said to Paul, "Almost thou persuadest me to be a Christian." But Paul replied that "almost" wasn't enough: Agrippa would need to be "almost, and altogether" converted (Acts 26:28–29).

As also recorded in the book of Acts, Ananias and Sapphira had covenanted to live the law of consecration. So they "laid . . . at the apostles' feet" everything they had—*except* for "part of the price" from something they had sold. And tragedy followed (Acts 5:1–11). Almost was not enough.

Christ said to the rich young man who wanted to inherit eternal life, "Yet lackest thou one thing" (Luke 18:22). That is not just a story about riches. It is about whatever "one thing" might be our most vulnerable spiritual weakness. And the Lord has made it very clear—He "cannot look upon sin with the least degree of allowance" (D&C 1:31). Almost is not enough.

It just doesn't work to stand between the temple and the world, simultaneously reaching to touch Zion with one hand and Babylon with the other. If we try to do that, we are still "glued to the world." Alma understood the same idea: "Come ye out from the wicked . . . and touch not their unclean things" (Alma 5:57). Touching both the temple and the world may be "almost" righteous. That is certainly better than having both hands on

Babylon. But it isn't enough: We must put both hands on the temple and hold on for dear life.

If we haven't known generosity and grace by being generous and gracious ourselves, if we haven't known forgiveness by extending it to others, we won't recognize those gifts when the Lord extends them to us. The gifts may be right before us and we won't even see them. That is why Jesus said, "Blessed are the merciful: for they shall obtain mercy," because only those who have learned how to be merciful to others "shall obtain mercy" (Matthew 5:7); not because He won't otherwise extend mercy, but because He can't. When He offers mercy to us, if we haven't already offered it to others, we won't feel it enough to recognize it and take hold of it. So, ultimately, "If you have not chosen the Kingdom of God first, it will in the end make no difference what you have chosen instead."[2] It is not enough to draw near to Him with our lips if we are keeping our hearts even slightly away from Him (see Joseph Smith—History 1:19). And that's why almost isn't enough.

And yet . . . there are times, there are moments, when almost *could* be enough—when our desires and our imperfect offerings to the Lord bring us close enough to Him that He might give us the strength we still need. "For I know that he granteth unto men according to their *desires*" (Alma 29:4; emphasis added).

When the Savior appeared to the Nephites, He showed each of them His wounds; then He taught them for what must have been many hours. Much of what He taught was new to them. It was so much for them to take in, especially after they had quaked their way through three terrifying days of darkness before they witnessed His supernal descent from the heavens. So He could see that they were weary and needed a time of rest before He saw them again the next day. "I perceive that ye are weak," He said, "that ye cannot understand all my words. . . . Therefore, go ye unto your homes, and ponder upon the things which I have said, . . . and prepare your minds for the morrow" (3 Nephi 17:2–3).

But as He was about to leave them, He "beheld they were in tears, . . . as if they would ask him to tarry a little longer with them. And he said unto them: Behold, my bowels are filled with compassion towards you. Have ye any that are sick among you . . . , or that are afflicted in any manner? . . . For I see that your faith is sufficient that I should heal you." So they brought forth their afflicted ones. He healed them. Many of them bathed His feet with their tears. Then He asked for their little children to be brought forth. He prayed words too marvelous to write. The multitude was overcome with joy. And then angels came and ministered to their children: "Behold your little ones" (3 Nephi 17:23; see also verses 5–22).

This transcendent moment, this piercing of the veil, occurred when the people really weren't able to understand the words of Jesus. They were too spent, too weak, and too exhausted. But they wanted Him to stay with them more than they wanted rest, food, comfort, or anything else. The desire of their hearts to be "with you" was vastly greater than the understanding of their minds.

They could "almost" comprehend Him, but not quite. Yet their yearning to be in His presence ran so deep that *almost* was *all* they could do. They had reached the limits of their capacity, but not the limits of their faith, even sufficient faith to be healed. And His yearning for them was enough to close any remaining separation. So He stayed with them. Almost, for them, was enough.

The life story of John Murdock,[3] an unusually faithful if somewhat zealous convert in Kirtland, offers another illustration of when "almost" could be enough. In 1832 John's wife Julia died in giving birth to twins they had named Joseph and Julia. Emma

Smith also gave birth to twins that day, but both of them died. Emma had borne three children in four years and lost them all. Because John had three other children, because he was serving as a full-time missionary, and because both he and Joseph Smith deeply felt Emma's loneliness, John offered his twins to Joseph and Emma. They gave the twins the Smith name and raised them as their own.

Little Joseph later died from an illness made worse from exposure on the night when a mob dragged the Prophet from the child's sickbed, where he had been trying to comfort the little one. When John Murdock returned from his mission, he lived in the Smith home for a short time, but he couldn't let his young Julia know who he was. Emma wanted her to grow up as their child. Joseph agreed, but he told John that the truth would eventually emerge. So John was almost, but not quite, able to embrace his own child.

In the School of the Prophets, Joseph Smith promised the brethren that if they had enough faith and humility, they would see the Lord's face. John Murdock yearned for that blessing. On one occasion, he began to see the Savior's form, His garment, His hair, His countenance. Then, wrote John, "while I was endeavoring to comprehend the whole personage from head to feet, it slipped from me, and the vision was closed up." He almost saw the Lord.

John soon knew more sorrow. His six-year-old child died of cholera. He married a second time (Amoranda Turner), and she died eighteen months later. He married once more (Electa Allen); then she died in Nauvoo, along with two of their three children. After marrying the widowed Sarah Weire, John arrived in the Salt Lake Valley in 1847 and became a bishop in 1848. Then, in 1851, at age fifty-nine, he was called as the first mission president to Australia.

His mission was a discouraging time. The weather was harsh,

the people were too consumed by gold-rush fever to care about religion, Australia's "tyranny of distance" was difficult, and John's health was deteriorating. Besides all of that, the local people preferred the preaching of his younger companion, Charles Wandell. So John returned home early, probably feeling that he had failed.

At his home in Lehi, he received news about his daughter Julia, who had stayed in the Midwest with Emma Smith—the only daughter Emma had raised. He learned that when Julia had discovered her true parentage, she was sad and upset at John for having withheld the truth from her. He wrote to Julia, trying to explain, and he pled with her to come to Utah. But by then the health of Julia's husband was failing, so the two never met again. John died in 1871, and Julia died nine years later.

John Murdock lived a life of sacrifice and devotion to the Lord's work, but also a life filled with disappointments and sorrow. After returning from Australia in 1853, he wrote a sentence that applies tellingly to both his mission and his life: "I went as far as I could, and when I could go no farther, I sent others." Fulfillment so often seemed to elude him. He sacrificed the true personal affection he felt for his little Julia in order to honor Emma's wishes—for which Julia later, ironically, blamed him. His vision of the Savior was incomplete. He lost numerous family members in death, and he knew frustration as well as consecration in his Church service.

I thought of John Murdock when we attended the dedication of the Melbourne Australia Temple in 2000. I sensed his great interest, perhaps even his feeling of fulfillment, in what we were doing. He couldn't have imagined a day when there would be five temples in that vast and in some ways incorrigible land. There in the Pacific, my thoughts about all that John didn't quite realize in his lifetime recalled a poignant line from the stage play *South*

Pacific: "This nearly was mine." Did John only "nearly" see his faith rewarded? Given our lack of control over events and the agency of other people, I chose to believe that day that for John Murdock—who had been as fully engaged as he could be in the consecration of giving his heart to the Lord—almost was enough.

Throughout his life, John's desires were righteous ones, and his behavior, even though at times maybe a little rigid, matched those desires to the extent of his capacity. His story and others like it cause me to feel that what we most *desire* does play a major role in whether our almost is enough. When our righteous desires run deep enough, those desires will motivate us to put all we have on the altar of sacrifice, engaging ourselves fully in the growth process of faith. As we hold nothing back, the Lord gives us strength to move as far as we need to go—toward Home, toward becoming like Him.

One of the most powerful righteous desires is the longing to belong eternally to—to be *with*—those we love most. And in a stroke of great theological harmony, our desires to be with our family members fully reinforce our desires to be with the Savior and our Father. That hope gives us a double incentive to hold nothing back in making sure that our daily walk matches our eternal desires. And when we do that as fully as we are able, *almost* can be enough.

I have seen that longing to belong bear remarkable fruit in the lives of men and women who have suffered through hard, sometimes tragic, personal stories. One of my occasional assignments as a Seventy was to interview people who had previously been excommunicated from the Church, had returned to the Church through baptism, and had applied to the First Presidency for a restoration of their priesthood and temple blessings, including (where appropriate) their temple sealings.

When the interview was satisfactory, it was my solemn privilege to lay my hands on their heads and perform the ordinance of restoration of blessings, which allows a new membership record to be issued showing the original dates of a person's priesthood ordination, temple endowment, and temple sealing. Just watching that procedure was a tangible witness to me about the reality and the power of forgiveness and of the Savior's Atonement.

These interviews were understandably very personal and very searching. I would often find it natural to ask, "What was it that helped you come back?" With many variations on the theme, the most frequent answer was, "I wanted to be sealed to my family."

As just one example, I still remember a man whose occupation during his years of excommunication was that of sheepherding. When I asked what had helped him find the desire and strength to return, he said, "Night after night, after checking on the sheep a few times after dark, I would sit alone by my fire and watch the burning logs and think about my family. My wife and my children meant more to me than everything else I cared about put together—and my mistakes were keeping me from being with them in the eternities." He paused as if he were still looking into that fire; then he said, "So I just decided that nothing would separate me from them. And here I am."

The yearning to be "at one" with those we love does help us have the power to overcome the most potent opposing forces. When I was about seven years old, in the days before seat belts, I was in the back seat of our car as the whole family drove along a dusty gravel road toward a cabin in the mountains. Suddenly the car door next to my seat somehow came loose, and the door flew wide open. The next thing I knew, I was pitched from the car and landed on the gravel road, hitting my elbows first, then tumbling over a couple of times. I must not have been seriously hurt, because I remember jumping to my feet and running after the car as it kicked up clouds of dust and sped away from me. By the time my father could safely stop the car on that kind of road, I had sprinted what felt like a mile. I still remember crying as I ran, calling as loudly as I could, "Dad! Dad! Stop the car! Wait for me!"

When I finally reached the waiting car, I was shaking and crying—not from pain, but from the near-panic of feeling that I had been left behind by my family. As I climbed back into my seat, pulled the door shut, and tried to lock it, my older brother tersely explained to me how stupid it was to fall out of the car. Then he pointed at my arms and cried out urgently, "What happened to your elbows?" I remember looking down at my arms, which were bleeding badly. The skin was torn all around my elbows, and I could see ugly little gravel rocks embedded in my flesh. Suddenly it all began to hurt like blazes! Before long we reached a place where my mom could wash off the dirt amid even more pain, apply some ointment, and wrap my arms with bandages.

Looking back, the most remarkable fact to me about that experience is that I didn't notice any pain from the hamburger-like abrasions on my elbows while I was running after the car. I first felt the pain when I heard my brother's cry and looked at the blood. The pain of suddenly fearing separation from my family had clearly been more frightening and intense than the stinging physical pain I could have been feeling.

That incident is a metaphor for me about the power of our desire to be "at one" with our families. If that desire runs deep enough, it will be stronger than any other force in our lives, strong enough to subordinate our pains and shortfalls, strong enough to govern our behavior. In that way, our desire to be with them can outweigh all opposition and can help us transcend any of our own weakness or other forces that might stand in our way.

In *Man's Search for Meaning,* the Austrian psychiatrist Victor Frankl (who survived a Nazi concentration camp) wrote, "He who has a *why* to live for can bear almost any *how.*"[4] To illustrate his point, Frankl remembered that in his days of greatest doubt and fear as a prisoner of war, he learned to visualize his wife's face.[5] Simply thinking of returning to her gave him the "why," the compelling positive motivation to keep going in the midst of nearly hopeless circumstances.

The Lord offers His gifts not only to "those who love me and keep all my commandments," but also to "him that *seeketh so to do*" (D&C 46:9; emphasis added). Thus did He offer to the Nephites certain tender promises from the Sermon on the Mount, "if ye shall come unto me, *or shall desire to come unto me*" (3 Nephi 12:23; emphasis added).

In the long run, we are likely to receive what we really want most because our desires ultimately drive our lives. So we can have eternal life if we want it, so long as we don't want anything else more. When that desire is strong enough, it will take us *almost* all the way Home. Then the Rescuer, who has been with us every step of the way, will again reach for our hand. If we clasp our hand in His, He will, like the wagon master with Agnes Caldwell, give us the strength to make the final ascent up the mountain of the Lord.

> *But behold, he did deliver them*
> *because they did humble themselves before him;*
> *and . . . they cried mightily unto him . . .*
> *and thus doth the Lord work with his power*
> *. . . among the children of men, extending the arm of mercy*
> *towards them that put their trust in him.*
>
> (Mosiah 29:20)

NOTES

PREFACE

1. *Wilford Woodruff's Journal*, 9 vols., ed. Scott Kenney (Salt Lake City: Signature Books, 1984), 7:33 (spelling and capitalization in original).

PROLOGUE

1. "Jesus, the Very Thought of Thee," *Hymns* (Salt Lake City: The Church of Jesus Christ of Latter-day Saints, 1985), no. 141.

CHAPTER 1
CLARIFYING THE ATONEMENT CONVERSATION—AND HOW THE TEMPLE HELPS

1. Elder M. Russell Ballard, funeral service for Elder L. Tom Perry, June 5, 2015. Accessed online at https://www.lds.org/media-library/video/2015-06 -1000-funeral-service-for-elder-l-tom-perry?lang=eng.
2. "In Humility, Our Savior," *Hymns* (Salt Lake City: The Church of Jesus Christ of Latter-day Saints, 1985), no. 172.
3. Bruce C. Hafen, *A Disciple's Life: The Biography of Neal A. Maxwell* (Salt Lake City: Deseret Book, 2002), 502.
4. Jan Shipps, *Sojourner in the Promised Land: Forty Years among the Mormons* (Urbana: University of Illinois Press, 2000), 112.
5. See Carl Mosser, "And the Saints Go Marching On: The New Mormon Challenge for World Missions, Apologetics, and Theology," chapter 2 in *The New Mormon Challenge*, ed. Francis J. Beckwith, Carl Mosser, and Paul Owen (Grand Rapids: Zondervan, 2002).
6. Kenneth L. Woodward, "What Mormons Believe," *Newsweek*, September 1, 1980, 68.
7. Robert A. Rees, "The Fatal Embrace," *Sunstone*, January/February 1981, 2.
8. Kenneth L. Woodward, "Woodward Responds," *Sunstone*, January/February 1981, 3.

9. Dieter F. Uchtdorf, "The Gift of Grace," *Ensign*, May 2015, 107.

10. Kim Peterson email to Bruce C. Hafen, August 23, 2012.

11. Tad R. Callister, *The Infinite Atonement* (Salt Lake City: Deseret Book, 2000), 8–9.

12. Neal A. Maxwell, "Lest Ye Be Weary and Faint in Your Minds," *Ensign*, May 1991, 88.

13. See chapter 21 of this book.

14. *The Complete Discourses of Brigham Young*, 5 vols., ed. Richard S. Van Wagoner (Salt Lake City: Smith-Pettit Foundation, 2010), 1:276.

15. Allan Rau email to Bruce C. Hafen, June 25, 2012; emphasis added.

16. James E. Faust, "The Keys of the Kingdom," *Ensign*, November 1975, 56.

CHAPTER 2
THE PURPOSE OF CHRIST'S ATONEMENT: PROVIDING FOR OUR GROWTH

1. Susan Arrington Madsen, *I Walked to Zion: True Stories of Young Pioneers on the Mormon Trail* (Salt Lake City: Deseret Book, 1994), 57–59.

2. This phrase apparently originated with C. S. Lewis. See Sheldon Vanauken, *A Severe Mercy* (New York: Harper & Row, 1977), 20.

3. Salvation Army, Doctrine 5; available at http://www.salvationarmy.org.za/index .php/our-faith/doctrines-of-the-salvation-army; accessed 2 July 2014.

4. *Hymns* (Salt Lake City: The Church of Jesus Christ of Latter-day Saints, 1985), nos. 292, 301.

5. See Terryl L. Givens, "Lightning out of Heaven," BYU Devotional, November 2005, accessed online at speeches.byu.edu/talks/terryl-l-givens.

6. William Wordsworth, "Ode: On Intimations of Immortality."

7. For comments on how these terms relate to "natural man" and "fallen man," see chapter 4, note 1.

CHAPTER 3
HIS ATONEMENT: REDEEMING BLESSINGS

1. The terms *mercy* and *grace* are often used interchangeably, but each has its own meaning. "*Mercy* is the more general of the two concepts, having broad enough meaning to include grace within its scope." Mercy "refers both to an attribute of deity and to a universal law that allows [Christ] to pay the penalty of justice on [our] behalf. As one of [the Father's] central attributes, [his] mercy is in some sense the source of all our blessings," including his decision to become the father of our spirits, to create the earth, and to provide the plan of Salvation—which includes the Atonement. "*Grace,* on the other hand, is the *means* by which mercy enacts many of its miraculous effects, particularly the blessings of the Atonement" (Bruce C. Hafen, *The Broken Heart* [Salt Lake City: Deseret Book, 2008], 175–76). See also Bruce C. Hafen, "Grace" and "Justice and Mercy," in *The Encyclopedia of Mormonism*, 4 vols., ed. Daniel H. Ludlow (New York: The Macmillan Co., 1992), 2:560–63; 2:775–76.

2. The term *redeeming blessings* as used in this chapter includes the Lord's having redeemed us from (a) physical death (by the Resurrection) and from (b) spiritual death (by the forgiveness of our sins). Redemption from physical death is unconditional, but redemption from spiritual death is conditional—we must

repent to be redeemed from sin. This portion of the text uses *forgiveness* rather than *redemption* in order to include only the forgiveness portion of redemption with the other "conditional" blessings of the Atonement.

This use of *spiritual death* refers to the first spiritual death—being "cut off from the presence of the Lord" by sin (Alma 42:9) prior to repentance, baptism, and receiving the Holy Ghost. The term *spiritual death* can also refer to the permanent "second death" (Helaman 14:18) that comes upon the wicked and unrepentant sons of perdition after the Resurrection (see D&C 76:31–39; Alma 40:25–26).

3. See Craig A. Cardon, "The Savior Wants to Forgive," *Ensign,* May 2013, 15–18; Brad Wilcox, *The Continuous Atonement* (Salt Lake City: Deseret Book, 2011).

Chapter 4
His Atonement: Strengthening Blessings

1. Scriptural terms such as *the natural man* or *fallen man* might seem to imply that, because of the Fall, men and women are evil by nature—as other Christian churches teach. However, as we have seen, the Restoration teaches that humans are born "whole" or "innocent," not evil or depraved. It was only *after* the children of Adam and Eve had chosen to reject their parents' teachings about the Fall and the Atonement that "men began from that time forth to be carnal, sensual, and devilish." (Moses 5:13). For further discussion about the meaning of "the natural man" and related issues, see Jeffrey R. Holland, *Christ and the New Covenant,* (Salt Lake City: Deseret Book, 1997), 203–4; Bruce C. Hafen, *The Broken Heart* (Salt Lake City: Deseret Book, 2008), 143–45.

2. Neal A. Maxwell, *Lord Increase Our Faith* (Salt Lake City: Deseret Book, 1994), 84

3. From a sacrament meeting talk prepared by "Allison" on April 2, 2014, copy in files of author. Used by permission.

4. In its complete context, the Westminster Confession of Faith states: "9.3 Man, by his fall into a state of sin, hath wholly lost all ability of will to any spiritual good accompanying salvation: so as, a natural man, being altogether averse from that good, and dead in sin, is not able, by his own strength, to convert himself, or to prepare himself thereunto. 9.4 When God converts a sinner, and translates him into the state of grace, he freeth him from his natural bondage under sin; and, *by his grace alone, enables him freely to will and to do that which is spiritually good*" (www.opc.org/wcf.html; emphasis added).

5. The standard works contain more than five hundred references to some form of *strengthen* and fourteen references to some form of *enable*. The main source for the use of the term *enabling power* among Church members in recent years is probably from the definition of grace in the Bible Dictionary for the LDS edition of the scriptures, which states, among other things, "This grace is an enabling power that allows men and women to lay hold on eternal life and exaltation after they have expended their own best efforts." The Church began using this Bible Dictionary in 1979. The Church website says of it: "Many of [its] entries draw on the work of Bible scholars and are subject to reevaluation as new research or revelation comes to light. This dictionary is provided to help your study of the scriptures and is not intended as an official statement

of Church doctrine or an endorsement of the historical and cultural views set forth" (https://www.lds.org/scriptures/bd?lang=eng).

6. LDS scholar Brent J. Schmidt has shown that the ancient Greeks and New Testament writers generally understood that the term *charis*, meaning "grace," was reciprocal or covenantal in nature rather than a free gift. For example, in that ancient world, "Once individuals had received a gift of kindness from the gods or others, an obligation of reciprocity was established among people and their deities" (Schmidt, "Obliging Grace: The Reciprocal and Binding Obligations of Charis," [unpublished manuscript, 2012], 7). This understanding is consistent with how the "gift of grace" is typically presented in LDS teachings, which "implies that we must fulfill our reciprocal obligations by making and keeping sacred covenants" (ibid., 134).

7. Quoted in David O. McKay, "Pioneer Women," *Relief Society Magazine,* vol. 35, no. 1 (January 1948): 8.

8. See, for example, Neal A. Maxwell, "'From Whom All Blessings Flow,'" *Ensign,* May 1997, 11–12.

9. See also D&C 50:40–44: "I am in the Father and the Father in me; and inasmuch as ye have received me, ye are in me and I in you."

10. "How Firm a Foundation," *Hymns* (Salt Lake City: The Church of Jesus Christ of Latter-day Saints, 1985), no. 85.

Chapter 5
His Atonement: Perfecting Blessings

1. Elouise M. Bell, "Holiness," in *The Encyclopedia of Mormonism,* 4 vols., ed. Daniel H. Ludlow (New York: Macmillan, 1992), 2: 649.

2. Martha Maria Humphreys, quoted in Marjorie Newton, *Southern Cross Saints: The Mormons in Australia* (Laie: Institute for Polynesian Studies, Brigham Young University–Hawaii, 1991), 227.

3. See chapter 20 of this book.

4. Neal A. Maxwell, *All These Things Shall Give Thee Experience* (Salt Lake City: Deseret Book, 1979), 32, 34, 36.

5. Neal A. Maxwell, *A Time to Choose* (Salt Lake City: Deseret Book, 1972), 46.

6. Neal A. Maxwell, "'I Will Arise and Go to My Father,'" *Ensign,* September 1993, 67.

7. Neal A. Maxwell, "The Pathway of Discipleship," Brigham Young University fireside, January 4, 1998; available at http://speeches.byu.edu/?act =viewitem&id =619; accessed 2 July 2014.

8. For the story of Elder Maxwell's illness in the larger context of his life story, see Bruce C. Hafen, *A Disciple's Life: The Biography of Neal A. Maxwell* (Salt Lake City: Deseret Book, 2002). The quoted sentence is on page 562.

Chapter 6
The Temple Ordinances and the Two Priesthoods

1. "In his account of the dedication of the Kirtland Temple, the Prophet recorded in his journal, 'Presdt Williams also arose and testified that while Presdt Rigdon was making his first prayer an angel entered the window and seated himself between father Smith, and himself, and remained there during his prayer.'

Truman O. Angell later added, 'When the afternoon meeting assembled, Joseph, feeling very much elated, arose the first thing and said the Personage who had appeared in the morning was the Angel Peter come to accept the dedication.' President Heber C. Kimball even gave a description of Peter's appearance. 'They had a fair view of his person. He was a very tall personage, black eyes, white hair, and stoop shouldered; his garment was whole, extending to near his ankles; on his feet he had sandals. He was sent as a messenger to accept of the dedication'" (Scott C. Esplin, "Wondering at His Words: Peter's Influence on the Knowledge of Salvation for the Dead," in *The 43rd Annual Brigham Young University Sidney B Sperry Symposium: The Ministry of Peter, the Chief Apostle* [Salt Lake City: Deseret Book, 2014], 303).

2. The ordinances of baptism, receiving the Holy Ghost, receiving the Melchizedek Priesthood (for brethren), and the endowment and temple marriage are essential for salvation and exaltation. Thus in the temple these ordinances are performed for the dead. Other ordinances, such as patriarchal blessings, naming children, and administering to the sick are desirable but are not saving and exalting ordinances (see Immo Luschin, "Ordinances," in *The Encyclopedia of Mormonism*, 4 vols., ed. Daniel H. Ludlow [New York: Macmillan Co., 1992], 3:1032–33).

3. For use of the term "these two priesthoods," see D&C 84:33; 107:21. See also 107:1.

4. *Discourses of Brigham Young*, ed. John A. Widtsoe (Salt Lake City: Deseret Book, 1971), 416.

5. *Preach My Gospel: A Guide to Missionary Service* (Salt Lake City: The Church of Jesus Christ of Latter-day Saints, 2004), 1.

6. Russell M. Nelson, "Begin with the End in Mind," Seminar for New Mission Presidents, June 22, 2014.

7. Stake conference talk, Orem Utah Sharon Stake, May 17, 2014.

8. David O. McKay, Los Angeles Temple Dedication, quoted in Truman G. Madsen, "House of Glory," BYU Ten-Stake Fireside address, March 5, 1972, 7.

9. John A. Widtsoe, "Temple Worship," *The Utah Genealogical and Historical Magazine,* vol. 12, no. 2, April 1921, 54–55; emphasis added.

10. *Teachings of the Presidents of the Church: Joseph Smith* (Salt Lake City: The Church of Jesus Christ of Latter-day Saints, 2007), 268.

11. Emily Utt email to Bruce C. Hafen, February 27, 2015.

12. For a description of the name, nature, and purpose of each of these rooms in the Salt Lake Temple, for example, see James E. Talmage, *The House of the Lord* (Salt Lake City: Bookcraft, 1962, a reprinting of the 1912 original edition), 183–92.

13. David A. Bednar, *Power to Become* (Salt Lake City: Deseret Book, 2014), 77; emphasis added.

Chapter 7
The Temple and the Doctrine of Sacrifice

1. "I Feel My Savior's Love," *Children's Songbook* (Salt Lake City: The Church of Jesus Christ of Latter-day Saints, 1989), 74–75.

2. James E. Talmage, *Jesus the Christ* (Salt Lake City: Deseret Book, 1983), 621.

3. Neal A. Maxwell, "'Deny Yourselves of All Ungodliness,'" *Ensign,* May 1995, 68; emphasis added.

4. *Lectures on Faith* (Salt Lake City: Deseret Book, 1985), 69. See also chapter 19 of this book.

5. See chapters 19 and 20 of this book for a more complete discussion of consecration and sanctification.

6. Neal A. Maxwell, *All These Things Shall Give Thee Experience* (Salt Lake City: Deseret Book, 1979), 32, 34.

Chapter 8
The Temple and the Power of Godliness Made Manifest

1. Truman G. Madsen, "The Temple and the Atonement," 1994 (online version).

2. Clark D. Webb, "Mysteries of God," in *The Encyclopedia of Mormonism*, 4 vols., ed. Daniel H. Ludlow (New York: MacMillan Co., 1992), 2:978.

3. *Teachings of the Presidents of the Church: Joseph Smith* (Salt Lake City: The Church of Jesus Christ of Latter-day Saints, 2007), 109.

4. *The Teachings of Harold B. Lee*, ed. Clyde J. Williams (Salt Lake City: Bookcraft, 1996), 575.

5. D. Todd Christofferson, "Free Forever to Act for Themselves," *Ensign*, November 2014, 18.

6. See chapter 20, "Sanctification."

7. Thomas S. Monson, "Blessings of the Temple," *Ensign*, May 2015, 91–92.

8. Bruce C. and Marie K. Hafen, "'Fear Not, I Am with Thee': Christ's Atonement and Our Personal Growth," in *The Lord Will Give Grace and Glory: Talks from the 2014 BYU Women's Conference* (Salt Lake City: Deseret Book, 2015), 157.

9. Daniel L. Belnap, "Introduction: Latter-day Saints and the Perception of Ritual," in *By Our Rites of Worship: Latter-day Saint Views on Ritual in Scripture, History, and Practice*, ed. Daniel L. Belnap (Salt Lake City: Deseret Book, 2013), 4–5; emphasis added. See also D&C 67:10-12; Hebrews 12:14.

10. *Teachings of the Prophet Joseph Smith*, ed. Joseph Fielding Smith (Salt Lake City: Deseret News Press, 1938), 324; emphasis added.

11. Richard Lyman Bushman, *Joseph Smith: Rough Stone Rolling* (New York: Alfred A. Knopf, 2005), 451.

12. Joseph F. Smith, *Gospel Doctrine: Sermons and Writings of Joseph F. Smith* (Salt Lake City: Deseret Book, 1986), 126–27.

Chapter 9
The Blessings of Temple Sealings

1. "Those portions of [the Abrahamic Covenant] which pertain to personal exaltation and eternal increase are renewed with [those who enter] the order of celestial marriage; through that order the participating parties become inheritors of all the blessings of Abraham" (Bruce R. McConkie, *Mormon Doctrine: A Compendium of the Gospel* [Salt Lake City: Bookcraft, 1966], 13).

2. Carlos E. Asay, *In the Lord's Service: A Guide to Spiritual Development* (Salt Lake City: Deseret Book, 1990), 11.

3. This statement assumes, of course, that the spouse will eventually be sealed to another worthy eternal companion, since a sealing between husband and wife is, along with personal faithfulness, essential to receive the blessings of exaltation.

4. Joseph Fielding Smith, *Doctrines of Salvation: Sermons and Writings of Joseph*

Fielding Smith, 3 vols., ed. Bruce R. McConkie (Salt Lake City: Bookcraft, 1954–56), 3:246–47.

5. Bruce R. McConkie, *A New Witness for the Articles of Faith* (Salt Lake City: Deseret Book, 1985), 144.

6. "If you would become a son or a daughter of God and an heir of the kingdom, then you must go to the house of the Lord and receive the blessings . . . which cannot be obtained elsewhere. . . . The ordinances of the temple, the endowment and sealings, pertain to exaltation in the celestial kingdom. . . . The Lord has made it possible for us to become members of the Church of the Firstborn, by receiving the blessings of the house of the Lord and overcoming all things. Thus we become heirs, 'priests and kings,' who have received of his fullness . . . who shall 'dwell in the presence of God and his Christ forever' . . . with full exaltation. . . .[Temple sealers] seal upon us the keys and powers which, through our obedience, entitle us to become sons and daughters and members of the Church of the Firstborn, receiving all things in the kingdom. This is what we can get in the temple, so that we become members of the family, sons and daughters of God, not servants. . . . No person can receive an exaltation in the celestial kingdom without the ordinances of the temple. The endowments are for advancement in that kingdom, and the sealings for our perfection, provided we keep our covenants and obligations" (Joseph Fielding Smith, *Doctrines of Salvation,* 2:41–45. See also Bruce R. McConkie, *Mormon Doctrine,* 13).

7. *Teachings of the Prophet Joseph Smith,* ed. Joseph Fielding Smith (Salt Lake City: Deseret News Press, 1938), 354.

8. Spencer W. Kimball, *The Miracle of Forgiveness* (Salt Lake City: Bookcraft, 1969), 5.

9. Heber J. Grant, Anthony W. Ivins, Charles W. Nibley, "'Mormon' View of Evolution," in *Messages of the First Presidency,* 6 vols., ed. James R. Clark (Salt Lake City: Bookcraft, 1971), 5:244.

10. "While the revelations leave no doubt as to the existence of intelligent matter prior to its being organized" as the spirit children of our Heavenly Father, the Lord has not revealed whether, prior to our spirit birth, we existed as individual beings with identity and agency, or whether these characteristics "essentially came together" from some primal elements "for each individual at the spirit birth" (Paul Nolan Hyde, "Intelligences," in *The Encyclopedia of Mormonism,* 4 vols., ed. Daniel H. Ludlow [New York: Macmillan Company, 1992], 2:693). This source summarizes the writings of LDS leaders on both points of view, concluding that "the question of whether prespirit intelligence had individual . . . consciousness remains unanswered" (ibid).

11. Terryl L. Givens, *Wrestling with the Angel: The Foundations of Mormon Thought—Cosmos, God, and Humanity* (New York: Oxford University Press, 2014), 163.

12. John Taylor, *An Examination into and an Elucidation of the Great Principle of the Mediation and Atonement of Our Lord and Savior Jesus Christ* (Salt Lake City: Deseret News Press, 1882), 140–41.

13. Truman G. Madsen, "The Temple and the Atonement," *Maxwell Institute Publications,* 1994.

14. William Shakespeare, *King Lear,* Act IV, scene vii.

Chapter 10
The Ascending Journey of True Followers—
Engaging Christ's Atonement

1. For a brief and readable summary of the book of Revelation, see Gaye Strathearn, "Revelation: John's Message of Comfort and Hope," in *The Testimony of John the Beloved* (Salt Lake City: Deseret Book, 1998), 281–300. Her essay also offers interpretations of some phrases quoted in this chapter, such as hidden manna, white stone, new name, white robes, pillar in God's temple, second death, and having the names of God and of Christ written upon oneself.
2. Gerrit W. Gong, "Temple Mirrors of Eternity: A Testimony of Family," *Ensign,* November 2010, 38.
3. Elder Bruce R. McConkie affirms that Eve, along with Adam, received all of the ordinances required for salvation and exaltation: "Before the fall Eve was sealed to Adam in the new and everlasting covenant of marriage . . . (Moses 3:20-25) [and] Eve is a joint-participant with Adam . . . and will inherit jointly with him all the blessings appertaining to his . . . exaltation" (*Mormon Doctrine,* 2nd ed. [Salt Lake City: Bookcraft, 1958], 224–25).

Chapter 11
Waiting Upon the Lord

1. Brent H. Nielson, "Waiting for the Prodigal," *Ensign,* May 2015, 102.
2. Harrison R. Merrill, "Let This Be Heaven," *The Relief Society Magazine,* vol. 15, no. 8 (August 1928): 410.
3. Orson F. Whitney, *The Life of Heber C. Kimball* (Salt Lake City: Bookcraft, 1945), 188.
4. "Be Still, My Soul," *Hymns* (Salt Lake City: The Church of Jesus Christ of Latter-day Saints, 1985), no. 124; emphasis added.
5. F. Enzio Busche, *Yearning for the Living God* (Salt Lake City: Deseret Book, 2004), 115–16.
6. Ibid., 116.
7. Ibid., 117.
8. "Praise to the Man," *Hymns,* no. 27.
9. James E. Talmage, *Jesus the Christ* (Salt Lake City: Deseret Book, 1983), 313–14; emphasis added.

Chapter 12
Expectations

1. Dennis E. Simmons, "But If Not . . . ," *Ensign,* May 2004, 73; emphasis added.
2. "How Firm a Foundation," *Hymns* (Salt Lake City: The Church of Jesus Christ of Latter-day Saints, 1985), no. 85.
3. "Lina Sandell-Berg: Songs out of Tragedy," *Christianity.com.*
4. Ibid.

Chapter 13
Marriage, At-one-ment, and the Temple

1. Bruce C. Hafen, *Covenant Hearts: Why Marriage Matters and How to Make It Last* (Salt Lake City: Deseret Book, 2005).

2. Dell Van Orden, "Pres. Hinckley Notes His 85th Birthday, Reminisces about Life," *Church News*, June 24, 1995, accessed online; emphasis added.

3. Lisa Ann Jackson, "News of the Church: Strong Families Key to Future, President Hinckley Tells Colorado Forum," *Ensign*, July 2003, 75.

4. Caitlin Flanagan, "Is There Hope for the American Marriage?," *Time*, 13 July 2009, 45.

5. In 2001, for example, the New York Times reported a "powerful consensus" among social scientists that "from a child's point of view . . . the most support-ive household is one with two biological parents in a low-conflict marriage" (Blaine Hardin, "2-Parent Families Rise after Change in Welfare Laws," *New York Times*, August 12, 2001, accessed online).

6. Obergefell v. Hodges, June 26, 2015.

7. The Court based its decision on four principles, the first of which was indi-vidual autonomy. The other principles included the importance of marriage to the two people involved, providing stability to children already being reared by a same-gender couple, and giving same-gender couples access to marriage as the keystone of the nation's legal and social order. See ibid.

8. Ibid.

9. "Response to the Supreme Court Decision Legalizing Same-Sex Marriage in the United States," Statement of the Council of the First Presidency and Quorum of the Twelve Apostles, June 29, 2015, mormonnewsroom.org.

10. See census.gov/compendia/statab/2011/tables/11s1335.pdf; see also Alan J. Hawkins, *The Forever Initiative: A Feasible Public Policy Agenda to Help Couples Form and Sustain Healthy Marriages and Relationships* (2013), 19.

11. See "'Disastrous' Illegitimacy Trends," *Washington Times,* December 1, 2006, washingtontimes.com/news/2006/dec/01/20061201-084845-1917r/.

12. See *The State of Our Unions: Marriage in America 2012* (2012), 101, 102.

13. See "One-Parent and Two-Parent Families 1960–2012," Office of Financial Management, ofm.wa.gov/trends/social/fig204.asp.

14. See David Brooks, "The Cost of Relativism," *The New York Times*, March 10, 2015.

15. See Karen S. Peterson, "Why Men Drag Their Feet down the Aisle," *USA Today*, June 28, 2002

16. See Noelle Knox, "Nordic Family Ties Don't Mean Tying the Knot," *USA Today*, December 16, 2004, 15; usatoday30.usatoday.com/news/world/2004-12-15 -marriage_x.htm.

17. Report of the Mission of Inquiry on the Family and the Rights of Children, a study commission appointed by the National Assembly of France, January 25, 2006, 32.

18. "The marriage apocalypse may be coming. Talk to any millennial [ages 18–29] and you can envision an America virtually marriage-free, with everyone happily single" (Carol Costello, "Ready for the Marriage Apocalypse?" http://www.cnn .com/2015/04/07/opinions/costello-marriage-millennials/).

19. See Hafen, *Covenant Hearts*, 226–27.

20. Flanagan, "Hope for the American Marriage," 47.

21. Robert D. Putnam, *Our Kids: The American Dream in Crisis* (New York: Simon and Schuster, 2015), 26–29.

22. Ibid., 56–60.

23. Ibid., 104–8.

24. Brooks, "The Cost of Relativism"; emphasis added.

25. "The Family: A Proclamation to the World," *Ensign*, November 1995, 101.

Chapter 14
The Temple and the Natural Order of Marriage

1. For some thoughtful counsel about divorce among Latter-day Saints, see James E. Faust, "Father, Come Home," *Ensign*, May 1993, 37.

2. Hugh Nibley, *Eloquent Witness: Nibley on Himself, Others, and the Temple*, vol. 17 in The Collected Works of Hugh Nibley series, ed. Stephen D. Ricks (Salt Lake City: Deseret Book, 2008), 312–13; see also Hugh Nibley, "Temples: Meanings and Functions of Temples," in *The Encyclopedia of Mormonism*, 4 vols., ed. Daniel H. Ludlow (New York: The Macmillan Co., 1992), 4:1458–59.

3. "The Family: A Proclamation to the World," *Ensign*, November 1995, 101.

4. Bruce R. McConkie, *The Promised Messiah* (Salt Lake City: Deseret Book, 1978), 378, 453.

5. Joseph F. Smith, John R. Winder, and Anthon H. Lund to Christine Eggleston, January 28, 1902, First Presidency letterpress copybooks, LDS Church History Library.

Chapter 15
Missionary Work, the Temple, and Real Growth

1. *Handbook 2: Administering the Church* (Salt Lake City: The Church of Jesus Christ of Latter-day Saints, 2010), 5.2.3.

2. New and Returning Member Progress Form, https://www.lds.org/bc/content/shared/english/wwlt/hasten/PD50020824-member-progress-form-eng.pdf.

3. Abby Hafen email to her family, January 14, 2015.

4. *Preach My Gospel: A Guide to Missionary Service* (Salt Lake City: The Church of Jesus Christ of Latter-day Saints, 2004), 1.

6. John L. Hart, "Prophet Breaks Ground for New Temples," *Church News*, November 23, 1996; accessed online.

7. Bruce C. Hafen, *A Disciple's Life: The Biography of Neal A. Maxwell* (Salt Lake City: Deseret Book, 2002), 466.

8. Ibid.

9. Russell M. Nelson, "Begin with the End in Mind," Seminar for New Mission Presidents, June 22, 2014.

10. Dallin H. Oaks, "The Parable of the Sower," *Ensign*, May 2015, 35.

Chapter 16
Keep the Covenants and the Covenants Will Keep You

1. Jeffrey R. Holland, "A Handful of Meal and a Little Oil," *Ensign*, May 1996.

2. Felix Mendelssohn, *Elijah* (New York: G. Schirmer Inc., 1986), 41.

3. Susa Young Gates, *Lydia Knight's History* (Salt Lake City: Juvenile Instructor Office, 1883), 23.

4. Ibid., 25.

5. Karen Lynn Davidson and Jill Mulvay Derr, *Eliza: The Life and Faith of Eliza R. Snow* (Salt Lake City: Deseret Book, 2013), 22.

6. James E. Talmage, *The House of the Lord,* rev. ed. (Salt Lake City: Deseret Book, 1976), 84.

7. Neal A. Maxwell, "Overcome . . . Even as I Also Overcame," *Ensign,* May 1987, 71; emphasis added.

8. Boyd K. Packer, *Let Not Your Heart Be Troubled* (Salt Lake City: Bookcraft, 1991), 257.

9. Richard Lyman Bushman, *Joseph Smith: Rough Stone Rolling* (New York: Alfred A. Knopf, 2005), 53.

10. Ibid., 59–60.

11. Jeffrey D. Keith, "Feeling the Atonement," BYU Devotional, October 9, 2001.

12. Bushman, *Rough Stone Rolling,* 114.

13. William G. Hartley, *They Are My Friends: A History of the Joseph Knight Family, 1825–1850* (Provo, Utah: Grandin Books, 1986), 148.

14. Ibid., 115.

15. Ibid., 156.

16. Gates, *Lydia Knight's History,* 69.

17. Ibid.

18. Ibid., 69–70.

19. Ibid., 70

20. Ibid., 71–72.

21. Patriarchal Blessing, April 3, 1836, Kirtland, Church Archives.

22. J. William Knight, *The Jesse Knight Family: Jesse Knight, His Forebears and Family* (Salt Lake City: Deseret News Press, 1940), 21.

23. Gates, *Lydia Knight's History,* 74–75.

24. *Letters and Papers of Lydia Knight and Newel Knight,* 28–29, Church History Library.

25. Gates, *Lydia Knight's History,* 76.

26. Ibid.

27. Ibid., 77.

28. Ibid., 79.

29. Ibid., 77.

30. Jan Jansak Williams and LaRea Gibbons Strebe, "Lydia Knight: 'God Rules' Was Her Motto," *Ensign,* August 1977, 52.

31. Knight, *Jesse Knight Family,* 21–23.

32. Gates, *Lydia Knight's History,* 100.

33. Williams and Strebe, "Lydia Knight," 52.

34. Knight, *Jesse Knight Family,* 24.

35. Vilate Raile, "Pioneers," in *The Relief Society Magazine: A Legacy Remembered 1914–1970,* ed. Carol L. Clark (Salt Lake City: Deseret Book, 1982), 19.

36. "Come, Come, Ye Saints," *Hymns* (Salt Lake City: The Church of Jesus Christ of Latter-day Saints, 1985), no. 30.

CHAPTER 17
THE REACH OF THE SEALING POWER

1. J. William Knight, *The Jesse Knight Family: Jesse Knight, His Forebears and Family* (Salt Lake City: Deseret News Press, 1940), 33.

2. Ibid., 34.

3. Ibid., 35–36.

4. Ibid., 37.

5. Jeffrey D. Keith, "Feeling the Atonement," BYU Devotional, October 9, 2001.

6. Knight, *Jesse Knight Family,* 39.

7. Ibid., 84.

8. This estimate uses the "economic power"' standard—the equivalent current value as a share of the nation's gross domestic product. See Measuringworth. com.

9. Keith, "Feeling the Atonement."

10. Knight, *Jesse Knight Family,* 86.

11. In Conference Report, April 1929, 110. Also quoted in note 12 below.

12. James E. Faust, "Dear Are the Sheep That Have Wandered," *Ensign,* May 2003, 62.

13. Norman Maclean, *A River Runs Through It and Other Stories* (Chicago: University of Chicago Press, 1976), 102.

14. Ibid., 81. Some of the quoted language is based on the film version.

15. Colleen McDannel and Bernhard Lang, *Heaven: A History* (New Haven: Yale University Press, 1988).

16. Terryl L. Givens and Fiona Givens, *The God Who Weeps* (Salt Lake City: Deseret Book, 2012).

17. Brigham Young, in *Journal of Discourses,* 26 vols. (London: Latter-day Saints' Book Depot, 1854–1886), 4:268.

Chapter 18
Saviors on Mount Zion: Restoring the Generations

1. See *Teachings of the Prophet Joseph Smith,* ed. Joseph Fielding Smith (Salt Lake City: Deseret News Press, 1938), 337–38.

2. Ibid., 330.

3. Bruce Feiler, "The Stories That Bind Us," *The New York Times,* March 15, 2013.

4. Ibid.

5. One source found that up to 80 percent of women perpetrators of child sexual abuse were themselves abused as children (see David C. Pruden, *Lead My People,* audio CD [n.p.: Pilgrimage, 2005]).

6. M. Catherine Thomas, "When Our Reaching Reaches His," in *Women and the Power Within: To See Life Steadily and See It Whole,* eds. Dawn Hall Anderson and Marie Cornwall (Salt Lake City: Deseret Book, 1991), 186–89.

7. Allen E. Bergin, "Three Contributions of a Spiritual Perspective to Counseling, Psychotherapy, and Behavior Change," *Counseling and Values,* vol. 33, no. 1 (Oct. 1988): 28–30.

Chapter 19
Consecration

1. *Teachings of Gordon B. Hinckley* (Salt Lake City: Deseret Book, 1997), 139–40.

2. *Preparing to Enter the Holy Temple* (Salt Lake City: Intellectual Reserve, Inc., 2002), 35.

3. *Teachings of Gordon B. Hinckley,* 147.

4. See Blaine M. Yorgason, Richard A. Schmutz, and Douglas D. Alder, *All That*

Was Promised: The St. George Temple and the Unfolding of the Restoration (Salt Lake City: Deseret Book, 2013), 252. This book contains a very readable account of the settlement of St. George and the story of building the temple there. It also provides a detailed account of Joseph Smith's final charge to the Twelve shortly before the martryrdom in 1844, including Joseph's request of Brigham Young to establish the complete practice of temple ordinances for the living and the dead.

5. See ibid., 256.

6. See ibid., 282–85.

7. Richard E. Bennett, "'Line upon Line, Line, Precept upon Precept': Reflections on the 1877 Commencement of the Performance of Endowments and Sealings of the Dead," *BYU Studies,* vol. 44, no. 3 (2005): 57.

8. Yorgason, Schmutz, and Alder, *All That Was Promised,* 32.

9. Ibid., 31.

10. Ibid.

11. Ibid., 30.

12. Ibid., 31.

13. George A. Smith, in *Journal of Discourses,* 26 vols. (London: Latter-day Saints' Book Depot, 1854–1886) 9:116.

14. Wilford Woodruff, in Conference Report, April 1898, 89; emphasis added.

15. "P. P. Pratt's Proclamation," *The Latter-day Saints' Millennial Star,* vol. 5, no. 10 (March 1845): 151.

16. Yorgason, Schmutz, and Alder, *All That Was Promised,* 14.

17. Church members were able to receive endowments and sealings for the living in the Council House, and later in the Endowment House, in Salt Lake City from 1851 to 1885 (Karen Lynn Davidson and Jill Mulvay Derr, *Eliza: The Life and Faith of Eliza R. Snow* [Salt Lake City: Deseret Book, 2013], 86–87), but because those buildings were not dedicated temples, no endowments for the dead or child-to-parent sealings for the dead were completed until the St. George Temple was dedicated in 1877.

18. Lyman Hafen, *Where Two Streams Meet: The Personal History of a Town* (St. George, Utah: Tonaquint Press, 2011), 47–49.

19. See L. A. Fleming, "The Settlements on the Muddy, 1865 to 1871: 'A Godforsaken Place,'" *Utah Historical Quarterly,* vol. 35, no. 2 (Spring 1967): 147–72.

20. Bruce C. Hafen conversation with Bill Cox, October 6, 2002.

21. Melvin S. Tagg, "The Life of Edward James Wood, Church Patriot" (MS thesis, BYU, 1959), 10.

22. Quoted in Bruce C. Hafen, *A Disciple's Life: The Biography of Neal A. Maxwell* (Salt Lake City: Deseret Book, 2002), 527.

23. Neal A. Maxwell, "Consecrate Thy Performance," *Ensign,* May 2002, 36, 39.

24. Neal A. Maxwell, "Why Not Now?," *Ensign,* November 1974, 13.

25. Brigham Young, in *Journal of Discourses,* 18:304.

26. Allan Rau email to Bruce C. Hafen, June 25, 2012.

27. *Lectures on Faith* (Salt Lake City: Deseret Book, 1985), 69.

28. Ibid., 71; emphasis added.

29. Brigham Young, in *Journal of Discourses,* 5:294.

30. Bennett, "Line upon Line," 57.

CHAPTER 20
SANCTIFICATION

1. D. Todd Christofferson, "Justification and Sanctification," *Ensign,* June 2001, 18.

2. Ibid., 22.

3. "There Is Sunshine in My Soul," *Hymns* (Salt Lake City: The Church of Jesus Christ of Latter-day Saints, 1985), no. 227.

4. Christofferson, "Justification and Sanctification," 18.

5. "Sanctification is the process of becoming a saint, holy and spiritually clean and pure" (C. Eric Ott, "Sanctification," in *The Encyclopedia of Mormonism,* ed. Daniel H. Ludlow [New York: The Macmillan Company, 1992], 3:1259.

6. Mary Karr, "Who the Meek Are Not," *The Atlantic Monthly,* May 2002. Used by permission.

7. Abby Li email to Bruce C. Hafen, March 9, 2015.

8. Scott Crump, "The Oquirrh Mountains," in *Utah History Encyclopedia,* uen.org.

9. Elizabeth Barrett Browning (1806–1861), "Aurora Leigh."

CHAPTER 21
WHEN "ALMOST" IS ENOUGH

1. "The submission of one's will is really the only uniquely personal thing we have to place on God's altar. The many other things we 'give' . . . are actually the things He has already given or loaned to us" (Neal A. Maxwell, "'Swallowed Up in the Will of the Father,'" *Ensign,* November 1995, 24).

2. William Law (English clergyman, 1686–1761), accessed from http://www.brainyquote.com/quotes/quotes/w/williamlaw158259.html.

3. See Marjorie Newton, "Father of Joseph's Daughter: John Murdock," *Journal of Mormon History,* vol. 18, no. 2 (Fall 1992): 177–93.

4. Viktor Frankl, *Man's Search for Meaning: An Introduction to Logotherapy* (New York: Washington Square Press, 1959, 1963), xiii. Frankl was quoting Friedrich Nietzsche.

5. Ibid., 58.

INDEX

Aaronic Priesthood: ordinances and principles of, 54, 56, 218; differences between Melchizedek Priesthood and, 55; consecration and, 218

Abed-nego, 115

Abuse, 5–6, 38–39, 200–201

Acceptance, of Lord, 50–52

Accidents, 37–38

Adam and Eve, 25–26, 31, 63, 92–95, 143–46. *See also* Fall of Adam

Adoption, doctrine of, 78–81

Adversity. *See* Opposition; Trials; Tribulation, overcome by Adam and Eve

Afterlife, 189–90

Agency, 95, 186

Ahnfelt, Oscar, 126

Allen, Electa, 243

Animal sacrifice, 63–64

Apostasy, 26

Asay, Carlos E., 77

Atonement of Jesus Christ: increased attention and insight on, 4–6; need for doctrinal clarity regarding, 6–11; casualness regarding, 11–17; temple as anchor for understanding and applying, 18–21; understanding doctrine of, 24–25; purpose of, 25–28; scope and blessings of, 29–30, 94; unconditional blessings of, 30–31; conditional blessings of, 31–33; strength through, 34–45, 116–17; perfecting blessings of, 46–52; blessings of, through higher ordinances, 61–62; eternal family made possible through, 129–30; sealing made possible through, 193

Attitude, 95, 119–20, 208–15, 226

Attributes of Divinity, 227–28

Averett, Elisha, 209

Bailey, Calvin, 173

Baker, Bonnie, 122–23

Baptism, 56, 57–58

Beckett, Samuel, 100

Bednar, David A., 61

Belnap, Daniel, 71

Belonging, 128–30, 245–48

Bennett, Richard, 208

Bergin, Allen, 200

Blessings: of Atonement, 29–30; unconditional, of Atonement, 30–31; conditional, of Atonement, 31–33; strengthening, of

263

Atonement, 34–45; perfecting, 46–52; of temple sealings, 75–83; expectations for, 112; faith based in trust rather than, 125–27; of sacrifice, 220–21; of sanctification, 223–27, 237–38; restoration of, 245–46

Brass plates, 194–95

Brigham Young University, 183

Broken heart, sacrifice of, 64, 66, 146–48, 217–18

Brooks, David, 139

Browning, Elizabeth Barrett, 237

Burnand, Eugene, 106

Burton, Theodore M., 108

Busche, F. Enzio, 107–9

Bushman, Richard, 71, 171

"But if not . . . ," 115–18

Caldwell, Agnes, 22–24, 42–43

Callings, 220

Callister, Tad R., 14

Cannon, David H., 211–12

Cannon, Wilhelmina, 211–13

Car, author thrown from, 246–47

Casualness, regarding Atonement, 11–17

Caterpillar, 103–4

Change, repentance and, 32–34

Charity, 47

Childbearing, unmet expectations in, 118–19

Children: wayward, 39–40, 180–92; of unmarried parents, 136–37; concern for, 140–41; iniquity of fathers visited upon, 198–99

Children of Christ, 78–83

Christofferson, D. Todd, 69, 222

Church activity, versus consecration, 216–20

Church of Jesus Christ of Latter-day Saints, The: expectations for, 114; "real growth" in, 159–62; Jesse Knight saves credit of, 182–83; teachings of, on afterlife, 190

Churchill, Winston, 215

Civil rights movement, 132

Cocoon, 103–4

Cohabitation, 136–37

Consecration: sanctification and, 204–5; versus sacrifice, 205–7; historical context of, 207–8; of pioneers, 208–14; conversion and, 214–15; versus church activity, 216–20; builds confidence in God, 220–21; adequate, 239–45

Contrite spirit: broken heart and, xiv–xvi; sacrifice of, 64, 66, 146–48, 217–18

Conversion, degrees of, 214–15

Converts, 153–66

Cookie Monster, 99

Covenants: and conditional blessings of Atonement, 40–42; observing, by sacrifice, 167–70; as two-way promise, 170; Knight family and, 170–79; of Jesse Knight, 181–84; as dynamic and interactive, 236

Cowdery, Oliver, 54, 193

Culture, and convert retention, 161–62

Dalton, John, 177

"Day by Day," 125

Dead, redemption of, 194

Degrees of glory, vision of, 91–92

Deliverance, of disciples, 97–98

Desires, righteous, 245

Discrimination, 132

Divorce, 133–34, 136

Dixie Cotton Mission, 213

Doctrine: misunderstanding, 11–16; understanding, 24–25

Dortmund, Germany, 108–9

Dragon, in vision of John, 88–89

Elijah, 167–68, 193, 194

Empathy, of Jesus Christ, 45, 49

Enabling power, 27, 41–42

Endowment: lessons of, 19, 59; importance of, 56; and mysteries of godliness, 68–69; of early Saints, 71; and convert retention, 160; performed in St. George Temple, 207

Enduring to the end, 57–58
Especially For Youth (EFY), 72
Exaltation, 56, 59, 77, 79, 80–81,
    239–41
Excommunication, 245–46
Expectations: for blessings, 112;
    problem of rising, 113–14; and
    accepting Lord's will, 115–18;
    dealing with unmet, 118–23; and
    faith based in trust, 125–27

Fairness, 12–13
Faith: as first principle of gospel, 56,
    57–58; facing fear with, 117–18;
    based in trust, 125–27
Fall of Adam, 25–26, 31, 143–45
Family: problems facing, 130–31;
    and importance of norms, 139;
    dysfunction passed through,
    198–99; transitional figures in,
    199–202; healing, in temple, 202–
    3; and desire to belong, 245–48
"Family: A Proclamation to the World,
    The," 130–31
Family histories, 194–99
Family law, 132–34
Faust, James E., 20, 185, 186
Fawcett, William, 209–10
Fear, facing, with faith, 117–18
Feiler, Bruce, 196
First principles and ordinances of
    gospel, 56, 57–58
Forgiveness, 31–33, 44, 202–3,
    232–33, 241
Frankl, Victor, 248
Freedom of religion, 135–36

Garden of Eden, 143
Gardner, Robert, 209
Gates, Susa Young, 177
Generosity, 241
Germany, prejudice against Church in,
    108–9
Givens, Terryl, 190
God: love of, 11, 189; sons of,
    79–80; nature of, 80, 190–91;
    will of, 115–18; love for, 168;

consecration builds confidence in,
    220–21
Godhood, 6–9, 16
Godliness: mysteries of, 68–69; and
    forsaking ungodliness, 69; through
    Atonement, 69–70, 81; and
    relationship with Jesus Christ,
    70–73; and entering into "rest
    of the Lord," 73–74; and joy
    in marriage, 149; temple and
    sanctified, 228–36
Gold plates, 171
Gong, Gerrit W., 91
Goodly parents, 197–98
Grace: conditional, 7–8, 16, 42–43;
    understanding purpose of,
    26–27; as unconditional gift of
    Atonement, 30; repentance and,
    31–33; succoring dimension
    of, 43–44; perfecting, 46–48;
    sanctification and, 223–24;
    recognizing, 241
Grant, Heber J., 181–83
Gratitude, 168
Great Apostasy, 26

Hafen, John G., 165
Hafen, Jon Orval, 196–97
Hafen, Mike, 188–89
Hafen, Orval, 196–97, 214–15
Handkerchief, of Lydia Knight, 174
Hanks, Marion D., 229
Healing: through Atonement, 5–6; of
    Hyrum Knight, 176
Heaven, 189–90
Helsinki Finland Temple, 106–7
Hinckley, Gordon B.: impact of, on
    Australian Saint, 51; on families,
    130, 138; on new Church
    members, 157, 158; on widow's
    mite, 205–6; on sacrifice and
    consecration, 206–7
Hinckley, Marjorie P., 113
Holland, Jeffrey R., 112, 168
Holy Ghost, 35
Home teaching, 108
Horses, well-broken, xiii–xiv, 234–35

"How Firm a Foundation," 45
Human nature, 26–27
"Humbug" claim, 182–83
Humility, 224–26
Humphreys, Martha, 46
Hunter, Howard W., 191–92

"In Humility, Our Savior," 4
Independence, in marriage, 144–45
Individual interests, versus social
    interests, 132–35
Instant gratification, 98–99
Israel/Israelites: adoption into house of,
    78–79; sacrifices offered by, 146

Jesus Christ: relationship with,
    34–35; succoring of, 43–45,
    116–17; empathy of, 45, 49; being
    accepted of, 50–52; godliness
    and relationship with, 70–73;
    becoming children of, 78–83;
    waits upon the Lord, 102–3;
    trusting in, 110–11; submits
    to will of God, 117; sacrifices
    pointing toward, 145–46; as
    transitional figure, 201–2;
    becoming like, 226–27; Nephites
    desire to be with, 241–42. See also
    Atonement of Jesus Christ
John the Revelator, 88–92, 106
Justice, 12–13, 185
Justification, 222–23

Karr, Mary, 234–35
Kartchner, Ray, 179
Kauper, Kurt, 108–9
Keeler, Joseph, 183
Keeler, Robert, 162–63
Keith, Jeffrey, 182, 184
Kimball, Heber C., 105–6
Kimball, Spencer W., 79–80
Kirtland Temple, 54, 60, 97, 169
Knight, Amanda, 181
Knight, Hyrum, 176
Knight, Jennie, 181
Knight, Jesse, 180–87

Knight, Joseph Jr., 172
Knight, Joseph Sr., 170–73
Knight, Lydia Goldthwaite, 168–69,
    173–79, 181, 185–86
Knight, Minnie, 181–82
Knight, Newel, 172, 173–76, 178–79
Knight, Polly, 170–73
Knight, Vincent, 168–69
Knight, William, 181, 182

Law(s): and social interests, 132; shift in
    family, 132–34; regarding same-sex
    marriage, 135–36
Lee, Harold B., 68–69
Lehi, 194–95
Love: of God, 11, 189; for wayward
    children, 187–89

Madsen, Truman, 68, 81–82
Manna, 89
Marriage: unmet expectations in,
    120–21; opposition to, 128–30;
    collapse of, 131–32; and shift
    in family law, 132–34; same-
    sex, 134–36; effects of changes
    regarding, 136–37; effects of
    collapse of, 138–40; and concern
    for children, 140–41; importance
    of, 142–43; of Adam and Eve,
    143–45; sacrifice and, 145–49;
    authentic joy in, 149–51. See also
    Sealing
Maxwell, Neal A.: on opposition, 17;
    and sanctifying effects of adversity,
    48–50; on sacrifice, 64; and "real
    growth," 159–60; on keeping
    covenants, 170; on consecrated
    disciples, 216; meekness and,
    233–35
McClellen, James, 178
McConkie, Bruce R., 79, 146
McKay, David O., 59
Meekness, xiv, 224–26, 233–36
Melchizedek Priesthood, 54, 55–56,
    218
Member Progress form, 154–57
Mercy: severe, 23–24, 110–11; as

unconditional gift of Atonement, 30; repentance and, 31–33; offering and receiving, 241

Meshach, 115

Mining, 182–83

Missionary work, 155–66, 219–20

Missouri, persecution in, 224

Mistakes, learning from, 36–38

Monson, Thomas S., 70

Mortality: and need for Atonement, 25–28; weakness as part of, 36; mistakes as part of, 36–37; knowledge regarding purpose of, 71; overcoming opposition in, 87; conditions in, 93

Mosser, Carl, 7

Motherhood, unmet expectations in, 118–19

Mt. Trumbull, Arizona, 214–15

Murdock, John, 242–45

Murdock, Julia, 242

Nebuchadnezzar, 115

Nelson, Russell M., 57, 160

Nephi, 152–53

Nephites, 241–42

New and Returning Member Progress form, 154–57

New Church members, 153–66

Nibley, Hugh, 142

Nielson, Brent H., 100

No-fault divorce, 133–34

Norms, 139–40

Oaks, Dallin H., 161

Obedience, 17, 63–64

Opposition: purpose of, 27–28; struggling with, 39–40; overcoming, 87; of Christ's true followers in vision of John, 90–91. See also Trials; Tribulation, overcome by Adam and Eve

Oquirrh Mountain Utah Temple, 236–37

Oquirrh Mountains, 236–37

Ordinances: as symbolic of Atonement, 18–20; of Aaronic and Melchizedek Priesthoods, 54; completion through living higher, 59–60; ascending room-to-room pattern in, 60–61; blessings of Atonement through higher, 61–62; in similitude of Christ's sacrifice, 63–67; and relationship with Jesus Christ, 71–73; as reminder of Christ's sacrifice, 116; proxy, 194, 199; as dynamic and interactive, 236. See also Temple

Original sin, 31

Overcoming: as theme of Revelation, 87; and temple allusions in vision of John, 88–92; Adam and Eve and, 92–95; temple worship and, 96; and waiting on Lord, 97–98

Packer, Boyd K., 170

Parable of the sower, 161

Parents, goodly, 197–98

Patience, 98–111

Paul, 117–18, 154

Perfecting blessings, 46–52, 62, 69–70

Perfection, 149–51

Perry, L. Tom, 3–4

Persecution, of early Saints, 224

Personal histories, 194–99

Peter, 53–54, 82–83, 106

Pioneers, 22–24, 44–45, 208–15

"Pioneers" (Raile), 178

Plan of salvation, 131

Plates of brass, 194–95

Premortal existence, 79–80

Priesthood: restoration of, 53–54; differences between Aaronic and Melchizedek, 55–56; and ascending room-to-room pattern of temple ordinances, 60–61; given to Adam, 94; consecration and, 218. See also Aaronic Priesthood; Melchizedek Priesthood; Ordinances

Progression. See Spiritual progression

Pulsipher, John, 210

Putnam, Robert, 138

Raile, Vilate, 178
Rau, Allan, 20
Reading, Natasha, 165
Redemption, 30–31, 62, 194. *See also* Salvation
Religious freedom, 135–36
Repentance, 31–33, 44, 56, 57–58
Rest in the Lord, 102
Rest of the Lord, 73–74
Restoration of blessings, 245–46
Resurrection, 30–31
Revelation, book of, 87–92
Reynolds, Noel, 57–58
Reynolds, Sydney, 57–58
Righteous desires, 245
River Runs Through It, A, 188–89
Roundy, Jared, 182

Sacrament, 3–4, 71–72
Sacrifice(s): ordinances in similitude of Christ's, 63–67; of Adam and Eve, 94; for Dortmund chapel, 108–9; and marriage, 145–49; and perfecting grace, 149–51; observing covenants by, 167–70; Knight family and, 170–79; versus consecration, 205–7; of pioneers, 208–14; blessings of, 220–21; of John Murdock, 243–44
St. George Utah Temple: Wilford Woodruff on, xii; pattern for ordinances in, 60; Lydia Knight serves in, 178; endowments performed in, 207; construction of, 210; blessings for patrons of, 229–34
St. George, Utah, 105, 208–13
Salvation, 56, 59, 239–41. *See also* Redemption
Same-sex attraction, 121–22
Same-sex marriage, 134–36
Sanctification: and Atonement's perfecting blessings, 46–52; consecration and, 204–5; justification and, 222–23; conditions for, 223–27; and attributes of Divinity, 227–28;

temple and, 228–36; blessings of, 237–38
Sandell-Berg, Lina, 124–26
Satan: yielding to, 35; in vision of John, 88–89; as opposition to Christ's true followers, 90; overcome by Adam and Eve, 92–95
Saviors on Mount Zion, 194, 199, 202
Sealing: and offering broken heart and contrite spirit, 19; sacrifice and, 66–67; blessings of, 75–83; and convert retention, 159–60; and wayward children, 180–92. *See also* Marriage
Sealing power, restoration of, 150–51, 193
Sego lily, 212, 214
Selfishness, 82–83
Severe mercy, 23–24, 110–11
Shadrach, 115
Shipps, Jan, 6–7
Silence, 107
Simmons, Dennis E., 115
Smith, Emma, 243, 244
Smith, George A., 209, 210
Smith, Joseph: priesthood conferred upon, 54; on spiritual progression, 59–60; on mysteries of godliness, 68; on knowledge of purpose of mortality, 71; on exaltation, 79; sustained by Lydia Goldthwaite Knight, 168–69; Knight family and, 170–74; and restoration of sealing power, 193; on temple work for dead, 194; and temple ordinance work, 210–11
Smith, Joseph F., 66, 74
Smith, Joseph (son of Joseph Smith), 243
Smith, Julia, 243, 244
Snow, Eliza R., 169
Social interests, versus individual interests, 132–35
Social media, 113–14
Sons of God, 79–80
Sower, parable of, 161
Spirits, 79–80

Spiritual progression: discourse regarding Atonement and, 6–9; conditions for, 16; and purpose of Atonement, 25–28; forces affecting, 35–37; Joseph Smith on, 59–60; and ascending room-to-room pattern of temple ordinances, 60–61; Nephi's teachings on, 152–53; of new Church members, 153–66

Spiritual receptivity, deepening, 103–4

Stockholm, Sweden, stake conference in, 123–24

Stout, Joseph Allen, 209

Strength: through Atonement, 34–45, 62, 116–17; through trials, 110–11

Stress, and family histories, 195–96

Succor, 43–45, 116–17

Suffering, 12, 48–50

Swedish hymn, 124–26

Talmage, James E., 64, 111

Taproots, 153–54

Taylor, John, 80–81

Technology, 113–14

Temple: as anchor for understanding and applying Atonement, 18–21; as goal of missionary work, 155–66; and healing family, 202–3; and attitude of sanctified godliness, 228–36; placement and pull of, 238. See also Ordinances

Thomas, Catherine, 199–200

Timing, 97–98

Transitional figures, 199–202

Tree of life, 89

Trials: spiritual growth through, 8–9, 17; struggling with, 39–40; strength through, 40–41, 44–45, 110–11; of disciples, 97–98; and family histories, 195–96. See also Opposition; Tribulation, overcome by Adam and Eve

Tribulation, overcome by Adam and Eve, 92–95

Trust, faith based in, 125–27

Turner, Amoranda, 243

Uchtdorf, Dieter F., 13

Ungodliness, forsaking, 69, 149

United order, 208

Urim and Thummim, 171

Usterud, Jennifer, 123–26

Waiting for Godot (Beckett), 100

Waiting upon the Lord, 98–111

Wandell, Charles, 244

Wayward children, 39–40, 180–92

Weaknesses, struggling with, 36

Weire, Sarah, 243

Whitney, Orson F., 184–85

"Who the Meek Are Not" (Karr), 234–35

Widow of Zarephath, 167–68

Widow's mite, 205–6

Widtsoe, John A., 59

Will of God, 115–18

Willie Handcart Company, 22–24

Wolfart, Friedrich, 162–66

Wolfart, Irina, 164

Wolfart, Petra, 165

Wolfart, Philipp, 165

Wolfart, Renate, 162–66

Wolfart, Volker, 164, 165

Wood, Elizabeth, 213–14

Wood, William, 213

Woodruff, Wilford, xii, 183

Woodward, Kenneth, 9–10

Works, 7–8

Young, Brigham: on obedience, 17; on endowment, 56; counsels Lydia Knight, 176–77; on God, 190–91; and united order, 207–8; and temple ordinance work, 210–11; on lusting after things of world, 218, 221

Youth, 82–83

Zarephath, widow of, 167–68